The Real ALMA MAHLER

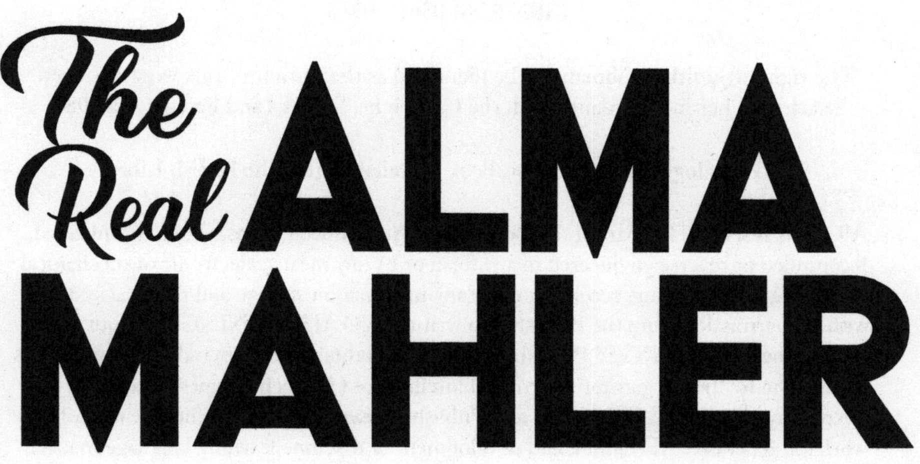

COMPOSER, SOCIALITE, REBEL AND INFLUENCER

JUDITH GROHMANN

AN IMPRINT OF PEN & SWORD BOOKS LTD.
YORKSHIRE – PHILADELPHIA

First published in Great Britain in 2025 by
Pen & Sword History
An imprint of
Pen & Sword Books Ltd
Yorkshire - Philadelphia

ISBN 978 1 03613 100 5

A CIP catalogue record for this book is available from the British Library.

Typeset in INDIA by IMPEC eSolutions
Printed and bound in England by CPI Group (UK) Ltd, Croydon, CRO 4YY

The Publisher's authorised representative in the EU for product safety is Authorised Rep Compliance Ltd., Ground Floor, 71 Lower Baggot Street, Dublin D02 P593, Ireland.
www.arccompliance.com

For a complete list of Pen & Sword titles please contact:

PEN & SWORD BOOKS LIMITED
George House, Units 12 & 13, Beevor Street,
Off Pontefract Road, Barnsley, S71 1HN, UK
E-mail: enquiries@pen-and-sword.co.uk
Website: www.pen-and-sword.co.uk

or

PEN AND SWORD BOOKS
1950 Lawrence Road, Havertown, PA 19083, USA
E-mail: uspen-and-sword@casematepublishers.com
Website: www.penandswordbooks.com

Become so very free that your whole existence is an act of rebellion.

Albert Camus

Contents

Acknowledgements

With this book, my publisher has once again given me the great opportunity to delve into the life of one of the most fascinating Austrian women of the last century – one who was far ahead of her time.

I would like to extend my heartfelt gratitude to the following people who helped me navigate the depths of this captivating subject:

First and foremost, my partner in crime at Pen & Sword, if I may say so, Ms Heather Williams. Heather, who shares a deep love for Austria, was the brilliant mind behind the idea of writing about an influential Austrian woman. She has given me the incredible opportunity to once again uncover many lesser-known aspects of history – this time through the magnetic and charismatic figure of Alma Mahler-Werfel – and to bring them to life not only for British and American readers, but for international readers.

Second, my heartfelt thanks to Karyn Burnham, whose editorial expertise, precision, and thoughtful questions helped refine this manuscript into its final form. Her care and an eye as sharp as a lynx's have made this book stronger on every level.

Third, a special thank you to my dear friend Brigitte Peytier-Nollen for her beautiful artistic contribution to the cover of this book. Her incredible talent and dedication to capturing Alma Mahler's essence have added a unique and powerful visual dimension to this project. Her passion for painting, coupled with her success as a sought-after artist, makes this collaboration all the more meaningful. In addition to her artistic work, Brigitte Peytier-Nollen also served as Proviseure in France and later at the Collège International Marie-de-France in Montréal and at the Lycée Français de Vienne, further reflecting her remarkable versatility and dedication.

Fourth, my dear friend Nadège Labrousse, who served as Attachée for French language cooperation at the French Embassy in Austria before becoming a teacher at the Lycée Français de Vienne. She not only provided me with key books and took one of the photographs included in this volume, but also encouraged me constantly to write the best possible account of Alma's extraordinary life.

Fifth, I am deeply grateful to University Professor Dr Christian Utz, esteemed musicologist and music theorist at the University of Music and Performing Arts in Graz, as well as President and Chairman of the International Gustav Mahler Society in Vienna. His insights into the lives of Alma and Gustav provided invaluable guidance, and our discussions in Vienna were both inspiring and illuminating.

Sixth, the wonderful Dr Anthony Raumann, Chairman of the Gustav Mahler Society in London, whose generosity made it possible for me to meet Marina Fistoulari-Mahler and exchange a few words with her during my visit to London in September 2024.

Seventh, Peter George Mahler, Gustav Mahler's third cousin twice removed, who enriched this book with his invaluable advice and a wonderful photograph that brings history to life.

Finally, my deepest thanks go to the entire team at Pen & Sword. Without their dedication, this book would never have made its way into the hands of readers around the world.

Prologue

In an Upper East Side apartment, where the golden light of late afternoon fell softly through the window, a woman has found solace. The brown building with its large black windows at 120 East 73rd Street, a testament to her triumphs and losses, was her sanctuary – a reflection of her troubled past and the deep loneliness that accompanied it. With a keen eye for beauty, she had decorated her two rooms with the elegance of a bygone era, and every corner told stories of illustrious gatherings and deep loneliness. The walls, adorned with paintings by famous artists from Europe and the United States, testified to the cultural milieu in which she moved with grace.

She grew up in a distinguished family immersed in the vibrant cultural climate of the Austro-Hungarian Empire, where artistic brilliance and intellectual zeal flourished, and now she absorbed the rich heritage that surrounded her. This world was shaped by the passionate debates of famous philosophers, the melodic compositions of celebrated musicians, and the innovative visions of groundbreaking artists. Every moment of her upbringing was marked by the complexities of a life at the intersection of creativity and intellect, allowing her to enjoy the intricacies between relationships and the myriad influences that shaped her identity. Her life was a complex web of music, art, and society in which she served simultaneously as muse, lover, and influential figure. In the salons of turn-of-the-century Vienna, she embodied the spirit of a modern woman who, above all, defied convention, creating a legacy as multifaceted as the art and ideas that now filled her home in New York and later reverberated through the centuries.

Today she wears a flowing black dress that speaks of both grief and fulfilment, falling gracefully over her figure – a striking contrast to the grey curls pinned atop her head. Her features tell a story of deep love, great loss and special creativity. An artist, philanthropist, and socialite, she was a rebel of her time, unyielding in her pursuits, and an influential figure in her circle.

In this sanctuary, she often reflected on the important stages of her life – her remarkable acquaintances, the moments of love and loss, and the deep motivations that had driven her existence. As soon as she reflected on her past, a bittersweet smile touched her lips; memories of joy and longing danced in her mind. With coffee in mind, she gracefully rises to fetch a cup from the living room, letting the rich aroma fill the air as she savours the first soothing sip.

Her gaze falls on her desk, where a fountain pen filled with her beloved lavender ink waits for her, eager to capture the delicate weave of her life. She has spent countless afternoons sorting through her documents – letters, notes, photographs – to write her memoirs, a labour of love that sheds light on her eventful life, marked above all by famous husbands, influential friends and all the passions that always fuelled her mind.

> I live on the third floor of my old house in the heart of New York, in two rooms. One bespeaks the power of words, the other that of music. I have two firms to administer, I say when I am asked why I keep so busy at my age.
>
> But I still have champagne for my friends when something calls for a celebration – and something always does. For I believe in joy as the sovereign remedy for sickness and the sole preservative of youth.
>
> From May to November my living room faces the green tops of great trees. Books line it from floor to ceiling: the German classics that Max Burckhard gave me as a girl, Werfel's works in all languages, the works of all the friends I have made over the years and of the great spirits I have admired over the centuries, from Plato to Bernard Shaw. Between the bookcases hang paintings by Oskar Kokoschka: my portrait, the colts of Tre Croci, and the six fans that remained after Walter Gropius burned the seventh in a jealous rage. And among the photographs in this room are two of my daughter Anna's portrait heads of Schönberg and Franz Werfel.
>
> My bedroom contains my desk, which is never clean, and my piano, all of my music, and in the corner a steel safe with the manuscripts of Mahler, Bruckner and others. On the mantel and on the walls I have the exquisitely carved baroque figures I brought back from Vienna in 1947. One of the pictures in this room looks slightly incongruous: it is

> Ludwig Bemelmans' scene of his novel, *Now I Lay Me Down to Sleep*, which he brought me after Werfels' death. There are the photographs of my children, and there is a drawing of Thomas Mann's head, which he gave me on one of my birthdays. And there are my father's paintings of the Dalmatian coast and the Austrian mountains, and of the Vienna Woods.
>
> Someone asked me what I loved most in my rooms. Everything, I had to answer. For these two rooms, if one looks carefully, hold all my life.
>
> My life was beautiful. God gave me to know the works of genius in our time before they left the hands of their creators.
>
> And if for a while I was able to hold the stirrups of these horse-men of light, my being has been justified and blessed. Everything, I feel, is simultaneous. Time does not pass. My father's death is as alive in me as Gustav Mahler's, or as Manon's, or Franz Werfel's. There is to me no past apart from the present, but, as the poet has written, there is a land of the living and a land of the dead, and the bridge is love.[1]

Since her childhood, her life had been closely intertwined with high society, with the salons of Vienna buzzing with conversations between revolutionary artists, radical thinkers and famous musicians. Growing up and surrounded by the intellectual giants and creative visionaries of her time, she absorbed their revolutionary ideas and artistic philosophies, which flowed around her like a stream and profoundly shaped her worldview.

This immersion in a very special world sparked her passion for the arts and awakened in her a deep appreciation for the transformative power of creativity.

Influenced by the dynamic exchanges in these circles, she quickly learned to navigate complex relationships and developed a keen understanding of social dynamics. The marriages she later entered into were not mere connections; they were alliances that bound her even more closely to influential figures and gave her access to a wider range of artistic expression and social impact. Each of these connections deepened her determination to make a significant contribution to the cultural fabric of her time and urged her to pursue her own artistic ambitions while encouraging the creative endeavours of those around her. These encounters ignited her passion for art and culture and also cemented her status as a major player in the cultural renaissance of her time.

But right now, she leaned back in her chair. The warmth of the cup enveloped her, offering her a moment of comfort. Ready to delve into the pages, she prepared to explore the interwoven narratives that had shaped her journey – this sanctuary of memories, dreams, and her relentless search for identity.

She owned a charming four-storey building just a ten-minute walk from Central Park, where she had four apartments for herself. She had taken care to ensure that each room reflected a facet of her life. One served as a drawing room for friends, while another became her retreat for solitude and study. Upstairs, in the two additional apartments, lived her former domestic staff and guests who were lucky enough to be invited by her.

As soon as this woman, known as Alma Mahler-Werfel, entered a room, heads turned toward her. Her magnetic presence and charismatic aura provided an electric charge at every meeting. A true femme fatale, she simultaneously aroused fascination, admiration and love, enchanting those around her in a matter of moments.

At just 19 years old, with her clear skin, enigmatic smile, lustrous flowing hair and piercing blue eyes, Alma was often hailed as 'the most beautiful girl in Vienna'. Over the years, many men sought her favour and courted her attentions, drawn by her magnetic presence and enigmatic charm. Yet few ever truly captured her heart, remaining on the periphery of her complex emotional world. Alma moved through her social circles with both allure and guarded independence, navigating her relationships on her own terms.

Her personality was as changeable as the city itself; one moment she was the imposing 'Grande Dame' – regal and commanding – the next she radiated a serene warmth that revealed the gentle femininity of a true Viennese woman. This duality made it difficult for even her harshest critics to dislike her. Some compared her to a demigod, worshipped by admirers who brought her gifts, while others despised her.

Her life was a constant interplay between public adoration and private reflection. But behind her confident exterior and enchanting beauty lay a deeply introspective mind attuned to the mysteries of life and death. When the music and applause had long since died down, in moments of solitude, she would reflect on the transience of time and be haunted by memories of the people she had lost. Yet these reflections did not diminish her vitality; rather, they enhanced it, giving her presence a melancholy depth. As if she were carrying the weight of history on her delicate shoulders.

Even in her later years, Alma Mahler-Werfel's connection to the great artists of her time remained unshakable. Her rooms, filled with relics of a living past – manuscripts, paintings and letters from her closest companions – became a sanctuary of creativity. These relics spoke not only of a bygone era, but of a spirit that still influenced the present. Each of her steps was a dance between memory and renewal, a testament to a life lived to the full, embracing both the beauty and tragedy of existence.

Throughout her life, Alma embodied the spirit of a true Renaissance woman – celebrated, criticised, and often polarising. Born into a privileged, cultured family in the Austro-Hungarian Empire, she was a muse who enchanted great artists and sparked countless creative souls. Her legacy, marked by complex relationships with prominent figures, reflected a remarkable journey of love, artistry and ambition. To this day her spirit lives on and resonates through the art she created, the lives she touched, and the people she empowered and mentored – those she inspired not only through love, but also through her guidance and vision.

This is Alma's story…

Chapter 1

Alma's Childhood – Attentive and Born into an Artistic Family

On the day Jakob Emil Schindler married his wife Anna Sofie von Bergen, everything was already in the making. Anna Sofie – the 21-year-old daughter of a Hamburg brewery family that had lost its entire fortune in 1871 – had come to Vienna to complete her studies in music and theatre at the Conservatory. There, she honed her skills as a soprano; as a soubrette, she focused particularly on the comic genre. On 4 February 1879, the day of their wedding, Anna was already three months pregnant with their first child. Although the couple could not have been happier, their marriage began in cramped conditions.

At 37, Jakob Emil Schindler came from a long line of cotton spinning-mill operator manufacturers rooted in the village of Fischamend in Lower Austria since the seventeenth century, but he was heavily burdened by debt. In Vienna's charming 4th district, Wieden, Jakob Emil shared a small bachelor apartment on Mayerhofgasse with his 20-year-old colleague, Julius Viktor Berger.

Though an artist by trade, Jakob Emil was also a dreamer. Nevertheless, originally meant to pursue a military career, he had entered the Vienna Academy of Fine Arts in 1860 and became a student of Albert Zimmermann. Zimmermann hailed from the southeastern corner of Saxony, situated in the border triangle of Germany, Poland and the Czech Republic. Renowned as a master of heroic-historical landscape painting, he often selected motifs for his magnificently stylised landscapes from the majestic mountain scenery. His works frequently featured biblical figures, and he also created nature portraits that captured the essence of the outdoors with a poetic play of light. He became a very good teacher and mentor to Jakob Emil Schindler.

Over the years, Jakob Emil Schindler travelled to Italy, Dalmatia, France and Holland, drawing inspiration from fellow artists. His keen eye for new motifs appealed to the wealthy nobility, who eagerly supported him. Over time, he became known throughout the Habsburg Empire as the most famous Austrian landscape painter of his era, celebrated for his detailed oil paintings.

Upon her arrival in Vienna, Anna Sofie had quickly landed a role in a minor operetta, where her cheerfulness and beauty instantly captivated Jakob Emil. And now they were married. But with their marriage in the Church of the Holy Guardian Angels – today the *Paulanerkirche* – Anna's music career and Jakob Emil's occasional stints as a tenor in the *Künstlerhaus Theatre* were now over. However, their union seemed to be a particularly happy one.

Anna approached every extravagance that Jakob Emil indulged in with wisdom and common sense. She managed the household with routine and diligence, caring for friends, guests, students, and beneficiaries who increasingly visited them as her husband's fame grew. Among the most frequent guests were Jakob Emil's elegant, white-haired mother Maria Anna, and Carl Moll – an aspiring artist with a keen business acumen. He held a special place as a favourite student and assistant to his instructor.

Carl Moll had attended private schools but faced challenges that kept him away from classes for years due to temporary anaemia. He later pursued his artistic education at the Academy of Fine Arts starting in 1879, eventually studying under Emil Jakob Schindler, with whom he built a close relationship. In this school of 'seeing', Moll created light-flooded landscape paintings of romantic naturalism, alongside architectural studies, still lifes, and interiors. The growth of his artistic ability and the influence of Schindler shaped his career. During this time, Carl Moll deepened his bond with the whole family, becoming an integral part of their artistic circle and household.

It was on a sunny Sunday, 31 August 1879, with a mild 19°C, that Anna and her beloved husband, Jakob Emil, welcomed a little girl into the world. They named her Alma Margaretha Maria Schindler. On one hand, Jakob Emil was enchanted by the little girl, but on the other, he was suddenly plagued by self-doubt. He questioned whether he was the right person for a small family and if his modest income would allow him to support them in the cramped apartment he shared with his artist friend. In his diary at the time, he wrote:

> I tell Anna that I love her, but I don't feel anything about it yet. It is possible, even probable, that this will change; it has been different at

> times. When I think about it carefully, I know that my circumstances are to blame for this unnatural lovelessness.[1]

Jakob Emil Schindler increasingly suffered with self-doubt, blaming himself for not being able to offer his family more – especially more comfort. That winter, he fell ill with diphtheria, a throat infection; he survived, but was left with paralysis for the rest of his life. His doctors sent him to East Frisia in Germany for treatment, where the climate helped him recover wonderfully.

To the outside world, Anna von Bergen-Schindler appeared to be the most loyal of wives and a devoted mother, showering her daughter with love and care. However, beneath this façade lay a tumultuous reality, as Anna struggled to reconcile her public persona with her private life, torn between her responsibilities and her own desires. And so, during Jakob Emil's absence, she began an affair with Julius Viktor Berger, the man with whom they shared their apartment.

When Jakob Emil returned from East Frisia, Anna informed him that she was pregnant again. She tried to cleverly cover up the affair, but Jakob Emil became suspicious, knowing he had not been in Vienna during the month the child was conceived. Nevertheless, he concealed his feelings and, without protest, accepted little Margarethe Julie, born on 16 August 1880, as his daughter.

February of the following year marked a significant milestone for Jakob Emil: he received the prestigious Reichel Artist Prize, along with prize money of 1,500 guilders (equivalent to £20,036, €23,500 or $26,654 today). This award finally provided Jakob Emil with the opportunity to pay off his debts and move his family to a much larger apartment in another district at Mariahilfer Straße 37.

Like many musicians and artists, Jakob Emil taught his most promising students to support his family. In the autumn of 1881, the 21-year-old Carl Moll approached him, seeking his guidance as a mentor. Jakob Emil gladly accepted, bringing Carl along on family holidays to Bad Goisern in the Gmunden district of Salzkammergut. He also took Carl on study trips to Lundenburg in the South Moravian Region of the Czech Republic and to Weißenkirchen in der Wachau, a town in the Krems-Land district of Lower Austria.

Before long Carl Moll became an integral part of the family. While he greatly admired his teacher, his admiration soon extended to Anna. It wasn't long before they, too, became lovers, living in constant fear that Jakob Emil might eventually grow suspicious.

In the German language, there are two forms of addressing others: the familiar *DU* (you), used for close relationships, and the formal *Sie*, reserved for more polite and distant interactions. The word *Duzen* refers to using *du* and first names, typically with family, children, or close friends, while *Siezen* means addressing someone with *Sie* and titles like *Herr* (Mr) or *Frau* (Mrs). In contrast to English, where only 'you' is used, the German language differentiates based on the level of familiarity.

Officially, Carl Moll and Anna von Bergen-Schindler addressed each other formally, observing the social norm of *Siezen*. However, in their private correspondence, they often switched to the informal *Duzen*. Anna affectionately called him 'dear Mollchen', while Carl wooed her with poems and flowers, referring to her as his 'mistress'. Alma, still a young girl at the time, grew up in an atmosphere charged with suppressed feelings and dishonesty. Though too young to fully grasp the depth of the deception, children often possess a keen instinct for insincerity, and Alma could sense the tension between her mother and Carl.

Alma Mahler-Werfel's upbringing was marked by a profound contrast between the public and private spheres of her family life. While she may not have directly documented her thoughts about her mother's liaison with Carl Moll, children often have an instinct for the unspoken; they absorb the emotional undercurrents around them. Alma's childish innocence might have shielded her from the full extent of her mother's infidelities, yet the insincerity and tension within the household could not escape her notice. This duplicity may have fostered a sense of mistrust in relationships, shaping Alma's views on love and commitment as she navigated her own romantic entanglements later in life.

The influence of her mother's secret affair, coupled with the façade of familial loyalty, may have left Alma grappling with conflicting emotions – admiration for her mother's strength, alongside a sense of betrayal from the hidden truths that coloured their lives. This inner turmoil undoubtedly contributed to the depth and complexity found in Alma's own artistic expressions, echoing the struggles of love, loss, and the quest for authenticity in a world rife with pretence.

Presumably, Alma – who later always saw herself as a true 'father's daughter' (wholly aligned, both emotionally and artistically, with her father) felt a profound emotional bond with him. In contrast to the tensions and deceit that marked her mother's liaison with Carl Moll, Alma found in her father a sense of warmth and stability. Jakob Emil's artistic spirit and the emotional depth likely resonated with Alma, providing her with a model of authenticity that was otherwise lacking in her family life. This bond may have fostered in Alma a longing for genuine emotional expression, reinforcing her complex feelings about love, fidelity, and the artistry that intertwined their lives.

Alma would later describe Carl Moll as lacking both intelligence and talent:

> Carl Moll, my father's eternal student, moved from one apprenticeship to another, often pursuing a variety of eclectic opportunities, much to the detriment of his modest abilities. He vividly described his first impression of our home: 'A moderately large room, with abundant light flooding through the windows from afar, an 18th-century hall cupboard, and in a huge armchair, a beautiful old lady with silver-white sidelocks, two children – one brown-haired and the other blonde – reading fairy tales. Schindler's mother with her grandchildren.'[2]

While Anna took on the responsibility of educating their two daughters very strictly, Jakob Emil fostered an environment rich in imagination and love for Alma and Margarethe. As time went on, it became increasingly evident that Alma was emerging as his favourite daughter, his 'little princess'.

Jakob Emil was a dedicated artist, and after some time, he achieved material prosperity that inspired him to find a country house where his family could spend their summer holidays. In the winter of 1884, he unexpectedly came across Plankenberg Castle, a historic site located near the Lower Austrian town of Tulln. Over the centuries, the castle has served as a residence for numerous renowned and noble figures, as well as a reformatory for nobles and a convalescent home for workers. Jakob Emil was extremely enthusiastic about the simple three-storey palace and the expansive park that adjoined it, nestled among the foothills of the Vienna Woods and surrounded by extensive vineyards. He rented the property for 300 guilders per year, and although the park was neglected and the palace's interior required thorough cleaning and restoration, the family was able to move happily into their new home in the spring of 1885.

Alma and her sister Margarethe spent large parts of their childhood in this picturesque Austrian El Dorado. They played in the park and set up private rooms for their dolls in the jasmine arbours; their laughter and singing echoed through the gardens. Alma always relished the company of her family and friends in the countryside, though she found herself somewhat indifferent to the charms of nature. The vibrant pulse of city life captivated her far more than the quiet demands of rural living. Their home was never without animals – cats and dogs, especially Irish Setters – and while Alma could certainly appreciate the picturesque beauty of the surrounding countryside, she preferred to observe it from the comfort of a well-trodden path or the window of a car. The rustic simplicity of country life simply did not appeal to her. Her father, however, was a man of contrasting sensibilities. He held a deep appreciation for the verdant meadows and sprawling forests near Vienna, and his taste for luxury was unapologetic – much to the dismay of his wife, Anna, who was left to juggle the household finances both in Vienna and Lower Austria, often feeling overwhelmed by the strain of their limited means.

Emil Jakob developed a particularly close bond with his eldest daughter, Alma, perhaps because he instinctively felt that she would always remain loyal to him, unlike others in his life. Alma sat with him in his studio for hours, mesmerised by the way colours danced across the canvas under his skilled hands. She cherished these moments in Lower Austria, often reflecting on them with a sense of wonder:

> From Carl Moll's sayings, you can see that I lived like a princess in the most beautiful nature. My father became the discoverer of this very nature. To know Austria's landscapes, you only need to see my father's paintings … then you will understand them.[3]

In those tranquil hours, she felt enveloped by the vibrant essence of the countryside, as if each brushstroke captured not just the scenery, but the very spirit of the place. Her father's art transformed the mundane into the extraordinary, revealing the hidden beauty of the meadows and forests that surrounded them. Alma's admiration for him deepened with each masterpiece, as she saw how passionately he engaged with the world around him, drawing inspiration from every hue and shadow. The paintings became portals for her, transporting her into a realm where nature and artistry converged. She found joy in the simplicity of the moments spent in his studio, a safe haven where her dreams of creativity began to take shape, illuminated by the vibrant colours of her father's work and the profound love that connected them.

Alma's father was profoundly musical, possessing a beautiful tenor voice that rendered Schumann's songs with grace. His conversations were captivating, filled with insight and depth that mesmerised those around him. While she was sitting with him, captivated by the revealing hand that guided the brush across the canvas, she dreamed not just of wealth for its own sake, but of a life that could nurture creativity:

> I wanted to pave the way for creative people. I envisioned a grand garden in Italy, filled with white studios where inspiration could blossom. That was the life I longed for, a space where art and beauty flourished in harmony.[4]

When Alma and her sister Margarethe Julie (known as Gretl), were old enough to read, Jakob Emil took his two daughters aside and told them about *Faust*: 'This is the most beautiful book in the world. Read it and keep it,' he advised them. This, however, led to an argument with his wife, who thought it irresponsible to expose such a book to little girls. In their household, Jakob Emil clearly took on the role of the artistic and musical teacher, while Anna assumed the thankless task of strict governess.

While their father withdrew to paint, their mother would force them to study. Unfortunately, her teaching methods were far from effective: she once demanded that Alma and Gretl learn their multiplication tables in a single day. The effort was so taxing on Anna that she developed a throat problem from the constant screaming and had to seek medical treatment that evening. Instead of studying arithmetic with her mother, Alma preferred to play on a piano that her father had given her.

Alma was only 8 years old when her family set out on a journey lasting several months from Dalmatia to Greece. Crown Prince Rudolf, son of Emperor Franz Joseph I, had commissioned Jakob Emil to create certain ink and watercolour drawings of popular coastal locations. This project, aptly named 'The Austro-Hungarian Monarchy in Words and Pictures', provided the impetus for their travels. A prepaid order enabled Jakob Emil to cover the costs for his family, along with Carl Moll and a maid, allowing them to embark on this artistic adventure together.

In November 1887, they all travelled by ship from Trieste to Dubrovnik. Alma's excitement bubbled over as they explored the port city and its stunning surroundings, each new sight igniting her imagination. The coastal landscape, with its vibrant colours and enchanting vistas, became a source of inspiration for her budding creativity. As winter settled in, they moved on to Corfu, where they would spend the remainder of the season.

During their time in Corfu, Alma experienced the joys of childhood amid the beauty of the island. While her father immersed himself in his artistic work, she often wandered through the lush gardens, dreaming of the grand spaces she envisioned for herself. She later reflected: 'We had a piano brought from Corfu, and here I began composing and annotating at the age of 9. As I was the only musician in the house, I was able to discover what was mine without being challenged.'[5]

This first big trip awakened in Alma a lifelong desire for foreign countries, but she was happiest when she could stay at home and play the piano. Here she first began to feel how much music meant to her. The warm Mediterranean sun and fragrant flowers filled her days with wonder, contrasting sharply with her mother's insistence on maintaining discipline.

In March of the following year, the Schindlers returned to Dubrovnik, soaking in the last of the coastal charm before beginning their journey back to Vienna in May via Opatija. Each stop along the way added to Alma's treasure trove of memories and dreams, reinforcing her desire to cultivate a life steeped in art and creativity.

This journey, commissioned by the Austrian Crown Prince, suddenly made Jakob Emil Schindler famous. His artistic talent blossomed, earning him recognition as one of the leading painters of the Austro-Hungarian Monarchy. His work caught the attention of esteemed institutions, and by 1887, he became an honorary member of the Academy of Fine Arts in Vienna, followed closely by a similar accolade from the Munich Academy. His accolades continued to grow: in 1888, he was awarded the Silver State Medal, and by 1891, the Gold State Medal followed suit, culminating in a prestigious Large Gold Medal in Berlin.

The pinnacle of his career came in 1892 when he showcased a selection of his latest works at the *Künstlerhaus* in Vienna, a historic exhibition hall and cultural institution founded in 1861 that has long served as a hub for contemporary art, showcasing the works of leading Austrian artists and fostering artistic innovation. The exhibition of Jakob Emil Schindler's latest works in this famous and respected hall not only solidified his reputation but also marked a turning point in his financial success, drawing art enthusiasts and collectors eager to witness the brilliance of his artistry.

In the summer of 1892, the Schindler family set out for a long-awaited trip to the North Frisian island of Sylt, accompanied by Carl Moll and his family. It was a much-anticipated pleasure trip for Jakob Emil, who had finally settled his debts. Just before this trip, he had been a guest of his friend, Prince Regent Luitpold of Bavaria, in Munich. Luitpold delighted in taking his guests under a concealed waterfall, causing laughter and chaos as they tumbled about in surprise. However, the joviality had taken a toll on Jakob Emil; the jarring impact of the water had triggered his longstanding appendicitis.

Despite the severity of his condition, Jakob Emil travelled to Hamburg and then onward to Sylt. On 4 August 1892, the family arrived in Westerland and settled into the holiday rooms of the Knudsen house. The atmosphere was buoyant as they enjoyed the beach and took leisurely walks. But as the days passed, Carl Moll noticed that his mentor was increasingly in pain. The local spa doctor was at a loss, prompting Carl to reach out to the renowned surgeon, Professor Friedrich von Esmarch, in Kiel, who dispatched an assistant to Sylt. Tragically, it was already too late.

During the afternoon, while Alma and her sister Gretl enjoyed a little trip, feeling very grown up in a restaurant, Carl Moll's brother rushed in, urgency etched on his face. 'You need to come with me, quickly,' he urged. In that moment, Alma felt an undeniable certainty wash over her. 'I knew in my heart that Papa was dead,' she later recalled. It was 2 pm on 9 August 1892, just five days after their arrival on the largest German island in the North Sea, where her father always felt safe and blessed.

Anna and Carl Moll sought to shield Alma and Gretl from the shock of seeing their deceased father. They placed the two girls in the room adjacent to where Jakob Emil Schindler's body lay in an open coffin. Anna Schindler forbade her daughters from having a final glimpse of their father. However, the clever girls found a way. When no one was watching, they slipped into the room and approached the coffin, yearning for one last look at the man they had loved.

They stood before the coffin for what felt like an eternity. The man they gazed upon, who had always seemed large and powerful in their eyes, now appeared small and frail. For little Alma, the death of her beloved father was a terrible blow, and one that she had difficulty coping with. She had lost not only her childhood hero but also an important orientation in her life. When she looked at his lifeless body, she realised how significant he had been to her and always would be, as he had given her a perspective and understanding of art and culture like no other. By the next day, the newspapers were filled with tributes to Jakob Emil Schindler, even including a report in the *Sylter Kurzeitung* detailing his passing. An autopsy later revealed the truth for the family: Jakob Emil had indeed died of appendicitis.

After Schindler's death, arrangements were made for his body to be transported from Sylt to Austria during a time when cholera outbreaks and quarantine measures were being reported in Hamburg. To ensure the journey was discreet, his coffin was cleverly concealed in a piano case, allowing it to cross the border unnoticed. The difficulties of this transport, coupled with the harsh, stormy conditions of the Nordic seas, left a profound mark on Alma's memories.

The notion of death at sea weighed heavily on her, overshadowing her sense of pride that her father had a gold-embroidered bar towel placed on his coffin (a symbol of his status and respect in the artistic community) when he was laid to rest on 14 August 1892. Her mother's frantic cries and almost hysterical mourning disrupted Alma's reverie, complicating the grief that engulfed their family during this harrowing time.

Alma's life unfolded during a time when women's roles were rigidly defined, often relegating them to the background in the art world. With her father's death, she lost not only a guiding figure but also the nurturing environment that had supported her budding talent. The shadow of loss was ever-present in Alma's life. The family was forced to abandon Plankenberg Castle due to financial difficulties, leading them to live year-round on Mariahilfer Straße.

As early as 1894, just two years after his passing, the legacy of Jakob Emil Schindler was honoured in Vienna when the prestigious Schindlergasse (formerly known as Bergsteiggasse) in the noble Währing district was named in his honour, serving as a lasting tribute to the artist, whose profound influence on the cultural landscape of the city continued to resonate long after his death.

Then, on 14 October 1895, a striking monument to Jakob Emil Schindler, made by Edmund Helmer, was unveiled in his honour at the beautiful Stadtpark in the centre of Vienna. The monument depicted him sitting casually in a wide frock coat, one foot resting on a shawl, embodying the dignified impression he had left on those around him. This tribute placed him also in esteemed company, near the monuments of great composers like Franz Schubert, Wolfgang Amadeus Mozart and Johann Strauss. Alma was present at the unveiling of the monument and described the event as 'the marble revival of my father's features and the finally coming to the fore of my little person.'[6]

She vividly recalled the overwhelming emotions of the day, admitting that she almost fainted when the ceremony finally came to an end. But for as long as she lived, Alma would sent postcards featuring a picture of her father's monument to friends, always emphasising that this statue truly reflected her father's character.

Meanwhile, Anna Schindler and Carl Moll continued their tumultuous relationship, marrying in Vienna on 3 November 1895. While Moll felt it was his duty to provide for the family of his late mentor, 16-year-old Alma struggled to accept this union, perceiving it as a betrayal of her father's memory. This tension created a difficult dynamic between her and Carl Moll. Alma viewed him as a usurper of her father's legacy.

In a society that often undervalued women's contributions to the arts, Alma struggled with a deep sense of isolation. Although she had inherited her father's passion for music and art, the constraints of her circumstances pushed her to the margins. While coping with her grief and the complexities of her new family dynamic, Alma was determined to honour her father's memory by pursuing her own artistic path.

After their honeymoon visit to Anna's parents in Hamburg, Carl Moll purchased a house in the district of Wieden, in Theresianumgasse 6, where his atelier became a buzzing central hub for Vienna's leading artists, writers and architects, including Josef Hoffmann and Koloman Moser, both pioneers of the Wiener Werkstätte movement. This movement, one of the longest-lived design movements of the twentieth century, played a key role in the development of modernism, standing at the crossroads between traditional craftsmanship and an avant-garde aesthetic.

Together with his new wife, Anna, and his two stepdaughters, Alma and Gretl, Carl Moll settled into this beautiful home, designed by architect Julius Mayreder, which featured a spacious studio and a large garden, providing an inspiring environment for both artistic pursuits and family life. It was in this rich, artistic atmosphere that Alma began to develop her own tastes and perspectives. The atelier hosted long evenings filled with music, lively debates, and sumptuous dinners, drawing Alma into a world of creativity and intellectual exchange.

Although still young, Alma quickly grew to enjoy the steady flow of visitors in her parents' house. Seated with her parents in the atelier, she eagerly soaked up conversations about modern architecture and art. These experiences within Carl Moll's atelier, surrounded by Vienna's cultural elite, helped shape Alma's artistic sensibilities and prepared her for the influential role she would later play in cultural circles.

Despite her undeniable talent, she faced an uphill battle to carve out a place for herself in a world that seemed intent on limiting her potential. Alma's youth completely separated her from her surroundings; they became indifferent to her, and music became everything.

But conversely, Carl Moll's influence began to dominate. He tried to test his educational skills on Alma, which above all aroused an enormous hatred in her towards him, because he was anything but Alma's guiding star. Despite this tension, Alma's engagement with such a wide array of artistic forms – from music to architecture and theatre – would transform her into a complex, multifaceted figure sought after by some of the greatest minds of the twentieth century.

Even three years after the death of Alma's beloved father, she found herself navigating a sense of loss that profoundly influenced her artistic journey. The pivotal moment came when she began to immerse herself more deeply in music, using it both as a means of expression and a way to process the grief of losing her father. This not only marked the end of her childhood hero but also catalysed her deeper engagement with her own musical path.

Now her initial childish fascination with music had passed, Alma committed herself to serious piano study, using music as an emotional outlet. She poured her grief and longing into her playing, channelling her feelings into the keys as a way to honour her father's legacy. With each practice session, she discovered the transformative power of music, allowing it to fill the void left by her father's passing.

As Alma honed her skills, she began to embrace the role of a serious musician, driven by her desire to carve out her own identity in the world of art. This dedication to music became a vital part of her life, providing both solace and purpose during a tumultuous time.

Alma was less enchanted by the operas and operettas that captivated her mother, and instead found herself drawn to the music of her father's favourite composer, Robert Schumann. While her mother hoped to instil a love for the theatrical and light-hearted works that filled Vienna's cultural salons, Alma's focus lay elsewhere. Her private piano teachers tried to guide her toward popular repertoire, but she stubbornly refused to follow their lead. She approached music with a fierce independence, preferring to explore her own musical passions on her terms.

The truth was that Alma was constantly driven by a singular passion: she wanted to play for her father. She dismissed her teacher's ideas, and no school dared to impose strict rules on her, allowing the young girl to immerse herself entirely in music during her free time. Alma also quickly mastered the art of reading music, demonstrating an exceptional talent for improvisation that set her apart from her peers. She was even once invited to participate in a school concert, but the experience left such a mark on her that she vowed never to do it again.

Alma studied counterpoint under the guidance of the blind organist Josef Labor, who introduced her to essential literature and the operas of Richard Wagner. She fell in love with Wagner's works, immersing herself in his music by playing and singing her way through his operas. However, this passion came at a cost; her voice, a rich mezzo-soprano, began to suffer as a result. Despite this, Alma acquired an impressive knowledge of Wagner's music, demonstrating a deep dedication to her craft.

In 1894, at the age of 15, Alma was sent to a prestigious boarding school in Vienna. This marked a pivotal moment in her life, as she left the comfort of her home and family to begin her formal education, which further immersed her in the cultural atmosphere of the city. While her education encompassed both music and the arts, she often felt that the environment was restrictive. Many sources indicate that she struggled with the school's rigid structure and yearned to focus on her musical pursuits, especially in the wake of her father's death. This tension between attending school and feeling confined by it profoundly influenced her development as an artist, fuelling her desire to break free and embrace her true passions.

As Alma herself expressed: 'I lived in a musical miracle that invented itself. Following my father's example, I now sought the helpers of my youth in older men from our artistic circle.'[7]

Alma was confident she could handle things at home without any help, but as Carl Moll's influence grew stronger, she resented the way her mother now fawned over the man who once lingered on the sidelines of their family life. In her youth, Alma often felt like an outsider, yet whenever she stepped into a room, she became the undeniable centre of attention. It was not just her striking beauty; there was a magnetic aura about her, a quiet power that drew people in and commanded admiration wherever she went.

Later in life, when asked about the attention she received, Alma would laugh it off, claiming she felt awkward, even unattractive. Her modesty belied the reality, as her presence left a lasting impression on everyone around her. She still wore the dresses her mother carefully stitched together, but inside she quietly envied the rich girls, effortlessly flaunting their luxurious gowns from the city's finest boutiques.

Unfortunately, Alma's hearing was compromised early on, a lingering effect of a severe bout of measles during her childhood. At first, the impairment was barely noticeable, but as she matured, it became an undeniable restriction, quietly affecting various aspects of her daily life. Despite this, her musical acuity remained miraculously unaffected, allowing her to pursue her passion for music undeterred. In social circles, however, she devised an ingenious strategy to mask her condition – what she referred to in private as her Alma method. With laser-like focus, she would tune in to the words of the person closest to her, listening with such unwavering attention that the speaker often believed they were the only soul in the room. Her ability to create this illusion of undivided attention had an intoxicating effect, especially on the men who populated the artistic salons she frequented. They, of course, mistook her attentiveness for genuine affection or admiration, flattered to be the apparent centre of her world.

Alma's beauty and magnetic presence already made her the object of fascination, but her method of engagement only heightened the allure. Men flocked to her, captivated by what they saw as her intense interest, though not all of them had genuine intentions. Despite the constant attention, Alma was deeply self-conscious about her hearing loss, and though she appeared confident and charming in smaller gatherings, she was often plagued by anxiety at the thought of her weakness being exposed. This led her to avoid larger social occasions, where the noise and multitude of conversations would have made her vulnerability painfully apparent. Even though her charm and intelligence never wavered, the fear of discovery haunted her, adding a layer of complexity to her interactions with Vienna's elite.

Then there was this man: Max Burckhard. Not just the director of the Vienna Burgtheater, Burckhard was a cultural force – an eccentric whirlwind of intelligence and creativity, melding the roles of critic, author, scholar and stage director into one captivating persona. His unique blend of brilliance and idiosyncrasy set him apart, making him a magnet for the artistic elite of Vienna. A close friend of Emil Jakob Schindler, Burckhard possessed an acute sense of empathy and a profound understanding of the delicate emotions swirling around Alma after her father's passing.

Recognising her need for guidance and mentorship, he boldly took it upon himself to step into this pivotal role. One fateful day, he found himself at her family's door, offering his support with an air of determination. 'Let me help her find her voice,' he seemed to say, as he extended a lifeline of encouragement and inspiration. Anna and Carl Moll agreed.

And so it happened that Burckhard introduced Alma to the philosophical depths of Friedrich Nietzsche, immersing her in the dense tapestry of his ideas at a time when she could only grasp the surface. Yet he was patient and perceptive, guiding her through the complexities of the text, teasing out its meanings like an experienced conductor drawing forth the nuances from an orchestra.

But his mentorship did not stop at philosophy. Burckhard understood the transformative power of the theatre. With an artist's intuition, he began sending her letters, which often contained tickets to the theatre, eagerly anticipating the performances that would further ignite her passion for the stage. After each show, they would engage in spirited discussions about the plays and their adaptations, enabling her to grasp the nuances between the written word and its theatrical interpretation. These tickets to the most riveting performances were priceless, each invitation an opportunity for exploration and discovery. Following these outings, he engaged Alma in spirited discussions, unravelling the magic of the stage. He taught her to see beyond the script, to appreciate the delicate interplay between the written word and its vibrant theatrical execution.

Through his mentorship, Alma's world expanded, filling with rich narratives and bold characters that ignited her imagination. In the intimate setting of their conversations, she began to weave her own artistic aspirations, inspired by the rich tapestry of life unfolding around her. Burckhard's influence became the catalyst for her artistic evolution, propelling her into a realm where her talents could flourish and her voice could resonate.

With a keen eye for talent and a deep appreciation for beauty, Burckhard introduced Alma to the exquisite poetry of Rainer Maria Rilke, whose evocative verses captivated her imagination. Rilke's words, rich with emotion and complexity, opened new avenues of thought for Alma, helping her navigate her feelings and aspirations. Through these literary explorations, she found a voice that resonated with her inner self, allowing her to express the tumult of her young heart.

While their connection was undeniably profound, there is no indication that Burckhard sought a romantic relationship with the enchanting young Alma. At 42, he was struck by her remarkable beauty and artistic potential, yet his intentions remained rooted in friendship and guidance. This relationship was one of mutual respect; Burckhard's admiration for Alma was a testament to his belief in her talent and future.

For Alma, the friendship with Burckhard represented a sanctuary during her formative years. The exchanges with him were not merely academic; they were infused with Burckhard's wisdom and enthusiasm, leaving Alma inspired and hungry for more knowledge.

Years later, as she reminisced about this influential period, Alma would fondly recall the warmth of Burckhard's mentorship. His attention, thoughtful and sincere, provided her with the validation she craved during her tumultuous teenage years. Burckhard's unwavering belief in her potential illuminated her path, nurturing her creative spirit and solidifying her identity as an artist. In her innocent way, she cherished the bond they shared, recognising that his guidance had not only shaped her artistic pursuits but had also played a crucial role in helping her navigate the complexities of her young life. Through Burckhardt, Alma entered a vibrant world of theatre, poetry and philosophical enquiry – one that would forever enrich her artistic sensibilities and prepare her for the challenges and triumphs that lay ahead.

During this time – in early 1895 – as the Burgtheater director visited her stepfather's atelier, Alma was still 15 years old. She recalled those visits with a mix of nostalgia and longing, feeling both inspired and isolated by the cultural world that surrounded her. At this age, Alma also embarked on her first literary adventure, curating her very own personal library. She recalled later:

> I began to venture out on my own, grateful that my mother was often too preoccupied to notice. Concealed beneath an old cape, I would sneak children's books to a quaint antiquarian bookshop, where I would indulge in the works of Dehmel, Bierbaum, Rilke, and Liliencron. Before long, I had amassed a delightful collection of books, a secret treasure trove that no one was allowed to discover.[8]

For Christmas, Burckhard orchestrated a delightful surprise that would become a cherished memory for Alma. Two of his devoted servants arrived at the Moll family residence, their arms laden with large, elegantly crafted laundry baskets filled to the brim with an exquisite collection of classic literature. Each volume was a masterpiece in its finest edition, bound in rich leather and adorned with gilded lettering that gleamed invitingly in the soft glow of the winter light.

This thoughtful and extravagant gesture did more than merely fill her home with books; it ignited a fervent passion for literature within Alma that would flourish in the years to come. In the midst of the turbulence that accompanied her mother's new marriage, these books became her sanctuary – a world where she could escape, explore and dream. They provided solace and a sense of belonging that she longed for, inviting her into the lives and thoughts of the great literary minds.

Under Burckhard's mentorship, Alma began to curate a vast and impressive library, a treasure trove of knowledge and imagination that reflected her evolving identity. Each book was a new adventure, each page turned was a step further into the labyrinth of her own mind, a source of immense pride that symbolised her independence and intellectual curiosity. She relished the idea of having her own collection, a private universe where she could immerse herself in the words of the greats and weave her aspirations into the narratives that surrounded her.

Alma often reflected on her intellectual journey, stating:

> My immediate surroundings felt so dull, and I had to seek out knowledge on my own. Max Burckhard was the first to truly engage with my restless mind. We were both wild Nietzscheans – he, a revolutionary modernist in spirit. Yet, I found him lacking as a man; his stoic reluctance often weighed heavily on me. While we generally agreed, that very consensus bored me over time.
>
> The peculiar dynamics between us – his strong masculinity, which initially irked me – led to our most colourful exchanges. I often deflected his intensity with a sharp quip, which only fuelled his frustration. He playfully dubbed me a 'coker' and would vanish from my life for stretches, only to return and reignite the same cycle of banter and tension.[9]

As Alma's library grew, so did her sense of independence. Each book was a key, unlocking doors to ideas and feelings that shaped the contours of her restless mind. The mentorship of men like Burckhard had opened new worlds for her, but Alma was always on the verge of wanting more – more intensity, more stimulation, more understanding of the unexplored territory that was her heart and mind. Burckhard had introduced her to the intellectual currents of her time, but Alma knew life had other things in store for her. If literature had ignited her soul, love and art would soon ignite her deepest passions, driving her to explore new realms of creativity and emotion.

Chapter 2

From Glamour Girl to Muse – Courted by Famous Admirers

As the months passed, Alma's intellectual appetite grew insatiable. She moved through Vienna's salons and theatres, always in search of conversations that could challenge and excite her. The mentorship of Max Burckhard had sharpened her mind and refined her taste, yet there was still a restlessness within her that no amount of literature or intellectual debate could fully satisfy. Alma felt on the brink of something greater – a transformation she could not yet define, but one she felt was coming.

Vienna itself was changing, too. The city was alive with artistic tension, as old traditions clashed with modern visions. Alma was drawn to this energy, sensing that the world she longed for, one of passion and avant-garde expression, was about to reveal itself.

It was not long before fate brought Alma into the orbit of Vienna's most progressive minds, a shift that would change not only the city's art scene but also her own life. These pivotal discussions took place in the home of her stepfather, Carl Moll, who played a central role in introducing Alma to this vibrant intellectual circle. What began as informal conversations in his home soon transformed into a defining movement for both Vienna's culture and Alma's personal journey. Among the men who gathered at Moll's house, there was one who would play a particularly important role in Alma's story.

In April 1897, Carl Moll hosted a gathering of a group of seventeen prominent artists from Vienna's burgeoning avant-garde scene at his home, including architects Josef Hoffmann and Koloman Moser, sculptor Franz Metzner and the painter Gustav Klimt. Over the course of the evening, these men discussed how to move forward artistically in a city where their visions were clashing with the conservatism of the *Künstlerhaus*. The Association of Fine Artists of Vienna, once a symbol of unity in the arts, had become increasingly divided. The management's unwillingness to embrace new, international art movements, had led to frustration and disappointment.

Carl Moll and his peers – visibly disillusioned with the outdated, historicist ideals that prevailed at the *Künstlerhaus* – decided that it was time for a radical change. Their inspiration came from the Munich Secession, a Bavarian group that had already taken a stand against the state art establishment and its rigid exhibition policies. That evening, they laid the foundation for a new association, one that would champion modernism and break from the confines of tradition: the Vienna Secession.

Vienna at the turn of the twentieth century was a vibrant cultural hub, where art, politics and gossip intermingled. Coffee houses served as essential gathering places for intellectuals, artists, and politicians, fostering discussions that shaped public opinion. While the atmosphere was often dominated by men, these venues provided a platform for exchanging ideas and opinions on both cultural and political matters. Gustav Klimt's work, particularly his symbolism and sensual themes, resonated deeply in this context, reflecting the societal changes and cultural tensions of the era.

Every man in Vienna had his favourite coffee house, a second home where he was known by name, and where the morning newspaper was laid out on his table as soon as he arrived. These Viennese coffee houses served as extensions of their apartments, places where friendships were forged and where time seemed to stretch into the quiet hum of conversation. Hours could be spent in these havens, surrounded by the city's intellectuals, artists, and thinkers.

And when young men gathered, sipping their coffee and exchanging ideas, there was often one name that came up – Alma Schindler. She was not merely a passing beauty; she was the kind of woman whose name lingered in the air, whose image stayed in men's minds long after their conversations were over. With her long, dark brown hair cascading over her shoulders and a tall, elegant frame draped in the voluminous skirts of the time, she was the embodiment of Viennese grace. Her pronounced chin gave her a distinctive allure, and her corseted waist accentuated her long legs, making her appear even taller and slimmer. But it was not just her beauty that captivated; it was the steel-blue intensity of her eyes – those expressive eyes that could pierce through the smoke-filled rooms of Vienna's coffee houses and hold a man's gaze longer than the finest cup of coffee.

Alma Schindler was not merely a passive observer of Vienna's vibrant art scene – she was an active participant, cultivating her own artistic talents. Alongside her music studies, she took lessons in drawing and sculpture, even earning a few awards for her small clay sculptures. Her stepfather Carl Moll, who was now a leading figure in the Viennese Secession, provided her with access to the avant-garde artists of the time. In his studio, Alma mingled with creative minds, soaking up the intellectual atmosphere that surrounded her.

Yet, as much as she explored visual arts, her heart truly belonged to music. When the Secession was founded, Alma was deeply intertwined with its ideals and vision. This group of artists sought to break away from the traditional norms of the established art world, creating a bold and independent movement. And Alma was captivated by their innovative ideas, regularly attending their meetings and identifying closely with their grand ambitions. It was exactly during this historical period that Gustav Klimt entered her life.

Klimt was elected president of the Vienna Secession, with Carl Moll as his vice president. It was a decisive moment in the history of Viennese art and a bold step toward modernism, and Alma, now 17, found herself in the midst of these transformative conversations. Alma was more than a beautiful presence at these gatherings, her youth and beauty making her an object of admiration, but it was her sharp mind and musical talent that truly set her apart. As the men came and went from Moll's house, planning the future of Viennese art, Klimt – already one of the most celebrated artists of his time – noticed her immediately. In Alma, Klimt saw not just a striking young woman, but someone whose intellect and potential rivalled the men in their circle. His admiration for her grew, and soon their connection became undeniable. Reflecting on these encounters, Alma would later write:

> I met Gustav Klimt at one of these meetings when I was very young. He was the most talented of them all, thirty-five years old, in the fullness of his strength, beautiful in every sense and already famous. His beauty and my fresh youth, his genius, my talents, our shared deep musicality, put us on the same note.[1]

Alma's vibrant presence and commitment to the arts did not go unnoticed by Klimt either. In fact, he was taken by Alma, more so than by any other society lady he had ever encountered. In a letter to Carl Moll, Klimt recalled their first meeting:

> I knew Alma from before, that is, I saw her once briefly at the unveiling of the Schindler monument, I liked her – just as we painters like a beautiful child – I saw her again in Carl Moll's house, I found her more beautiful than ever.[2]

Throughout 1898 Alma frequently crossed paths with Klimt, who was at the peak of his artistic prowess. At a tarot party hosted by Carl Moll, Alma noted, 'After dinner, we took black coffee in the studio, danced, and sang. Klimt is such a dear man,' capturing the light-hearted atmosphere they shared. Later that month, she described another meeting at a lunch with Gustav Klimt, Eugen Alfred Richard Jettel, Gotthard Kuehl, Julius Mayreder, and Olga Krieghammer. 'On the way home,' she wrote, 'Klimt said: I tell you what, let's change places, and sat down opposite me.' She found his playful banter both charming and frustrating, remarking, 'He is such a dear fellow. I was actually a little annoyed with him because he said I was spoilt by too much attention, conceited, and superficial.'

In Alma, Klimt recognised not just a pretty face but a vibrant spirit whose potential and talents could rival even the artistic men of their circle. This evolving connection was built over shared laughter and spirited conversations long before the beginning of a romantic connection between them. Whether at dance sessions, exhibitions, or intimate gatherings, their paths intertwined, deepening a bond that would profoundly influence both their lives.

Gustav Klimt indeed embodied the spirit of his time in Vienna, both in his artistic vision and personal style. His distinctive appearance, characterised by a full beard and elegantly tailored suits paired with flowing robes, when he was in his atelier to paint beautiful women, contributed to his enigmatic persona, setting him apart as a notable figure in Vienna's art scene.

Though Alma's journal entries from this time suggest a certain ambivalence towards Klimt, they also reveal a deep fascination. In fact, she was both fascinated and cautious. Just a few months later, on Wednesday, 19 October 1898, she wrote about a question that her very attentive sister Gretl had asked her:

> The epoch of Pettenkofen, Waldmüller, Makart, and Papa won't be surpassed easily. Not by a thousand Engelharts and Klimts. Tempora Mutantur. This afternoon, Gretl asked me, if I could swear, that I wasn't in love with Klimt. I said, 'Yes, I can.' That amounted to a solemn oath. I really can, and pride myself in being able to say so.[3]

Despite her assertions, Alma's diary entries hint at the allure Klimt held for her. Just a few weeks later, on Saturday, 12 November 1898, she wrote of her joy at speaking with Klimt: 'Today I actually spoke to Klimt. I'm so happy … I consider him handsome and brilliant … I made a few insinuations. He must have understood them.'[4]

In November 1898, Alma's diaries captured a playful exchange that revealed the growing bond between her and Klimt. She noted with a hint of amusement:

> Before dinner, Klimt looked at the seating plan, was offended that he wasn't sitting next to me, and asked if that was my doing. I denied it, telling him he'd be sitting opposite me. He asked me to be sure not to forget it, and he still keeps the place-cards with 'Alma and Klimt' in his wallet.[5]

This innocent banter underscored the chemistry developing between them, and Alma mused about Klimt's fondness for her, saying: 'I firmly believe that Klimt is fond of me. If he is not, then he is the greatest sham on earth.'[6] She longed for the chance to speak openly with him, writing: 'If only I could speak frankly with him. I hope the opportunity will arise one day. He's such a nice man.'[7]

Through her words, it was clear that beneath the light-heartedness lay a deeper yearning for connection, hinting at the affection that was quietly blossoming between them.

As the artistic circles buzzed in 1898, anticipation for the IVth Exhibition of the Association of Visual Artists of Austria Secession grew, with the official opening set for March 1899. Alma's diaries reveal the vibrant interactions that paved the way for this landmark event. On 25 March 1898 she wrote: 'At 12:00 we went to the Gartenbau-Gesellschaft to look at the pictures. I won the bet with Klimt. He was delightful. And we – he, I, and the critic Vincenti – went up to look for Thomas.'

She expressed hope, writing: 'I hope and believe that the exhibition will be well received. It's simply beautiful.'

In March 1899, during the IVth Exhibition, Gustav Klimt personally escorted Alma to one of his masterpieces, *Schubert at the Piano*. Klimt's attention made the moment all the more significant, and Alma, already captivated by both the artist and his work, considered it 'the best painting in the Secession'. It was in these moments, standing beside Klimt, that Alma felt the thrill of being part of Vienna's artistic pulse, a world where creativity and passion intertwined. On 12 March, a momentous day unfolded for Alma as she sat down to lunch at her mother's house. Reflecting on the ordinary setting, she noted the late afternoon light filtering through the windows, unaware that her life was about to change. In her diary, Alma recounted the atmosphere that day:

> Lunch with Hancke at Mama Moll's, and now it's late afternoon, early evening. A day I shall never forget. Mama Moll drove off to Hietzing, and we stayed behind with Mama. All of a sudden she said: 'Children, come over here and sit down; I have something to tell you. Have you noticed anything? No? Before long, you'll be getting a little brother or sister.'[8]

Alma's heart raced, and tears streamed down her face. Meanwhile, her sister Gretl laughed, but the news plunged Alma into a whirlwind of emotions. She imagined the future flashing before her eyes – her mother's family ties, the looming presence of the new sibling, and the turmoil it would bring. 'I'd never experienced anything of the kind; I almost fainted.' The news would eventually herald the arrival of little Maria, born on 9 August 1899, forever altering the dynamics of the Moll household.

These diary entries offer a fascinating window into Alma's inner world. Her complicated emotions towards Klimt reflect her burgeoning identity as a woman navigating Vienna's art circles, where intellect, beauty, and passion intertwined.

On 22 March 1899, the Moll family embarked on a much-anticipated trip to Italy, leaving from the Vienna Westbahnhof railway station. While they dreamed of art, culture and adventure, Alma's first impression of the city of Venice was far from favourable. She described the scene in her diaries: 'Snow flurries, water without end, grey on grey. Rain, snow, black gondolas cold and damp. You can scarcely imagine anything more depressing.'[9]

Despite the city's famed beauty, the reality was a stark contrast to her expectations. On a positive note, Alma confessed to flirting madly on this trip, igniting sparks of excitement along the way. She recounted charming encounters with a young Frenchman on the train from Vienna to Venice, followed by an Englishman upon arrival, and later, several handsome Italians. In her defence, she playfully noted that their youthful charm and the tiresome journey only whetted her appetite for adventure. Alma's flirtations with young men from various countries during her Italy trip reflect her youthful exuberance and desire for freedom. At just 20 years old, she was confidently exploring her identity and engaging with the romantic possibilities around her. These interactions showcase her emerging independence and willingness to embrace life's adventures, painting a vivid picture of a young woman stepping into her own, both personally and artistically. Her lively interactions reflected her zest for life and love amid the backdrop of Italy's allure.

From Venice, they travelled to Florence, a city that resonated deeply with Alma's artistic sensibilities. The exquisite architecture and rich history inspired her, and she found herself drawn to the masterpieces housed within the renowned Palazzo Pitti. It was here that she wrote fondly in her diary, reflecting on the profound impact of the art she encountered.

As they continued their journey, they ventured to Naples and she wrote in her diary: 'Naples is wonderful … and today there is such an atmosphere, such a scent in the hills, all around.'[10]

Then the family travelled to the stunning island of Capri, each destination enhancing Alma's passion for both art and life: '"*Vedere Napoli e voi murire*", the saying goes – in that case they should also say "Die, see Capri, and return to life." It is a veritable paradise here.'[11]

Finally, the Moll family arrived in Rome where, on 16 April, they attended a Vatican Mass, an experience that left a lasting impression on Alma's heart and spirit. Especially while she was flirting with a young man. Before the family left Rome, Alma once told Gustav Klimt about a strange dream she'd had: in it, he and Emilie Flöge – the sister of his sister-in-law and a celebrated fashion designer who would later become his muse – had a falling-out out. Alma said she briefly woke up, but then returned to the same dream. Klimt listened and asked her: 'And would that have improved the situation? There is plenty of room for improvement.' He looked at her thoughtfully and continued: 'I see. So you are thinking of getting married. I'd always thought you weren't like the other young ladies. So, you are contemplating marriage, are you?'

On 20 April Alma, her mother and Carl Moll visited Pisa, marvelling at the Leaning Tower before returning to Florence on 22 April. At Moll's suggestion, Gustav Klimt – who had remained in Rome – joined them in Florence on 25 April to continue the journey with the family. The air was electric, charged with unspoken emotions and artistic fervour. Alma, aware of Klimt's long-standing attachment to Emilie Flöge (who was married to his brother Ernst), was both intrigued and wary of his presence.

Their travels brought them to Genoa on Saturday, 29 April. The train rattled along the tracks, but for Alma, the journey to Genoa was charged with anticipation. Klimt, seated in a different compartment, was visibly frustrated at being separated from her. It was later that evening – in the quiet solitude of her hotel room – that the moment happened. Alma captured it vividly in her diary, her words filled with the intensity of her emotions and the significance of their connection.

> Left for Genoa at midday, changing trains at Pisa. Kl. was sitting in a different compartment and was furious at not being with us any longer. In Genoa, towards evening, I was standing alone in my room. Kl. came in:
>
> 'Are you on your own?'
>
> 'Yes.'
>
> And before I realised it, he'd taken me in his arms and kissed me. It only lasted a tenth of a second, for we heard a noise in the room next door. We went downstairs. That moment will remain indelibly imprinted on my mind. Halfway down, I turned round and went back up again. It's indescribable: to be kissed for the first time in my life, and that by the only person in the whole world that I love.
>
> In the evening we went for another stroll. When I came downstairs, Kl. Came up to me and whispered:
>
> 'Alma, my Alma.'

> Mama could not understand what was ailing me – I looked so dreadful.[12]

As their relationship deepened in Italy, Gustav Klimt became increasingly direct in his intentions. On 1 May, Alma wrote in her diary:

> This morning I bought Klimt the blouses. He held me and kissed me again. We were both terribly agitated. Later, he stood by me and said: There is only one thing for it, complete physical union. I staggered and had to steady myself on the banister. At 6:00 in Verona, he returned to the subject again: If two people are united, their happiness is assured. God won't object either.[13]

Despite Gustav Klimt's fervent advances, Alma remained resolute. That evening, she confronted him on the stairs, asking for a copy of the German play *Faust*, by Johann Wolfgang von Goethe, and firmly stating: 'From this book, I take my code of behaviour: do no favours without a ring on your finger. There's nobody I am more fond of than you. But that – not yet.'[14]

This exchange reveals not only Alma's self-respect and strength but also her clear moral compass, shaped by literature and societal expectations. As their time in Venice drew to a close, Alma was in a state of emotional turmoil, torn between passion and propriety.

Despite her intense feelings for Klimt, Alma maintained her dignity and resolve. She was clever, evading his advances with a witty, but firm retort. Alma clung to her guiding principle, a mantra she held dear: 'Do no favours without a ring on your finger.'[15]

Her ability to outwit his advances with intellect and resolve demonstrated not just strength, but a commitment to preserving her dignity in a world full of temptation.

Nevertheless, their interactions grew increasingly complicated, with Klimt oscillating between guilt and desire. On 4 May, after she had given him a photograph of herself, Alma recalled Klimt's reaction: 'So you've bought two copies of yourself ... both for you.'

Their moment was brief, but it carried a heavy undercurrent of longing. However, when Klimt expressed shame, whispering to Alma, 'What have

I done? I am so ashamed,' her response was decisive: 'Give me back my picture.' This conversation shows not only Alma's emotional intelligence, but also her awareness of the power dynamic between them. Even as Klimt pursued her relentlessly, she held firm to her values.

The situation came to a head when Carl Moll intervened, recognising the gossip their relationship had stirred. As Carl said, 'I know everything now. I know about your relationship. I find it disrespectful. Tomorrow, you, Alma, should tell him that the affair has got to end.' Alma's relationship with Klimt, once filled with artistic admiration, had turned into a public spectacle. She reflected on their last conversations, where Klimt continued to plead: 'Alma, don't be angry. I couldn't sleep all night. I felt as if I'd killed a little child.' This dramatic statement illustrates Klimt's emotional manipulation, as he tried to hold on to Alma through guilt.

Their farewell was symbolic, with Klimt beseeching her: 'Keep up a place in your heart for me, Alma, just a tiny one.' Yet, Alma's strength prevailed. Her ultimate decision to end their romantic entanglement – despite the deep connection – was a testament to her maturity. As they parted, Klimt looked at her one final time, and Alma recorded her overwhelming sorrow: 'All of a sudden, I could feel just what – suddenly – I had lost.'[16]

Klimt's departure marked the end of a pivotal chapter in Alma's life. Her diary reveals not only the depth of her feelings but also her remarkable resolve. The emotional struggle she endured and her decision to prioritise her independence over passion would define much of Alma's journey in the years to come. As she watched Klimt's train leave the station, she knew her life was now taking a different course – one that would be defined by her decisions, not the desires of others.

On 10 May, the family returned to Vienna and Alma captured her feelings in her diary:

> Vienna. How sad I am to be here. The closer I am to him, geographically, the greater the distance in my mind. Letter and sheet music from Oberstetter. On the letter he wrote: 'To my brilliant friend Alma – a souvenir of H.E. Oberstetter'. A most attractive ballad. Saw Mahler.[17]

For young women at the end of the nineteenth century, the challenges of growing up were vastly different from those faced in the twenty-first century.

Regular schooling, a high school education, or even university studies were almost unimaginable for girls of that time. Despite Alma's remarkable musical talent, she never progressed beyond the status of gifted amateur. This was not merely due to a lack of personal seriousness or discipline; rather, it stemmed from the absence of role models and societal limitations imposed on women's ambitions.

Nineteen-year-old Alma believed that women could not be geniuses, 'because they lack intellectual depth and philosophical education'. Her thoughts reflected the societal restrictions of her time, where women were often denied access to advanced education and intellectual development. Frustrated by these limitations, Alma expressed a deep yearning for a different reality, at one point confessing in her writings: 'Oh – just to be a man.'[18]

Every Tuesday for over five years, Alma made her way to Josef Labor's studio at Rosengasse 4. An esteemed Austrian pianist, organist, and composer of the late Romantic era, Labor was more than just a teacher, he was a fatherly figure who mentored many musical luminaries. Yet, as Alma progressed, she began to feel the constraints of his teachings. It became clear to her that if she wished to transcend her status as an amateur, she needed a more rigorous instructor.

In the spring of 1900, at the premiere of Alexander von Zemlinsky's cantata *Frühlingsbegräbnis* in the opulent Golden Hall of the Vienna Musikverein, the illustrious concert hall that had opened in 1870 and would become the home of the Vienna Philharmonic orchestra, Alma encountered the very composer who would change her life. Under Zemlinsky's expert guidance, she began to compose several songs, and what started as a student-teacher relationship gradually blossomed into a passionate love affair. Zemlinsky dedicated his *Five Songs Op. 7*, composed in 1899, to Alma, and she found herself captivated not only by his music but also by his sharp intellect and intense charisma.

Despite his less-than-classical appearance – described by Alma in her diary as 'a caricature – chinless, small, with bulging eyes and too crazy conducting' – Zemlinsky was completely enamoured with her, proclaiming, 'I want you – with every atom of my feelings!' In reality, Zemlinsky was of short stature, with a delicate frame that belied his powerful musical presence. He had small lips, a prominent nose, and large ears that stood out, giving him a distinctive profile. His expressive brown hair framed a face that was not conventionally handsome, but his intense gaze and passionate demeanour conveyed a magnetic charisma that drew people to him despite his unassuming appearance.

During their first meeting, the conversation quickly took a lively turn. They began discussing Schmedes with such fervour that Zemlinsky quipped, 'If we can think of someone with whom neither of us has a bone to pick, we'll down a glass of punch in their honour.' After some contemplation, they both settled on Gustav Mahler as their subject of admiration. They raised their glasses, toasting to him, and Alma expressed her deep veneration for Mahler, sharing her longing to meet him. Zemlinsky encouraged her, saying, 'Why don't you make an appointment with him at his office? He'd be terribly pleased.'[19] Alma replied with enthusiasm, 'I wouldn't mind if I did!' They were revelling in their shared admiration when suddenly, Dr Johann Nepomuk Fuchs, who was Zemlinsky's composition teacher at the Vienna Conservatoire from 1891–3, interjected, 'Mahler is a scoundrel.' The unexpected remark left both of them flabbergasted, momentarily silencing the excitement in the room.

About two weeks later, Alma encountered Zemlinsky again at a soirée, where her initial impression of him remained less than flattering – she thought him rather unremarkable. Yet, that evening sparked an intense conversation about Richard Wagner's *Tristan und Isolde*, a work Alma passionately adored. To her surprise, when she shared this admiration with Zemlinsky, his enthusiasm transformed her perception and so she noted in her diary that he suddenly appeared 'really pretty'. This newfound connection ignited a desire within Alma; she yearned to learn from Zemlinsky, wishing fervently that her mother would permit it.

Zemlinsky, recognising her talent and ambition, welcomed Alma into his circle of students that winter. Until then, he encouraged her to send him her compositions, hoping to assess her abilities more accurately. However, when he received her three songs, he was taken aback – his response was one of disappointment. 'There are so many mistakes in the three songs that my head is buzzing,' he wrote, underscoring his strict nature as a teacher. Zemlinsky's uncompromising standards were clear; he sought to guide Alma toward excellence, expecting nothing less from her.

He criticised his student's ideas, making it clear to Alma that her superficiality was hindering her success as a composer. Zemlinsky's strict approach caused a real storm of indignation in the Moll family household. Alma's mother, in particular, could not understand why her daughter would 'voluntarily give herself up to such an ugly person'. However, as the summer months passed, her perspective began to shift. Alma came to regard Zemlinsky as 'one of the nicest people I know'. Despite the tension in her home, she continued to take lessons with him, fully aware that he might never completely understand the choices she made. However, he soon expressed his disapproval of her 'superficial social life', demanding a choice: 'Either you compose or you go to social gatherings – one of the two. But choose what is closer to you.'

April 1901 marked a turning point in Alma's relationship with Zemlinsky. Their connection, which had until then been limited to the world of music, with her piano lessons, and the world of intellectual discourse, had suddenly begun to develop into something far more intense, but Alma was never one to shy away from facing her feelings head on. Her diary entries from this period capture her inner turmoil and her growing affection for the composer with raw, unbiased honesty. On 13 April, she wrote:

> I don't know – if someone asked me, 'Are you in love with Z.?' I wouldn't be embarrassed. I would definitely say yes. In fact, I have said this before – to Mie and Muhr, a few weeks ago. At the time, I simply said: I love – Z.[20]

Her openness is striking here, an openness that defies the social conventions of her time. Alma Schindler was, in fact, a very brave young woman, and she was not afraid to say what many of her friends might be reluctant to admit. She knew what she was feeling, and the intensity of her feelings was undeniable. 'Because I said it directly, no one believed me. That's how stupid people are. They understand innuendo more easily than the honest truth.'[21]

Even her frustration with those around her reflects a sense of isolation. Alma's inner world was rich and profound, and yet she felt misunderstood. In that moment, the simplicity of the truth was more scandalous than any subtle hint could ever be.

Then, just days later, on 18 April, the shifting dynamic between Alma and Zemlinsky escalated. Their relationship had crossed the threshold from the emotional to the physical, a moment she records in her diary with poignant imagery and emotional depth:

> With him, I am always the giver, the one who gives – and because I love him so deeply, I take advantage of my position. With outstretched arms, I want to shower him with golden flowers – until we reach the wall, that white wall that marks the point from which there is no return.[22]

In this passage, Alma's words flow like music, describing her desire not only to love, but to give completely, to envelop Zemlinsky in her affection. The metaphor of the white wall suggests the limits of their love, the barriers they may face but have not yet fully overcome. She reflects on the contrast between her former lover Gustav Klimt, and Alexander von Zemlinsky: 'With Klimt, I was always the one who got something from me. Why, I don't know. Does it have to do with outward appearance and the joy of victory that comes with it?'[23]

This comparison reveals Alma's need for a relationship in which she can be the active participant, the one who gives as much as she receives. With Zemlinsky, she finally feels able to take on that role. Then, in a tender moment of vulnerability, she recounts the event that cements their bond: 'He took me in his arms and kissed me. I kissed Z. yesterday too. I took his hands. I hugged him. He kept saying, "You have no idea what this means to me."'[24]

In that moment, Zemlinsky's reaction shows that their love was not one-sided. Alma's affection was reciprocated, and the kiss symbolised more than a physical act; it was the culmination of the deep emotional connection they had built over months. The intimacy between them had finally manifested in a way that could no longer be denied.

As April progressed, Alma's creative spirit suddenly blossomed alongside her budding relationship with Zemlinsky. On 19 April, she wrote in her diary: 'Worked well between Wednesday and today. I've written a whole rondo. Look forward to my dearest one.'[25]

Here, her enthusiasm for her work reflects not only her artistic drive, but also the anticipation of seeing Zemlinsky again. For Alma, music was a language that went beyond words, a means of expressing the feelings that she sometimes found difficult to put into words. When they finally met, the atmosphere was filled with a certain familiar intimacy: 'He came in, hand in hand with Maria. We sat down at the piano. I took his hand, we kissed, but I was already much calmer than the first time.'[26]

The calm she describes represents a change in her emotional world. The initial whirlwind of passion had turned into a deeper understanding, but beneath that calm lay a tumult of deep longing and great doubt. 'I don't think I'm capable of reaching the depths of truly intense passion. The ecstasy has evaporated so quickly.'[27]

These words reveal Alma's self-reflection. The passion of their initial connection was still there, but tempered by the realities of their relationship. The fiery desire that had once consumed her gave way to a more complex, thoughtful love. 'I still desperately long for him – but it's not as wild as in the first week.'[28]

Alma's admission of her longing shows the duality of love – its ability to inspire and yet leave one vulnerable. She longed for Zemlinsky's presence, but recognised the need for something deeper than just physical attraction. 'Anyway, it's his own fault – his constant questions have cooled my fire. He claims everything about me is hollow, not sincere or real.'[29]

The tension between them is palpable in these lines. Zemlinsky's probing nature challenged Alma, forcing her to confront aspects of herself that she might have preferred to avoid. His insight into her emotional world was both a gift and a burden, making her question her own authenticity.

'And he's not entirely wrong. He's so perceptive that he senses it. He keeps asking, "Tell me, do you really mean that?" And every time I answer, "Would

I say that otherwise?"'[30]

This exchange underscores the vulnerability of their relationship. Zemlinsky's relentless questioning not only reveals his deep interest in her, but also reflects his own insecurities. Alma's answers, tinged with a hint of defensiveness, reveal her struggle to maintain her identity while navigating the complexities of love.

As April continued to unfold, Alma found herself caught in a whirlwind of emotions that intensified with each passing day. In her diary entry of 25 April 1901, she expressed her honest thoughts about Zemlinsky:

> I've been considering whether to marry Z. With him, I believe I would regain my mental equilibrium. I feel so at one with him that I simply can't imagine ever leaving him … Hence when he's not with me, I feel my music trickling away. Should I write and tell him? Muhr's money is all well and good – but what so oaf! Yesterday Z. told me he would send me the ballet – I should be the first to hear it. How unbelievably happy that makes me! His love elates me! If only I'd met him earlier. I would have become an entirely different person.[31]

Yet, as much as she cherished these feelings, Alma could not ignore the thrill of attention from other suitors. The kisses exchanged with other men tantalised her with a sense of freedom, making her question the constraints of a devoted relationship. Would a life with Zemlinsky. mean sacrificing her adventurous spirit?

The thrill of her love for Zemlinsky was undeniable, yet it often manifested as a tumultuous rollercoaster ride. On one hand, she was consumed by thoughts of him; he occupied her mind like a haunting melody that would not fade. On the other hand, she found herself inflicting pain on him, a pattern that both puzzled and troubled her.

In her moments of reflection, Alma could not help but confront her harsher feelings. She admitted to herself that she saw him as unattractive, even going so far as to tell him he was ugly. Later, on 2 November 1901, she wrote another entry that revealed the depth of her affection for him:

> Today too – all my thoughts are centred on this one person, this ugly, sweet little man. I knew it yesterday at Spitzer's – he came in, I took his hands, even that was a pleasant thought. Nothing about him is disagreeable, unappetising, I love everything about him.[32]

In her diary, she recorded the cruel truth: she could have easily attracted a hundred other men, if she wished. This acknowledgment of her power only deepened her internal conflict. Beneath the surface of her arrogance lay a profound vulnerability, one that made her realise that Zemlinsky was suffering from the very arrogance she wielded as a shield.

His sensitivity and emotional depth became apparent as he frequently pleaded with her not to play with his feelings. His words revealed a fragility that Alma had not anticipated; it was clear that her jests and barbs cut deeper than she intended. Each plea from Zemlinsky pierced her conscience, urging her to consider the weight of her actions and their impact on his heart.

Amid this emotional turmoil, the lack of understanding from her friends and family added another layer of complexity to her situation. Alma's mother, Anna, even threatened not to let her daughter's admirer into the house anymore. Friends and family could not comprehend her attachment to Zemlinsky, often dismissing it as a folly unworthy of her talents and ambitions. This disconnect left Alma feeling increasingly isolated, navigating the rocky terrain of her emotions without a solid support system. As she grappled with the dichotomy of her feelings – desire intertwined with disdain – Alma stood at a crossroads, unsure of how to reconcile her love for Zemlinsky with the expectations and judgments of those around her.

In the quiet moments of her day, when she was alone with her thoughts, Alma felt the weight of her choices pressing down on her. Love, she realised, was not merely a beautiful emotion; it was a complex web of connection, vulnerability, and sometimes, self-inflicted pain. As the days turned into weeks, she knew she would have to confront these truths, lest they consume her entirely.

But as the days turned into months, the pendulum of their relationship suddenly swung in the opposite direction. After nearly a year of enduring Alma's relentless humiliation, Zemlinsky found himself at a breaking point. The once intoxicating thrill of their romance had become overshadowed by her harsh words and dismissive attitudes. With a heavy heart, he put pen to paper at the end of May 1901, hoping to convey the turmoil that had begun to fester inside him. In his letter, he laid bare his feelings:

> Finally, my pride is starting to rebel a little, and I'm telling you what I've suppressed for a long time and what I've often wanted to say: 'My love, you emphasise so often, as often as you can, how ridiculously little I am and have, how much makes me unsuitable to belong to you. Do you have so much to give, so infinitely much, that other beggars are against it? Love for love, I know nothing else.'[33]

His words dripped with vulnerability, exposing the deep wounds Alma had unwittingly inflicted. He wrestled with the very essence of his identity, questioning whether he could ever be enough in her eyes.

Yet, beneath the weight of his heartache lay a profound appreciation for her beauty, an acknowledgment of the magnetic allure that had first drawn him to her. But as he pondered their future, he could not help but ask, 'And later? In twenty years?' The haunting question lingered in the air, suggesting that love alone would not be sufficient to sustain their connection. He was beginning to see that beauty fades, and what remains should be built on something deeper, something that transcends mere appearance.

Alma, however, remained oblivious to the guilt that churned within him. She failed to grasp the true significance of Zemlinsky's words, lost in her own world of self-absorption and fantasy. Her response was one of confusion; she couldn't comprehend the gravity of the situation or the depth of his emotional struggle.

In a second letter, Zemlinsky was forced to be even more explicit. He sought to clarify his feelings, emphasising that he did not expect 'beauty' from Alma as a prerequisite for their love. Rather, he longed for the simple, yet profound gifts of love and trust.

> I am going out more and more because I am richer inside. Yes, I am. You are smiling? What do you get from inner wealth? Do you think I don't have more than that? So I am terribly ugly? So let's say I thank God now that I am like this.

In his raw honesty, Zemlinsky expressed gratitude for the connections he had formed with women who had seen beyond his exterior. 'Thank God that there have been so many girls who have reached my soul through my ugliness and never said a word to me about it, so that I know that I am still a person who cannot be looked down upon, who has some value.'

Alma, in her own way, struggled to navigate the conflicting emotions that arose from Zemlinsky's heartfelt confessions. She often took refuge in girlish fantasies, staging her relationship with him like a play, carefully crafted for an audience. Yet beneath this performative facade lay a desperate yearning. On the one hand, she begged to be suffocated by his kisses, intoxicated by the passion he offered. But on the other hand, she was blinded by her own self-interest and insecurities, unable to see the reality of their relationship.

This theatrical performance of feelings obscured her vision, preventing her from recognising the truth: she had long since outgrown her friendship with Zemlinsky. The very intimacy that had once drawn them together was now strained by her inability to reciprocate the love and understanding he so desperately needed. As she flitted between fantasies and reality, Alma risked losing not only Zemlinsky but also a part of herself, trapped in a cycle of desire and disdain.

Alma Schindler was drawn to Alexander von Zemlinsky in every way but one, driving him to the brink of madness. And he envisioned a woman who would retreat from public life for him, but such an arrangement was out of the question for Alma, who cherished her independence and vibrant social existence.

Two days later, Zemlinsky took a moment to reflect on Alma's recent words and actions, trying to decipher the emotional labyrinth that defined their relationship. He found himself grappling with her conflicting declarations:

> How heartfelt you write: 'I want to be the mother of your children – if it were true! It is not! I keep thinking about whether I should even come out this week. Perhaps it is good if you don't see me for a while.'[34]

Her words echoed in his mind, a haunting reminder of her elusive nature. On one hand, she expressed a desire for closeness, for a future intertwined with his own; yet on the other, there was a chilling detachment, a retreat into the shadows of uncertainty. This duality bewildered him. Was she merely playing a game, revelling in the power she held over him, or did she genuinely fear the vulnerability that love demanded? The thought of losing her was almost unbearable, yet her insistence on distancing herself felt like a cruel jest.

As he penned his thoughts in response he recognised the depth of his longing, but also the painful truth: Alma was as unpredictable as the tides, drawing him in with the promise of affection only to leave him stranded on the shore of doubt. Each word she wrote was a puzzle piece that failed to fit into the picture he desperately tried to create of their future.

There was another side to Alma Schindler, however – one that has resurfaced repeatedly in articles and biographies: the topic of antisemitism. And it remains deeply paradoxical. Though she had several Jewish friends and claimed to love Zemlinsky, Alma occasionally indulged in wild, antisemitic outbursts. Many of these tirades feel contrived as though borrowed from the prejudices of others and repeated as her own – echoing the ambient rhetoric of fin-de-siècle Vienna. Such attitudes were, disturbingly, part of the prevailing social convention and class consciousness among the bourgeoisie.

Alma teased Zemlinsky about what she thought were his ugly features, saying she could easily have 'hundred others' to replace him. She also noted that to marry Zemlinsky would mean she would 'bring short, degenerate Jew-children into the world'.

As Alma navigated her relationships, she often wielded antisemitism as a tool of power. In the mind of Karl Lueger, she viewed a person's Jewish descent not only as a point of contempt, but also as an opportunity to assert her own Aryan superiority. This reflected her pronounced will to dominate and belittle those around her, particularly the men who admired her. Beneath her bravado lay a deep yearning for love – not in the physical sense, but a desire to be worshipped and exalted by her admirers. This insatiable need for validation overshadowed her ability to form genuine emotional connections, showcasing a complex interplay of affection and manipulation.

As the relationship grew strained, Zemlinsky visited Alma less and less. It was a rather tumultuous period in her young life. Emotionally adrift and increasingly disillusioned with Zemlinsky, Alma was unknowingly approaching a turning point – a fateful encounter in November 1901, one that would challenge her convictions, awaken new longings, and ultimately redefine her understanding of love, relationships and power.

Chapter 3

Alma's Foray into Music – A Composer's Journey with Gustav Mahler

As the leaves fell and the air grew crisp, Alma sensed that change was in the air. The approaching winter would not only usher in a new season, but also a new chapter in her life. Little did she know the fates were aligning for an encounter that would alter her path irrevocably. November would prove to be a decisive month for a turning point that would lead her to the man who would change her life forever. It happened during an autumn afternoon in November 1901; Alma was strolling with her friends along the Vienna Ringstraße when she suddenly encountered Emil Zuckerkandl and his wife Berta.

Emil Zuckerkandl, a renowned Austro-Hungarian anatomist and physical anthropologist, was known for his brilliant mind and infectious humour and he told Alma Schindler: 'Mahler will be coming one of these days. Would you like to be there too?' In fact, Emil was well aware of Alma's interest in the composer. Alma, however, became brusque and replied immediately with a firm 'no'. She had already avoided a meeting with Mahler that summer. Her reluctance was due to the stories she had been told by her acquaintances – including rumours of secret love affairs. But Emil Zuckerkandl was nothing if not persistent, countering her dismissal with a spirited: 'Nonsense. I want it.' Alma remained resolute and their conversation abruptly ended with nothing agreed upon.

However, fate had other ideas. Exactly one week later, Emil's dear wife Berta Zuckerkandl, the esteemed writer, journalist, critic, and salonnière, wrote to inform Alma that Gustav Mahler had postponed his visit to the following Sunday, a day reserved for the Zuckerkandls' reception. Berta wrote that she had invited notable figures, including Gustav Klimt and Max Burckhard, along with a request for Alma to join them. Caught in a tangle of emotions, Alma hesitated but ultimately agreed.

And so it happened. The Austro-Bohemian composer Gustav Mahler had been appointed director of the Vienna Court Opera in 1897, and Alma first met him in the autumn of 1901. She was 22 and he was 41. Alma wrote in her diaries that she 'went to the invitation with a sense of embarrassment'. Mahler had recently returned from Paris, where he had performed with the Philharmonic Orchestra at the Austrian Embassy. In Paris he had met Sophie Clémenceau, the sister-in-law of the prominent French statesman Georges Clémenceau, and sister of Berta Zuckerkandl. He had arranged to meet her again at the Zuckerkandl family home in Vienna.

However, as always, things turned out differently than expected. When Mahler entered the Zuckerkandl apartment, his gaze fell upon the young Alma Schindler. It was not merely her pretty face or her alluring figure that caught his attention; rather, it was her voice, which seemed to resonate in the air with a captivating energy. Seated at the table next to Gustav Klimt and Max Burckhard, the trio was enveloped in laughter and animated conversation, while Mahler watched them from the corner of his eye until he could resist it no longer; he turned to them and asked: 'Are we not allowed to laugh along?'

Just then, a new guest arrived, full of excitement from having attended the concert of Czech violinist Jan Kubelik. The guest enquired whether Alma had heard Kubelik's performances, and she replied dismissively, 'I'm not interested in solo concerts.' From the other end of the table, Mahler – having been drawn back into the conversation – chimed in, 'Me neither'.

After dinner, the discussion shifted to the topic of beauty. Mahler started by expressing his admiration for Socrates' head. Alma, quick to join the discourse, added that she also found the head of the musician Alexander von Zemlinsky beautiful. Mahler dismissed this as far-fetched. Alma's fighting spirit was ignited, and she began to philosophise passionately about Zemlinsky. She then asked Mahler why he had no interest in performing the Hofmannsthal ballet. 'Because I don't understand it,' he replied candidly. Seizing the opportunity, Alma offered, 'I want to explain the content and meaning to you.' Mahler's interest was piqued, leaning in towards Alma, he responded, 'I'm very curious'.

'But not until you explain the meaning of the *Bride of Korea* to me,' she teased, prompting a hearty laugh from Mahler. As Alma described in her diary on Thursday, 7 November 1901:

> He said he found it very good of me that I spoke of Alex with such a respect, and it was also a good sign for Alex that when you know him better, you get to like him…
>
> I must say, I liked him immensely – although he's dreadfully restless. He stormed about the room like a savage. The fellow is made entirely of oxygen. When you go near him, you get burnt. Tomorrow I shall tell Alex some of this.[1]

Mahler invited Alma, Mrs Sophie Clémenceau and Berta Zuckerkandl to the rehearsal of *The Tales of Hoffman* at the Opera the next morning, and the three women accepted. However, before they parted ways, Mahler turned to Alma with a curious intensity and asked where she lived, and if he could accompany her. She hesitated, feeling a flutter of nerves; despite her internal tumult, with a polite smile and steady voice she declined his advance.

Undeterred, Mahler sought her assurance that she would attend the dress rehearsal in the morning. 'Yes, yes, if I have done a good job,' she teased, echoing the kind of phrase often told to children in Vienna: you earn a reward by being brave and well behaved. A playful glint lit her eyes as she turned to leave. But as she left him, doubt crept in. Had she been misunderstood? Her shyness meant she was rarely, or never, herself among strangers, usually concealing her true feelings with boldness.

Alma's stepfather Carl Moll spoke at length with her about her new acquaintance with Mahler. He launched into one of his theatrical monologues, speaking almost as if addressing an audience, 'Yes, but I tell you …' The rest of the Moll family found this kind of grandstanding tiresome. Beneath the performance, though, Carl's concern was genuine – he worried about the significant age difference and sensed that Mahler's commanding personality could easily overpower Alma's more sensitive and impressionable nature. The image of his bright, independent stepdaughter becoming the submissive companion of a much older and already powerful man, was not the future Moll had imagined for her. Alma reflected on Mahler's earlier comments about Alexander von Zemlinsky, whom he had dismissed as 'restricted', and on the ballet, which he had called 'unperformable'. Harsh though they were, his opinions did not diminish her fascination with him. On the contrary, she was flattered by the attention Mahler had bestowed on her. With a sense of finality, she wrote: 'But I met Gustav Mahler, and my years of apprenticeship came to a sudden end to make way for another, difficult and decisive task.'[2] By 'apprenticeship', Alma seemed to mean the formative period of her life – her studies, her youthful romances, her development as a composer. Now, with Mahler, she sensed she was stepping into a new and far more complicated role, though what that role would demand of her remained to be seen.

The following morning, Friday, 8 November, Alma went to the home of Emil and Berta Zuckerkandl and then made her way to the Opera, accompanied by Berta and Sophie Clémenceau. Mahler greeted them warmly, guiding them through the corridors to the auditorium. Interestingly, Alma noted in her diary that she had to carry her coat the entire way, but in her *Memories* book, she suggests that Mahler was attentive enough to carry her coat for her.[3] Regardless, Alma was struck by Mahler's kindness and charm during the rehearsal – he made two trips to check on his guests, making sure they were comfortable and could see well. As he took his leave, he reminded her of her promise to return for the performance, adding with a half-smile: 'Fräulein, don't forget: a man's word is as good as his bond.'[4]

When asked later about his first impression of Alma Schindler, Mahler admitted:

> I didn't care for her at first; I thought she was just a doll. But then I realised she is also very perceptive. Maybe my initial impression stemmed from the fact that one doesn't normally expect such a good-looking girl to take anything seriously.[5]

It seemed that Alma's love for Alexander von Zemlinsky was gradually waning after her encounter with Gustav Mahler. On 12 November, she confided in her diary: 'At home, I worked, but with no inclination or desire – entirely devoid of inclination (and desire!). I can't even think of writing to Alex. I feel absolutely nothing for him.'[6]

A week later, during an outing to the Opera with her mother, Alma spotted Mahler at the director's box. At first he did not recognise her, but she could not help but stare at him. Suddenly, their eyes met, and he acknowledged her. During the break, as Alma and her mother made their way into the foyer,

Mahler appeared, greeting them warmly. Alma introduced her mother, and he invited them both to tea in his office: 'We talked about everything under the sun – he is fascinating, kind.'[7] Mahler knew that the Moll family lived in a house at the Hohe Warte in the 19th district, called Döbling, and so he told Anna Moll that he loved to walk there. As a result, Anna invited him to visit; he pushed the boundaries a little further: 'I'd be happy to do that, but when?' and then immediately added 'Soon'. Anna replied, 'You must decide on the day.' Mahler got up to check his repertoire book and the following Saturday was agreed upon for their next meeting. Before they left, in a flash of boldness, Alma declared that she wanted to be hired as a conductor at the Opera. Taken aback and amused, Mahler replied that while he was not in the habit of appointing conductors so spontaneously, he was already seriously intrigued by her talent – and, in truth, he would like her in any case. Whether he meant romantically, artistically, or both, his words hung in the air: 'We stared at each other, stared, stared.'[8]

Mahler and Alma parted ways, but both felt that something had come into their lives – a spark, an unspoken connection, unexpected and deeply stirring. Despite the briefness of their encounter, the intensity of their exchange lingered. On 20 November, Alma finally confessed in her diary: 'It is just too dreadful; I should be ashamed of myself … but Mahler's picture is engraved in my heart.'[9]

The once vibrant connection she had with Zemlinsky had already begun to fade – a change that only deepened as Alma found herself increasingly drawn to Mahler. During his next visit, Zemlinsky noticed the shift in her demeanour; his affectionate words were fewer, and he refrained from kissing her, presenting her instead with a letter he had written – the same letter from Chapter 2 – as a form of explanation.

By this point, several weeks had passed since Alma's first encounter with Mahler at the opera. Her emotions had begun to settle, and she had openly acknowledged the depth of her feelings for him. It was during this period of reflection that Alma found herself in a conversation with the Burgtheater director and long-time mentor Max Burckhard, who, as a keen observer of human nature, immediately sensed the shift in Alma's heart. He discerned the complexities of her feelings for Gustav Mahler, a reality that seemed to elude Alma herself. Burckhard, the connoisseur of life and people, instantly felt the full, eventful truth, the power of which neither Mahler nor Alma could measure. And he analysed it out loud: '[Mahler] was completely madly in love, the other evening.'

'I didn't notice anything,' Alma replied.

'Well, what will you do, if he proposes to you?'

'I will accept,' Alma said, very calmly. She remained unaware that, following a gathering at a social event, Mahler had accompanied Burckhard home. There, he had enquired about her, eager to know more about the woman who had captured his attention. Burckhard, astute as always, chose to withhold details from Mahler, simply stating, 'Anyone, who knows Miss Schindler, knows who she is, and the others should not know.'

The Saturday following their meeting at the Opera, Mahler arrived in Döbling as arranged and stayed the whole evening – much to the delight of Anna Moll, who invited him for her famous 'Paprikahendl' (paprika chicken) dinner, together with Max Burckhard. He walked with Alma to the local post office in Döbling to call his sister, informing her that he would be staying longer and that she need not prepare anything for him. As they walked together through the gently falling snow, a quiet intimacy began to settle between them. In this serene setting, Mahler began a conversation about marriage, expressing his desire to unite their lives. His words were more than a proposal; they marked a turning point in their relationship, one that had deepened from mutual admiration to something far more personal. Alma's heart raced as she realised the significance of his words, feeling both exhilarated and frightened by the possibility of a future with the man who had so profoundly captured her.

> It is not so easy to marry someone like me. I am completely free; I have to be. I cannot be tied down materially anywhere. My position in the Opera is precarious, subject to change from one day to the next.[10]

Without enquiring about Alma's feelings, he dictated to her – as she would later describe it – his will, his life's command. Alma responded thoughtfully: 'What you say is self-evident to me. Don't forget that I am the child of artists, have always lived among artists, and ultimately feel like an artist myself. I've never viewed these matters any differently.'[11]

Silence enveloped them as they walked, and the tension of their conversation lingered. Once back at the house, they soon made their way to Alma's room, as if drawn by an unspoken understanding. There, Mahler kissed her, deepening the intimacy between them. He then returned to the topic of marriage, with Alma listening intently, processing his words. He had made his decision regarding their future.

After some time, they returned downstairs to join the other guests. The discussion turned that evening to the Friedrich Schiller, the German playwright, poet, philosopher and historian, a topic familiar to Mahler, but one that Alma found less engaging. That evening made Alma realise that Mahler was the only man who had the power to shape her life, and his value and significance towered far above those of all the men she had known to that point. Alma was electrified by Mahler's presence in their house in Döbling:

> Mahler was here – I can think of nothing but him. He had to make a telephone call, and we walked to Döbling together. He told me how much he liked me. I didn't confess my feelings, though. We spoke of many things – not everything. A barrier divides us – Alex. I am not certain, but I believe I love him (Mahler).[12]

This newfound admiration filled her with a sense of excitement and trepidation: 'A battle is raging within me. Alex against Mahler. My trust for Mahler is boundless.'[13]

Alma grappled again with her deep emotions, torn between the familiar comforts of Alexander von Zemlinsky and the captivating allure of Gustav Mahler.

On 1 December, excitement stirred within her as she immersed herself in Mahler's music, noting: 'Sang through the Mahler songs all morning. I am beginning to like some of them. It's pretty dour stuff.'[14] The complexity of his compositions began to resonate more and more with Alma, mirroring her own tumultuous feelings between the two men.

The following day, the tension that had been building between Alma and Mahler reached a climax:

> This afternoon: Mahler. He told me that he loved me – we kissed each other. My lips are sealed. His caresses are tender and agreeable, igniting something deep within me. If only I knew – him or the other. I must gradually get Alex out of my mind. I'm terribly sorry. If it weren't for all that, I would have gotten engaged today.[15]

The weight of her decision hung heavily in the air, a pivotal moment that could alter the course of her life forever. As Alma found herself caught between two towering figures in her life, Zemlinsky and Gustav Mahler, the tension of her conflicting emotions was palpable. Each man represented different facets of her identity – while Zemlinsky stood for the familiar comfort of love, Mahler represented the exciting possibility of a deep connection. Mahler's decisive kiss was not only an act of passion; it symbolised the change in Alma's feelings and her future life, but also the irresistible attraction of a man who not only captivated her, but also challenged her intellectually and artistically. This moment marked a critical turning point for Alma, as she wrestled with her loyalties and desires, caught between the safe haven of her past and the stormy seas of a future with Gustav Mahler.

Alma's heart became a whirlwind of emotions. On one hand, she was captivated by Mahler's artistic vision and the promise of a future intertwined with a man of such passion. On the other hand, the shadows of her previous love haunted her, reminding her of the affection she had once felt. She often found herself thinking: Could she truly leave Zemlinsky behind? Would she be able to forge a new identity alongside Mahler, or would she always carry the remnants of her past?

In moments of solitude, Alma would sit by her window, gazing at the snowy streets of Vienna, lost in thought. It was during these contemplative hours that she began to write again, her thoughts spilling onto the pages of her journal. She poured her heart into her entries, capturing the nuances of her changing feelings, the tension of love and loyalty, and the fear of losing herself in the process, so on 7 December 1901:

> Gustav was here. We kissed each other over and over again. In his embrace, I feel so warm. If only he still loved me as much – but

> I consider him fickle, dreadfully fickle. He tried to convert me, in many senses. I shan't be seeing him for nineteen days. On Monday, he is going to Berlin. I don't know what else to write, but my feelings are for him and against Alex. Never before have I watched the clock as avidly as today. I couldn't work for sheer longing.[16]

This passage reflected the complex emotional landscape Alma navigated as her relationship with Mahler deepened. The warmth of his embrace symbolises the magnetic pull she felt toward him, contrasted by her growing doubts about his commitment. Her description of his fickleness reveals an awareness of his unpredictability, suggesting that beneath the allure she sensed a potential for instability. This tension of her broader struggle between the safety of her past with Zemlinsky and the exhilarating yet uncertain path she could take with Mahler was emblematic.

The longing she expressed in her diary underscored the intensity of her feelings, while her inability to focus on her work highlighted the consuming nature of love and desire. Her thoughts drifted towards Mahler, illustrating how her heart was increasingly drawn away from her former life, caught in the tumult of passion and the anxiety of impending separation.

One of Alma and Mahler's first really intense conversations was about Jesus Christ. Although Alma had been raised Catholic, she later became very free-spirited through the influence of Schopenhauer and Nietzsche. Mahler fervently opposed this attitude, creating a strange paradox, which was: a Jew passionately advocating for Christ to a Christian.

As Alma navigated the intricate world of music, her perspective on Mahler began to evolve, shaped by both admiration and the criticisms of others. In the following weeks, Alma had numerous experiences with people from the world of music. For instance, on the day she met the music writer Ludwig Karpath, she sat at a table with him and conductor Adalbert von Goldschmidt, listening to their discussion.

But when the conversation turned to Mahler, Goldschmidt remarked dismissively, 'Oh, he's such a milk-faced man; he's no man, that fidgety man. And his music isn't music.'

Alma soon learned why Goldschmidt harboured such animosity toward Mahler: he had submitted his opera *Gaea*, which Mahler had rejected.

Karpath stood up to defend Mahler as a composer, revealing something that Alma could not yet know: 'I should know, because I made him in Vienna.'

This was enough for Alma. She relayed all the details of that evening to Mahler, who grew visibly annoyed as he listened. In the following days, Karpath came to the Opera, hoping to discuss a few matters with Mahler. During their meeting, Karpath grew irritated, because Mahler remained seated with an air of arrogance. But before Karpath could take his leave, Mahler stood up, walked in front of him, and extended his hand, saying, 'I must thank you for making me in Vienna.'

Karpath was stunned: 'Miss Alma Schindler told you that?' But Mahler responded that he did not know Alma Schindler at all. A few days later, the news of Alma's engagement to Mahler appeared in the newspaper.

The disparaging remarks made by Goldschmidt reflect the challenges Mahler faced in gaining acceptance among his contemporaries, who often viewed him as an outsider. Goldschmidt's disdain – labelling Mahler a 'milk-faced man' – exemplified a broader struggle that artists often endure: the friction between innovative expression and traditional expectations.

Alma's defence of Mahler, fuelled by her ever-growing affection, highlights her emerging role not only as his partner, but also as a supporter of his artistic journey. It was a crucial moment that foreshadowed her commitment to him, revealing her willingness to stand up for what she believed in, even when faced with opposition.

The incident with Ludwig Karpath further illuminated the complexities of Mahler's identity as a composer. Mahler's retort to Karpath, 'I must thank you for making me in Vienna,' was a powerful assertion of his artistic independence. It underscored the paradox of a man who, despite being maligned, retained a sense of self-worth and confidence in his musical vision.

On 8 December 1901 Gustav Mahler and Alma Schindler became engaged. The official announcement of their engagement appeared in the respected liberal newspaper *Neue Freie Presse* on 23 December, and Alma stepped into a new chapter of her life. One that would intertwine her future with Mahler's – both as a woman in love and as an artist in her own right, navigating a world filled with admiration, criticism and the quest for validation. 'From the moment of our engagement, his tone had changed dramatically, from that of an adoring lover to that of a mentor. At the same time, however, I lost my initial unconditional faith.'[17]

As the days progressed, the announcement of their engagement ignited whispers among their acquaintances in the Viennese music scene. Alma found herself at the centre of attention, her name now intertwined with that of the esteemed conductor. But while some celebrated the union, others expressed scepticism, suggesting that Mahler's intense dedication to his art would overshadow any potential for a shared life. Alma, however, felt an exhilarating sense of purpose; this relationship was a convergence of her artistic aspirations and romantic desires.

With Mahler, Alma experienced a profound intellectual connection, one that had been absent in her previous relationships. He challenged her thoughts and encouraged her to delve deeper into her creative pursuits. Yet the whispers of doubt lingered, fuelled by the lingering presence of Alexander von Zemlinsky. Despite her engagement, Alma grappled with her past feelings for Zemlinsky, who had been a steadfast companion in her life before Mahler's arrival.

In the early days of their domestic relationship, Mahler conducted *Die Zauberflöte* (*The Magic Flute*) by Mozart, exclusively for Alma. She watched from her service seat at the Opera, where she was given special access to the performance. After each act, Mahler would speak to the concertmaster, allowing him and Alma to exchange glances longer than the pieces actually lasted. Later, Alma wrote him letters expressing her impressions of the opera. And on 9 December, Gustav Mahler wrote to her:

> Dearest, please write to me about The Magic Flute as well. I can imagine that it might not make complete sense to you yet. You are still too much yourself. It was the same for me for a long time with the works you mention. But everything, even the most trivial thing, that you tell me about yourself is valuable and dear to me. Please make a great effort with your letters. Write down the words as they come to you.

In one of his last letters during his trips to Berlin and Dresden in mid-December 1901 – about four weeks after their first meeting at the Zuckerkandls' home – Mahler asked Alma to speak to her mother about his desire to marry her, hoping to be welcomed as a son upon his return. However, before his arrival, their first conflict arose.

Alma replied that she needed to work on her compositions, which had been her passion until then. This response infuriated Mahler; he could not accept that anything could be more important to her than writing him a letter. He subsequently sent her a long letter forbidding her to continue composing. Mahler did not understand that he was undermining the creativity central to Alma's identity. After reading his letter, Alma cried all night long.

With each passing day, the reality of her engagement loomed larger, prompting Alma to confront her innermost desires. The excitement of her new life with Mahler was tempered by the acknowledgment of the sacrifices she might have to make. As she stood at this crossroads, she knew that her decisions would shape her future in ways she could hardly foresee. Years later, in her autobiography, Alma would write:

> The asceticism that one dictates to oneself is right, but the asceticism that one is ordered to follow, as happened in my marriage to Gustav Mahler, irritated me to the limit of what I could bear. Incidentally, I had never shown Gustav Mahler a single note of my music.[18]

She told her mother what had happened. Anna, who really valued Mahler, was horrified and advised her daughter to end her relationship with this man. But this only made Alma calmer and more confident. She wrote Mahler a letter and promised that she would not compose anymore and from then on, she kept that promise.

She received a further letter from Mahler in which he softened his original demands. But still, the demands took their toll. Alma later noted:

> I buried my dream at that time. Perhaps it was better that way. I was able to live out the productive gifts I possessed in other, greater minds. But somewhere inside me, a wound burned that never completely healed.[19]

One day, while she was sitting at the piano, her stepfather appeared and confronted her with his opinion of Mahler. He said, that he 'was old, had debts, was sickly, had problems working at the Opera, was not handsome either, he also composed, but it didn't mean anything.' Alma's reaction, however, was different to what Carl Moll had expected; she started laughing loudly and he left her room disappointed.

After his return from Germany, Mahler came to her every day and stayed until late at night. Since there were no more buses or trams running, he had to walk home from the Hohe Warte in the 19th district to Rennweg in Vienna's 3rd district – a journey of nearly 7 kilometres (over 4 miles) that took him close to two hours on foot. He loved to do this, singing and whistling as he walked.

And yet, it was not Mahler's frailties that kept Alma at his side, nor was it the grand allure of his genius alone. It was something far more complex. Mahler, with all his contradictions – stern yet tender, commanding yet needy – had become part of her very identity. His daily visits filled her days, and though they often stretched long into the night, Alma found comfort in the routine of his presence. His footsteps, as he walked home through the deserted streets of Vienna, felt like an echo of their new, shared life together.

One day during their engagement, a delegation from the Philharmonic Orchestra approached Alma, hoping she might persuade Mahler to distance himself from the concertmaster, Arnold Rosé, whose growing influence they viewed as detrimental to the balance of power within the ensemble. At only 20 years old, this was a fascinating experience for her, revealing the power dynamics within the music world. It would not be the last time she was asked to intervene on Mahler's behalf. In later years, too, Alma would prevent injustices against him when she could. But in this instance, her intervention came too late; Mahler's relationship with the orchestra had already soured, leaving her powerless to change the outcome. This tension continued to affect Mahler's time with the Vienna Philharmonic, contributing to the ongoing struggles he faced within the orchestra.

With each passing day, as Mahler whistled through the night and Alma sat at her piano in silence, she knew that she had chosen this path. She might not compose her own music anymore, but in supporting Mahler she had become part of something far greater than herself.

The first Christmas of their engagement approached; it was a sacred time for Alma, steeped in cherished childhood memories. For Mahler, however, it felt foreign and alien, leading him to view Alma's excitement and expectations as mere empty phrases. Suspicion clouded his mind; he sensed danger lurking in every corner. For Alma, this marked the beginning of a period of suffering beyond compare. She soon noticed that everything Mahler had initially admired about her became a source of suspicion. Her hairstyle, her clothing, her conversations – all were scrutinised under his critical gaze. To him, they seemed far too worldly.

Alma recognised that his anguish stemmed from envy and the judgment of so-called friends, and it became torturous for her to endure this treatment. Several of Mahler's acquaintances looked down on the 20-year-old – condescendingly referring to her as 'girl'. They tested her intellect and understanding, probing to see if she could appreciate the artists and thinkers they admired, while attempting to mould her opinions to fit their narrow views.

Then came the grand Christmas celebration, where several of Mahler's friends were invited, along with their wives, ex-wives, and lovers to join him and Alma at his flat in the 3rd district. What was meant to be a festive occasion quickly developed into a miserable time for Alma.

'I will never forget the deceitful, solemn grandeur of that evening,' she later recalled. 'No one spoke, but evil, hostile eyes measured my every move.' A former girlfriend of Mahler approached her, asking how Alma felt about his music. Alma's response was sharp: 'I know very little, but what I do know, I don't like.'

Mahler burst into laughter, causing the guests to bow their heads in disapproval, while Alma's mother felt embarrassed by her daughter's bad behaviour. In the midst of this commotion, Mahler suddenly took Alma by the hand and led her into his sister Justine's small room. 'It was horrible out there; let's be alone for a bit,' he whispered, and in that intimate moment they found happiness again, even as the guests in the next room practically plotted Alma's downfall.

From January 1902 onward, the atmosphere surrounding Mahler and Alma grew increasingly hostile. Alma and her fiancé were subject to a persecution which only ceased when Mahler left the Vienna Opera in 1907. However, the intrigues aimed at tearing the couple apart had little effect; instead, they fostered a deeper bond between Mahler and Alma and pushed him further away from his so-called friends.

Meanwhile, preparations for their wedding were underway. Mahler was constantly tormented by the nagging question of whether marrying such a young woman was the right decision. He grappled with the fear that he was 'too old' for her. This anxiety never left him; instead, it manifested as nervousness and illness. He endured painful tensions and self-inflicted torment: on one hand, he longed for death, while on the other, he craved an exhilarating life.

At times, he would candidly express to Alma, 'Oh, if you had already had an affair or were a widow, then everything would be easier.' Such outbursts deeply pained Alma, who had always regarded her 'girlhood' as something special and beautiful. At that moment, she could not grasp that Mahler was merely voicing a societal expectation – the notion that an 'experienced woman' held significant value in their world.

Before the wedding, Alma was grossly underestimated by the short-sighted individuals surrounding Mahler. They believed the gap in their ages would render her a compliant instrument for their own ambitions, seeking to manipulate and consolidate their power over him. Alma was subjected to humiliation and denigration in an attempt to convince Mahler of her immaturity, a strategy intended to wound his pride. However, the detractors failed to account for Alma's own pride and her burning desire for independence.

As the pressure mounted, Mahler began to distance himself from his friends, increasingly fearful of confrontation. Ironically, the very mob that sought to undermine Alma ended up achieving the opposite of their intentions. Instead of breaking her spirit, they only solidified her resolve to assert her identity and autonomy.

Although bourgeois morality frowned upon premarital or extramarital sex, Alma was no longer a virgin when she married Mahler – just as her mother had not been when she married Emil Jakob Schindler. Gustav and Alma first had sex shortly after their engagement.

On 9 March 1902, Mahler and Alma exchanged vows in the *Karlskirche* in the heart of Vienna. It was pouring with rain that day; the groom arrived on foot in galoshes, while the bride arrived in a carriage accompanied by her family and witnesses. The lunch following the ceremony was brief, and soon after, they packed their bags and headed to the train station. On the journey to St Petersburg, a sense of relief washed over them. Mahler's depression seemed to lift. He had been invited to conduct three concerts in St Petersburg, making it the perfect destination for their honeymoon. However, halfway through the trip, he was struck by a severe migraine, pacing the aisles of the train, pale and in distress. As soon as the train stopped, he rushed outside, running around the platform to alleviate his discomfort. By the time they arrived in St Petersburg, he was suffering from chilblains, fever and hoarseness – not the ideal start to a honeymoon. Unfortunately, Alma caught his illness as well. Despite these setbacks, she later recalled it as the most beautiful three-week period of her life. From the sidelines, she listened to the concerts and watched as her husband, gradually recovering, conducted with an increasingly joyful demeanour. Alma noted in her diary that his face took on a divine expression. She felt it was her mission to remove all obstacles from his path and to live solely for him.

In St Petersburg, Mahler conducted works by Joseph Haydn, Franz Schubert, the funeral march from *Götterdämmerung*, and Beethoven's *Eroica Symphony*. The audience was delighted. A cousin of Mahler's, who lived in St Petersburg and held a high-ranking government position, showed the couple around the city. He offered excellent recommendations for restaurants and charming streets, took them to the Hermitage, and accompanied them to visit palaces. The River Neva, flowing from Lake Ladoga into the Neva Bay of the Baltic Sea, was still frozen, and many tram tracks were laid across it. In the evenings, ice skaters glided by, and Alma and Gustav watched them; there was grace, elegance, cheerfulness, and an air of luxury.

On some days, individual orchestra members were absent, and only later did Mahler learn that they had likely been sent to Siberia by the Tsarist authorities. During this period of political repression, many people, including dissidents, artists and intellectuals, were exiled or imprisoned for perceived disloyalty or activism. It was heartbreaking for Mahler, who understood the difficult plight of these musicians and the oppressive regime under which they lived.

Mahler and Alma also mingled with high society. During concert intervals, Alma was introduced to several grand dukes and noticed a certain liveliness and kindness in them, that she found lacking among the high nobility in Vienna, although the conversations were held in French. She also observed, that the writer Dostoyevsky was rarely spoken of, and people mostly turned up their noses at him.

On their way home to Vienna they stopped in Warsaw, where they were followed by a stranger who tried to entice them with promises of the city's nightlife, nightclubs and forbidden pleasures. Gustav and Alma managed to escape to the train station in a passing carriage. There, Alma gave her remaining Russian money to a Jewish man selling matches. Her husband was deeply pleased by this gesture of solidarity. Alma later said she learned a great deal from the old man and felt, in that moment, she fully understood the weight and suffering of the Jewish people.

Upon their return to Vienna, Alma and Gustav moved into their new apartment in the Auenbruggergasse next to Rennweg in the 3rd district, marking the beginning of a life together that would span six years of intense change, yet would remain deeply harmonious. The apartment was modest, consisting of three rooms and three closets, and it held many challenges for Alma. She was met with a household in complete disarray, weighed down by debts. Though Mahler had received a substantial severance payment from his time in Budapest and earned handsomely from his performances, his siblings' reckless spending drained his finances. Raised with a sense of modesty and financial discipline, Alma took it upon herself to restore order, making it her mission to see her husband debt-free.

Alma felt insecure around Gustav in the first few years of their marriage. After winning him over with her boldness, she later revealed that she felt her physical confidence undermined by her pregnancy. She became pregnant shortly after their marriage in 1902, a time when she was still adjusting to the intense demands of her relationship and the expectations placed on her. The rapid changes in her life during this time added to her feelings of uncertainty. Oddly, after what he considered his 'spiritual victory' over her – a period where he saw himself as having shaped her into the woman he always envisioned – Gustav seemed to overlook Alma. This 'victory' came at the cost of Alma's own sense of self. In his eyes, he had succeeded in making her the ideal partner, but his controlling behaviour stifled her individuality. Through their marriage appeared deeply harmonious on the surface, the internal dynamics were more complex. Alma's growing realisation that she needed to reclaim her independence created tension beneath the surface. It was only later, when Alma began to free herself from his controlling influence, that Mahler rediscovered his love for her.

Before he left Vienna, Mahler converted to Catholicism to avoid the career limitations imposed by his Jewish heritage in Europe at that time. Despite this shift, his daily routine remained unchanged throughout their six-year marriage. He followed a rigid schedule, rising each day at 6.30 am for a breakfast of coffee, butter, wholegrain bread, jam and milk, prepared by his cook. Lunch was always a simple affair – broth, lean foods, and no onions or spices. His entire diet, as Alma later noted, resembled 'sick food'.

The disillusionment of the young wife, who, like many women of her generation, had entered marriage practically unprepared for household management, dealing with servants, or child-rearing, began early. Each day, when Gustav came home for lunch, his clerk Karl Hassinger informed her of his arrival. When he rang the bell, Alma would place the pot of soup on the stove, then open the front door on the fourth floor – just enough time to get the soup boiling. When Gustav ate at home Alma was not permitted to speak, as he needed to concentrate on his thoughts, his problems, and the new ideas that occupied him even at mealtime.

Even during vacations, Alma's life largely revolved around her husband's needs. Since Mahler composed in the summer, they retreated to a refuge in the countryside away from Vienna – first to Stainbach on Lake Attersee in Upper Austria, then to Altaussee in Styria, before finally moving to their own holiday home in Maiernigg, Carinthia. The 'Villa Mahler', situated directly on Lake Wörthersee, was nestled between the forest and the lake, a location so enchanting that Alma never grew accustomed to its beauty, but found it delightful again and again. The villa featured two magnificent stone terraces: an open one on the main floor and a covered loggia below, both offering sweeping views of the lake, which seemed to smile back through every window. The towering spruces and alders of the forest peeked in everywhere. Mahler's balcony in front of the attic was like a watchtower overlooking it all. 'It's too beautiful,' he would say, 'you can't deny yourself it.'[20]

Mahler had a composing hut built so he could work without interruption. It was a simple room furnished with a table, an armchair, a sofa, and a piano. In Maiernigg their days followed a strict routine: Gustav composed in the mornings, and the afternoons were reserved for sports like swimming, rowing, and mountain hiking. After meals, Gustav used to spend about half an hour in conversation with Alma. In the afternoons, they engaged in physical activity, or hiked for three to four hours daily, regardless of the weather. Alma often grew exhausted, but if she put her arms around Gustav he would express his love for her, renewing her energy to continue.

During their first summer together in 1903, just a few months after their wedding, Gustav was noticeably very relaxed and grounded, undistracted by his ambitions or the incessant demands of his work at the Opera. Even if letters arrived from Vienna, he left them unanswered, savouring the peacefulness of Carinthia. And he was always the first to share his new compositions with Alma – like the *Fifth Symphony* – seeking her thoughts on them.

However, during this summer, Alma, already five months pregnant, struggled to keep pace with her husband. The joy she had envisioned for this time together did not come to fruition. Gustav's adherence to his routine, established during his bachelor days, seemed inflexible. It often felt as if his wife were merely an adornment, expected to fit into his schedule and conform to his wishes. Alma grew more critical of their marriage during this time but resisted the idea of surrendering without a fight. That summer, she also experienced some emotional ups and downs, which Gustav noticed. In response, he turned to his usual method of expression and composed a song as a gift to her: *Liebst Du um Schönheit (If You Love for Beauty)*, set to a poem by Friedrich Rückert. Alma was delighted by the gesture, though it did not resolve her underlying dissatisfaction.

On 3 November 1902, their first daughter, Maria Anna, first daughter, was born following a challenging breech birth. Mahler was instantly captivated by the little girl, lovingly nicknaming her 'Putzi'. Alma, however, struggled to embrace her new role as a mother; she found it difficult to connect with her firstborn as she had once imagined she would. To her distress, she sensed an emotional distance towards the child, and despite her efforts, she was never able to foster the close, loving bond she had envisioned.

Alma felt increasingly neglected by Gustav, and her frustrations simmered until they erupted in a fierce argument at the end of December. She craved more attention from him – ideally as much, if not more, than he lavished on their daughter. The strain pushed their relationship to a breaking point. Gustav, however, responded with a blunt insensitivity that stung deeply, telling Alma, 'If your dreams of blossoming flowers aren't coming true, that's entirely up to you.'

Mahler's career was marked by highs and lows. Initially, everyone wanted to be close to him, offering advice and connections. However, as soon as it became clear that he had his own inflexible vision, many withdrew; in recent years he had found himself surrounded by critics and adversaries. Each morning, Gustav and Alma opened the newspapers with trepidation, bracing themselves for the critics.

During this period, the Mahlers maintained a good relationship with Richard Strauss, the Bavarian composer and conductor, and his wife, the German soprano Pauline Strauss-de Ahna. Mahler and Strauss could spend hours debating musical nuances – variations, tempos – while Alma found herself less captivated by Pauline, whose mood swings were often challenging.

They were also frequent visitors at the home of Anna Moll on the Hohe Warte, and it was there one day that Alma's childhood friend Alfred Roller joined them. Roller, a set designer, shared with Mahler his enthusiasm for Wagner's *Tristan und Isolde*, describing his ideas and concepts from years of watching performances. Impressed, Mahler appointed Roller to stage *Tristan*, which resulted in a highly acclaimed production and eventually led Roller to head the set design department at the Opera.

Mahler's sister Justine resented Alma, pursuing her with relentless jealousy. For nine years, Justine had shared an apartment with her brother, advising and reprimanding him as she saw fit. But with Alma's arrival, Justine felt her influence slipping away.

In January 1903, Mahler excitedly shared with Alma news of a new opera that had captured his interest: *Louise* by Gustave Charpentier, an homage to the city of Paris and its vibrant Montmartre district.

Mahler was determined to stage *Louise* in Vienna and invited Charpentier to join the rehearsals and attend the premiere. However, Charpentier found the production disappointing; as a surrealist, his vision clashed with Mahler's and the director's interpretations. Recognising this disconnect, Mahler decided to postpone the premiere, allowing Charpentier to make adjustments, to better align with his vision. Charpentier reworked the production, giving it a less noble tone. He added striking elements: the seducer wore a red light bulb under his tailcoat to symbolise his heart, while the ballerina danced endlessly in a short ballet tutu, cast in a vivid purple cone of light to reflect the bohemian spirit of Montmartre.

The experience was eye-opening for Mahler, teaching him a new sense of playfulness and self-irony. Reflecting on the production later, he admitted, 'I was wrong there; the author must know better.'[21]

From the premiere onwards, the Mahlers generously offered Charpentier their box. But soon, they were advised against entering it, as Charpentier had started inviting 'the underworld' – in particular, a woman he was enamoured with, whom he now brought to the box daily. While the friendship with Charpentier endured, they did never see each other again. When Alma visited Paris in 1926 and tried to reconnect with Charpentier, she discovered his address had changed. Thanks to extensive efforts by the Austrian embassy to track him down, she eventually located the new address, but was ultimately not allowed to see him.

In mid-June 1904, Mahler conducted the *Second Symphony* in the former bishop's church, the Basel Minster, and Alma found the performance magnificent; it was perfectly suited to the venue, with its wreath of lights, high ceiling and resonant music.

During the summer, the Mahler family returned to their house in Maiernigg, where they relished the tranquillity. Gustav Mahler began working on his *Sixth Symphony* there, but he also devoted himself to his beloved little daughter, frequently carrying her around, singing and dancing with her.

They were both delighted to receive a letter from the composer Hans Pfitzner, who sent them an original manuscript – which thrilled Mahler. Upon returning to Vienna in the autumn of 1901, Alma examined the piano score of Pfitzner's opera *Die Rose vom Liebesgarten (The Rose from the Garden of Love)* and was extremely enthusiastic about it. When she placed the opera on her piano stand, Mahler, who habitually played whatever was there, was swept away by the music. He premiered the opera on 21 November in Vienna, and Alma noted that for the first time, she felt she had a positive influence on her husband.

Mahler and Alma experienced jealousy towards each other. Initially, Alma felt more jealousy than her husband. She envied his past, which she naively deemed very reprehensible, while he was jealous of Alma's future – a sentiment she would come to understand later.

In June 1904, Alma was expecting their second child. In the months leading up to the birth, she and Gustav would often walk to Belvedere Palace or around the Ringstraße, at least three times after lunch. However, as the weeks progressed, this became increasingly difficult for Alma, and Gustav found himself walking alone, quickly returning to his wife out of concern for her well-being.

Alma and Gustav enjoyed many exciting evenings with friends, including Max Burckhard, who introduced them to his friend, German author Gerhart Hauptmann, and his wife, Margarete. The men would engage in lively discussions, creating a vibrant atmosphere.

A stay in Abbazia (now Opatija, Croatia) brought the family closer together than before, yet Mahler continued to work tirelessly, even on vacation. Alma never witnessed him truly relax. On 14 June, the couple returned to Vienna and took a horse-drawn carriage to the Prater. Upon their return to the apartment, they encountered friends and decided to attend a performance of *Der arme Heinrich (Poor Henry)* by the author Hartmann von Aue at the Burgtheater.

On the night of 15 June, Alma awoke with the realisation she was going into labour. She roused her husband, who immediately called for a midwife. The birth occurred at noon, a significant moment for Alma: midday, in the middle of the week, in the middle of the month, and in the middle of the year – an emblematic sign for them. They adored their child, whom they named 'Anna Justine', from the very beginning. Her affectionate nickname was 'Gucki', as she gazed at her parents with such curiosity through her bright blue eyes.

Mahler travelled extensively with his children and wife, finding it difficult to be away from his family. He shared a wonderful bond with each of his daughters, making faces with them, telling stories, and sharing jokes.

The summer of 1904 was blissful and free of conflict, with everyone feeling very happy. As the holidays drew to a close, Mahler played his now-completed *Sixth Symphony* for Alma. She made it a priority to dedicate time to her husband. Alma later expressed that 'no work had flowed from her husband's heart as much as this one'. In that moment, they both cried tears of joy.

The *Sixth Symphony* stands out as Mahler's most persona, and deeply prophetic, work. The routine of everyday life – careful management of household expenses, childcare and daily responsibilities – had worn down some of the passion between Alma and Gustav. However, his love, subdued by the struggles and practicalities of life, was waiting for a chance to reemerge.

Around this time, Roller was commissioned to direct a new production of *Fidelio* for the Vienna Opera. The production boasted stunning decor and innovative reinterpretations, with the powerful Leonore overture now serving as transitional music to the finale.

Alma, feeding their youngest child, was determined to attend the final rehearsals. Hidden in a theatre box, she would dash out every half hour to check on her children by phone. In late September, Mahler asked her to stop breastfeeding so she could attend the premiere of his *Fifth Symphony* in Cologne – a performance she was determined not to miss. But nature was unforgiving; the sudden weaning made her ill, forcing her to stay behind. Mahler travelled alone to Cologne, where the premiere on 19 October was well received by the German audience. Continuing his tour, he went on to Amsterdam to conduct the *Second* and *Fourth* symphonies, returning to Vienna by morning to share his experiences with Alma over breakfast before heading to work at the Opera. His schedule included conducting twice weekly and managing both new productions and premieres. The *Third Symphony*'s December premiere in Vienna was a great success, meriting an encore. To celebrate, he often invited the orchestra to a beer night at *Zur Goldenen Birne* in the Vienna-Mariahilf district – a gesture of appreciation to the musicians he valued so highly.

During the Christmas holiday season, they attended intimate gatherings and dinners with friends, as well as refined soirées with high society – one of the few 'parties' they frequented in Vienna. Their strolls through the city always attracted attention: 'There's Mahler with his wife,' people would whisper – their appearance created quite a stir.

Mahler with his mercurial character, sometimes changed his opinions by the day, a trait that Alma learned to accept. She was pained by her unfulfilled desire to compose, having promised him during their engagement that she would set it aside. Now, though, she travelled everywhere with her music in tow, there was never time to write. The disappointment often overwhelmed her, and in those moments, Gustav would gently place his hand on her head and whisper: 'Because not all flowered dreams come to fruition?'

At the end of January 1905, Alma and her husband attended a concert featuring works by Alexander von Zemlinsky and Arnold Schönberg. The program included *The Mermaid*, a fantasy for large orchestra in three movements, and Schönberg's symphonic poem *Pelleas and Melisande*. That evening, Alma recognised the difference between Zemlinsky's charming ideas and abilities and the stronger, more daring qualities she saw in Arnold Schönberg, whom she considered a very interesting man. Reflecting on her past, she remembered Zemlinsky as her composition teacher and recalled how she had first met Schönberg through him, when he was still Zemlinsky's student. Zemlinsky had once advised her – though she did not particularly like Schönberg at the time – 'Just keep an eye on him; the world will talk about him one day.'

Years later, now married to Mahler, Alma encountered Schönberg again, only to hear him dismissively comment, 'How could Mahler manage the *Fourth* when he couldn't even handle the *First*?' Alma thought this was 'a typical Schönberg remark', and yet she found it interesting that Schönberg would later become one of Mahler's most devoted advocates.

Through Zemlinsky's introduction, Schönberg began visiting the Mahlers' home, sparking a unique friendship among the three men. Zemlinsky's excessive pride often led to curt remarks toward Mahler, despite his underlying admiration. Schönberg, meanwhile, seemed to channel a youthful rebellion against the 'older' artist, whom he also held in high regard. Their meetings typically began with a meal, followed by an intense discussion at the piano, where personalities clashed. Schönberg's paradoxical comments met with Mahler's reprimands, and after a tense exchange, Schönberg would storm out, with Zemlinsky trailing behind, shaking his head. Mahler, exasperated, asked Alma not to invite 'that arrogant fellow' again, while Schönberg, muttering on the stairs, vowed not to return. Yet, within weeks, Mahler found himself inviting Schönberg and Zemlinsky back. Referring to them as 'Eisele and Beisele', Mahler resumed their debates, which both Schönberg and Zemlinsky had secretly been hoping for.

In the summer of 1905, Mahler completed his *Seventh Symphony*, having already laid out what he called its essential construction sketches by mid-1904, a testament to his methodical approach.

Each morning, the couple's eldest child would go into her father's study to talk with him. These sessions went on for a long time, and Maria Anna would often emerge with her cheeks covered in jam. Their conversations brought father and daughter closer, and Alma secretly delighted in watching their connection. Maria Anna was very much her father's child – beautifully stubborn, both guarded and affectionate, with dark curls and large blue eyes. Mahler would say, 'The artist is like a hunter in the dark; he doesn't know what he will hit, or if he will hit at all.' For him, education could only happen through example; he believed that setting a good example was everything.

The summer holidays were always dedicated to Mahler's work and peace of mind. Everyone moved silently, and the children were forbidden from laughing loudly or shouting. Alma wrote later that they all lived in service of his work, but she always felt it was the right way to live.

In 1907, Alma returned from Rome feeling unwell and exhausted. Their younger daughter, Anna, was also weak, with a fever and symptoms of scarlet fever. After Anna recovered, the family travelled to Maiernigg, their usual summer retreat, where Mahler had just resigned from his position at the Vienna Opera. Soon after arriving, however, their elder daughter, Maria Anna, showed alarming symptoms of both scarlet fever and diphtheria – an illness that seemed incurable from the outset. For two weeks, Gustav and Alma hovered by her side in fear. On the last day, Maria Anna underwent an emergency tracheotomy, and after preparing the setup with the English nanny, Alma retreated to the lakeshore in utter despair. She screamed into the silence, alone with her anguish, until the English nanny came and simply told her, 'It's over'. On 5 July 1907, Maria Anna passed away.

Alma and Gustav were devastated, joined in their grief by Alma's mother, Anna Moll. When Gustav invited them for a quiet walk along the lakeshore, the depth of their sorrow overwhelmed Anna, and she collapsed from what appeared to be a heart attack. Alma tended to her mother as best as she could and, amid the heartbreak, watched as her beloved daughter's coffin was taken away. The couple was in a state of shock. As Alma later wrote, she fainted, and the doctor, who attended her, discovered her heart had been weakened by emotional and physical strain. He prescribed complete rest. Gustav, too, underwent a medical examination, and the physician gave him a grave warning: 'You must take great care of your heart.' This marked, as Alma later reflected, the beginning of the end for Gustav Mahler.

His tenure at the Vienna Opera had recently ended, their child had died, and now this diagnosis – a narrowing of the mitral valve opening (mitral stenosis), which placed serious strain on the heart. They felt unmoored, both emotionally and physically. While they still had their residences in Vienna and Maiernigg, the loss of stability, routine, and a sense of belonging left them feeling effectively 'homeless'. Seeking clarity, Mahler visited Dr Friedrich Kovacs, a respected Viennese cardiologist, who confirmed the diagnosis and emphasised that he must avoid all strenuous physical activity – including mountain climbing, cycling and swimming.

Alma, determined to support him, gathered their essentials, and together they journeyed to Schluderbach in the Tyrolean Alps. In this majestic landscape, surrounded by nature, they found some solace, beginning to envision a new way forward and to make peace with the future that awaited them.

After the summer of grief, autumn swept through the country, bringing unexpected news. Several letters arrived, including one from Heinrich Conried, the director of the Metropolitan Opera in New York. An Austrian by birth who had made his career in Germany before moving to America, Conried had been leading the Metropolitan Opera since 1903 and offered Mahler a position. Mahler viewed this as a sign of fate and was summoned to Berlin to sign a contract for four months during the 1907–8 season. The program included three new productions and two or three concerts.

In late autumn, Mahler conducted his favourite operas for the last time at the Vienna Opera, performed his *Second Symphony* at the *Konzerthaus*, and on 15 October, conducted Beethoven's *Fidelio*. During his final days in Vienna, friends – including Alexander von Zemlinsky and Arnold Schönberg – wanted to meet with him. They gathered at a tavern in Grinzing, called *Der Schutzengel* (the Guardian Angel), from where Mahler did not return home until late. He recounted the evening's events to Alma, and they shared many laughs together.

Then it was soon time to bid farewell to Vienna. Friends shed tears as they said goodbye to Alma, Gustav and their little daughter Anna, now the only child they had. The family looked forward to a new life far away from Austria, trying to leave behind the grief of recent loss that had overwhelmed them just months before. Mahler remarked during the trip that the opera repertoire was over and expressed relief at not having to witness its decline. They travelled via Paris to Cherbourg and boarded a ship named *Amerika*, with the *Marseillaise* playing in the background.

Upon arriving in New York, Gustav and Alma Mahler were immediately introduced to the opera director and invited to lunch. Mahler learned he would conduct *Tristan und Isolde* as his first opera. Working with the American orchestra turned out to be both effortless and enjoyable, a refreshing change from the dynamics in Vienna. Alma later recalled that the orchestra, the singers, and the opera house, were magnificent. The performance proved to be one of the most dazzling in the Metropolitan Opera's history, receiving tremendous applause.

Despite the success, memories of their deceased daughter, Maria Anna, lingered. Mahler was often nervous, irritable and visibly saddened. He took special care of his heart, resting in bed for a few hours each day. Alma, too, suffered physically and emotionally. After collapsing suddenly, two New York doctors prescribed her a four-week rest cure. Nonetheless, Alma and Gustav felt they were in good hands in America.

When the season in New York ended, the ensemble travelled to Boston, and then in winter to Philadelphia, where *Tristan und Isolde* was again performed. They stayed in the US for only three months that first year, but during that time, a significant friendship was formed. Through Otto Hermann Kahn, a principal sponsor of the Metropolitan Opera, they met Dr Joseph Fraenkel. His deep admiration for Mahler made him an important friend and supporter for both Gustav and Alma.

In May 1908, the couple returned to Austria, travelling via Cuxhaven to Wiesbaden, where Mahler conducted his *First Symphony*. Alma noticed he looked considerably older. From Germany, they continued to Vienna, where she and her mother, Anna, went on to Toblach in South Tyrol to find a summer residence, following Dr Friedrich Kovacs's advice. They eventually found a house just outside the town, then returned to Vienna to pack before moving to Toblach with Gustav and their daughter. Finally, peace and quiet settled over the couple, with only occasional visits breaking the calm – and these visits often turned into joyful musical gatherings.

In the winter of 1908 they returned to America, as Mahler had accepted a new contract, extending through 1909, as a concert conductor. Two prominent New York society figures, Minnie Untermyer and Mary Seney Sheldon, proposed founding an orchestra for Mahler, and they raised a substantial sum of $100,000 to make it happen. As concert director, Mahler now had an orchestra created specifically for him, fulfilling one of his long-held dreams.

The year 1909 began with the project of a very special tribute to Mahler due to his departure from the Vienna State Opera in 1907. At the end of April 1909, several sittings at Auguste Rodin's atelier took place, where he was creating a bust of Mahler – a project commissioned by Carl Moll and made possible in great part by Sophie Clémenceau, the Parisian *salonnière* and sister of Berta Zuckerkandl. On 1 October, the Mahler family packed up their belongings in Vienna, put their furniture into storage, and left their shared apartment behind as they returned to New York. Mahler was thrilled to be free from Opera, and his new position allowed him to travel across the United States, conducting concerts in cities such as Philadelphia, Springfield and Buffalo.

In November, the Mahlers received an invitation from the West-Roosevelt family in Oyster Bay and enjoyed their time there. Shortly afterwards, after dining with investment banker, collector, philanthropist and patron of the arts, Otto Hermann Kahn, they were invited to a séance led by the medium Eusapia Palladino. The experience left Mahler more disturbed than impressed. Later, with his own orchestra established, Mahler's first concert rehearsal attracted a notable visitor with the name of Louis Comfort Tiffany, who requested permission to attend incognito.

Together, Gustav and Alma attended many plays, operas and concerts, always seated in boxes of honour and given special seats. Concert after concert in the USA followed, and soon it was already summer 1910. Alma brought her husband back to Toblach in South Tyrol while she herself went to Tobelbad, a small, fashionable health resort in Styria, to cure her nerves, as she later wrote. Her husband's heart condition put her under a huge amount of strain because she organised everything related to his life; she made everything easier for him and ensured he had as little stress as possible. It was clearly too much for her. This was a time with no computers or mobile phones – only landlines and stationery for writing letters.

In Tobelbad, Alma was introduced to Walter Gropius, who fell immediately in love with her. But everyday life quickly caught up with her, and life with Mahler went on. Then came a letter – one Walter Gropius had written to Alma, mistakenly delivered to Mahler. They talked it through, but from that moment, Mahler's love grew more dramatic, even obsessive. He demanded that Alma leave the door to her room open at night, just so he could hear her breathing.

Later, after another incident in which Walter Gropius ambushed Alma under a bridge and she accompanied him to the train station to say goodbye, something unexpected happened: the bond between husband and wife deepened. Mahler clung to her with even greater fervour, and Alma, despite the emotional chaos, stayed.

As Mahler's anxieties mounted, he took an extraordinary step to address the turmoil in his marriage. In August 1910, while in Leiden, he sought out Sigmund Freud, the famed psychoanalyst, hoping to gain insight into the emotional turbulence that haunted his marriage. Their conversation – which took place during a long walk through the streets of Leiden – would leave a lasting impression on Mahler.

He unburdened himself to Freud, revealing the deeply rooted insecurities that consumed him: fear of abandonment, a gnawing sense of inadequacy as a husband, and the struggle to reconcile Alma's creative ambitions with his own towering ego. Freud listened, then responded with brutal clarity: 'How can you chain a young woman to you in such a state?' He laid out the psychological dynamics of Mahler's relationship:

> I know your wife. She loved her father and can only seek and love that type. Her age, which you fear so much, is precisely what makes you attractive to your wife. Don't worry! You love your mother; you have sought her type in every woman. Your mother was angry and suffering, and you unconsciously wanted the same from your wife![22]

Freud's insights helped Mahler recognise the emotional toll his dominance had taken on Alma. For the first time, he began to see her not merely as his wife, but as an individual with her own voice, desires, and unrealised potential. The session marked a shift in their relationship – subtle, but real.

Yet Mahler's inner turmoil did not vanish. Around the same time, while working on his *Tenth Symphony*, he began scribbling anguished notes to Alma directly onto the manuscript pages – desperate outpourings of love, jealousy, and despair. Alma later reflected on this period with painful honesty:

> Although I had often despaired over my life in recent years, I could never have imagined a life without Mahler. Least of all with another man. I had sometimes thought about leaving, alone, somewhere, starting anew, but always without any desire for anyone. Mahler was and remained the central point of my existence.[23]

Freud's words may have reached them both, but the wounds ran deep. And Alma later recalled:

> And how right he was in both cases! Gustav Mahler's mother was called Marie. When we met, he wanted to rename me Marie, although he had difficulty pronouncing the 'R'. When he got to know me, he wanted me to be 'more sad' – these were his words. When he complained that I had unfortunately not experienced much sadness, my mother replied: 'Calm down, life will take care of you!'[24]

Freud's analysis brought some relief to Mahler, though he reportedly dismissed the notion of his fixation on his mother. For Alma, this period reinforced her understanding of their complex bond and the deep psychological forces that shaped their lives together.

In the autumn, new tours with Mahler were booked in America: this time to Seattle, Buffalo, Springfield, then back to New York and Brooklyn, and then on to the country. Before Christmas, Mahler suffered a slight relapse of a sore throat. The illness faded quickly and did not alarm either of them – though, in hindsight, it should have.

At Christmas 1910, Gustav surprised Alma for the first time with a huge gift: under a cloth covered with many roses, she found many small presents, including perfume and two gift vouchers – things that he would never ordinarily have given. The two of them went for walks arm in arm during Christmastime, or Alma sent him with Anna ('Gucki', a sweet nickname meaning something like 'little looker' or 'peekaboo girl', from the Austrian dialect word *gucken* – 'to look'), to Central Park to play and throw snow at each other. A magnificent image.

At the beginning of 1911, Alma and Gustav were often visited by a young woman who tried to convert them to occultism. Fortunately, she was unsuccessful. On 20 February, Gustav again developed a fever and a sore throat, but he was determined to conduct the next day. During the break, he was very weak and had a headache, but he forced himself to continue conducting. He was given an aspirin and felt better. Eight days later the fever returned, and after collapsing, Mahler consulted a doctor. The same doctor appeared again the next morning – his hair grey with worry – and told Mahler that he had just buried a friend. The next three months were marked by fluctuating periods of strength and weakness. Alma became his nurse because he was noticeably frailer. When he felt better, he would lie on the sofa in the living room; when worse, he stayed in bed and Alma fed him. Two blood tests were also carried out during this time, and each time the fever seemed to disappear. Mahler's personal physician, the well-known Austro-American endocrinologist and neurologist Joseph Fraenkel, along with a panel of doctors from New York, were keen to bring him back to Europe so their bacteriologist colleagues could examine him more closely. Cabins were booked on a ship, and Dr Fraenkel travelled with Alma, their younger daughter Anna and Mahler, who was lying on a stretcher.

When they arrived in Paris, they went to the Hotel Elysée: there, Gustav had chills and collapsed. A doctor was called in and ordered him to be transferred immediately to a sanatorium on rue Dupont. From there, as Alma describes it, things went steadily downhill for him. While Gustav hoped that he would soon feel better – 'God grant that I get well, then things can still be good' – his condition continued to deteriorate, and so Alma telegraphed her favourite doctor, the internist Dr Franz Chvostek Jr., and he advised her to return to Vienna with her husband immediately, because 'you never know what might happen next'.

When they arrived in Vienna, they went straight to the Löw Sanatorium in the 9th district of Alsergrund in an ambulance, and moved into a huge room with a veranda. Mahler clearly felt at home there. He received a white basket from the Vienna Philharmonic as a gift, and his closest friends visited him. He constantly called his wife 'My Almschi' in a very thin voice. He said goodbye to his daughter and hugged her tightly: 'Be good to everyone, my child!' He was extremely emaciated, had a swelling on his leg, and suddenly had breathing difficulties and uremia. Despite his pain, Mahler shouted 'Mozart' twice, and Alma asked Dr Franz Chvostek Jr. to start injecting her husband with morphine. From then on, his death struggle began and he started gasping for air.

On 18 May 1911, while a hurricane-like storm swept through the city at midnight, Gustav Mahler, the Austro-Bohemian Romantic composer, and one of the leading conductors of his generation, died peacefully in Vienna. Alma was not allowed to go into the death chamber. But her stepfather Carl was fetched by the doctors and stayed with Gustav until the end. Alma was devastated and asked herself thousands of questions: 'Do I have to live without HIM now? I felt like I had been thrown out of a speeding train onto a foreign plain. What am I supposed to do on earth now?'[25]

Alma mourned with all her heart for the man she loved so much. She had his picture on her bed and spoke each day to him. During those dark days, her internist came by and diagnosed her with pneumonia. Alma had to take it easy, otherwise she would soon follow her Gustav. Secretly Alma hoped to follow her husband. She continued to live, but noted that against the backdrop of her grief, 'a whole, free life could never again arise'.[26] His death, the greatness of his face, which became more and more beautiful, close to death – she never wanted to and would never forget it.

Yet, amid her sorrow, the world continued to turn, and Alma would find herself on the cusp of a new chapter, grappling with the legacy of her husband and the demands of her own life. Little did she know that the years ahead would be shaped by her struggle to navigate the depths of her loss, while forging her own path as a woman and an artist in a world that seemed to have changed irrevocably.

Chapter 4

Widowhood and Femme Fatale – Alma's Love Affairs after Mahler

With Gustav Mahler's passing in spring 1911, Alma found herself at a painful crossroads, bearing the weight of profound grief while still facing the unfolding future. She had lost the man she loved, felt completely uprooted, and – as she later explained – she could hardly believe he had abandoned her. At 30, Alma still had her whole life ahead. Although sorrow lingered, her spirit was gradually drawn back to life's beauty, often through music. Recovering from her illness, she found that music captivated her once more. Her days, once defined by Gustav's presence, were now reshaped by the innocence and energy of her young 6-year-old daughter Anna, who became her daily companion at the piano. Alma began to reclaim her passions and discovered new sources of joy and connection. What emerged at the end was a tender companionship between mother and daughter, marked by hours spent at the piano, where, together, they began to weave a new melody of resilience and renewal. Together, they spent entire days at the piano, where their cook often had to pull them away to eat. Yet, each time they returned, with laughter and song, to their shared refuge in melody, where even the simplest meals seemed to taste better when seasoned by music. With a shared love of music, Anna distracted Alma from her grief and brought her unexpected moments of joy.

But after Gustav's passing, Alma was not left entirely alone; she found herself surrounded by those who cared for her and her late husband. Among them was Dr Joseph Fraenkel, who had become a beloved figure in New York's medical community. Born in Vienna and emigrating to the United States, he initially served the poor in a disadvantaged district before gaining recognition among wealthier patients. His reputation attracted the attention of German-American banker and philanthropist Jakob Heinrich Schiff, who soon offered Fraenkel a position at Montefiore Hospital. There, he became the hospital's director and the family doctor for New York's elite, while still treating poor patients free of charge. In return – Alma later quipped – he ripped off millionaires for their notes, illustrating Fraenkel's dual nature as both a compassionate healer and a savvy professional.

After Gustav's death, Fraenkel travelled to Vienna to see Alma again, expressing his deep affection for her by proposing marriage. Alma, however, rejected his offer. Despite his persistent affection, Fraenkel's visits only served as a reminder of her grief, leading Alma to feel the need to escape from him. 'Wandering on', as she described it, became her refuge, and she began to seek solace in her own emotional landscape. On a ship to Corfu, she encountered an Albanian minister who imparted a saying that resonated with her: 'It is not the murderer who is guilty, but the murdered.'[1]

This phrase lingered in her mind, reflecting her complex feelings of loss and responsibility. Meanwhile, her life was filled with possibilities, yet her focus remained largely on music. One composer who courted her attention was the Monaco-born German Franz Schreker, who was emerging as a significant opera composer in Germany after Wagner. Alma and Schreker attended opera performances together, while she noted his 'strange mixture of intellect and constitutional ignorance'.[2] Yet, he ultimately played no substantial role in her life, and after a brief period together, she chose to leave him behind as she continued her journey of self-discovery. With each interaction, Alma navigated her grief and the new reality of her life, creating a delicate balance between remembrance and the pursuit of her own path.

In the autumn of that year, Alma moved with her 7-year-old daughter Anna to an apartment on Elisabethstraße, her first time building an independent life in downtown Vienna. Her initial public appearance after Gustav's passing took place just weeks later, on 20 November, in Bavaria, where the Munich Philharmonic Orchestra performed Mahler's *The Song of the Earth* posthumously in the Munich Tonhalle under the baton of Bruno Walter. Alma was deeply moved by the piece's great success.

On her way back to Vienna, Alma encountered Paul Kammerer, a biologist with a passion for music and a profound admiration for her late husband. Kammerer, who was connected with some of Vienna's most prominent circles, including conductor and composer Bruno Walter, sociologist Rudolf Goldscheid, composers Alban Berg and Franz Schreker, philosopher Ludwig

Erik Tesar, and even Albert Einstein, soon became captivated by Alma. He saw in her a 'brilliant Viennese woman' of a rare type. Initially, Kammerer lent his support to Alma's efforts to establish the Gustav Mahler Foundation, which she intended to use to help young musicians with funds from Mahler's estate.

Kammerer's feelings for Alma soon intensified. Although married, he sought every opportunity to spend time with her, inviting her to his Biological Research Institute in the Vienna Prater, where he encouraged her to engage in scientific observations as a distraction from her grief. Alma found this new pursuit intriguing, meticulously recording the behaviours of various animals. She observed, for instance, whether a praying mantis would lose its memory when it shed its skin. She also cared for mealworms, which she found unsettling.

As time passed, Kammerer's adoration for Alma grew more fervent, expressed through numerous letters and emotional declarations. He once forced a kiss on her, and often threatened, as he left her apartment, to end his life at Mahler's grave if she did not return his affection. He even claimed that Mahler had appeared to him. Although initially disturbed by these assertions, Alma gradually became accustomed to Kammerer's dramatic sentiments.

In an effort to restore stability, Alma decided to speak with Kammerer's wife, Felicitas Maria Theodora von Wiedersperg. She advised Felicitas to involve herself more deeply in her husband's work and even suggested she take away the gun he frequently brandished, fearing it might lead to tragedy. Following Alma's intervention, the Kammerers' marriage seemed to improve.

Early in 1912, Carl Moll told Alma about an emerging artist named Oskar Kokoschka, who was making waves in the Viennese art scene. He encouraged her to have the young artist paint her portrait. Alma, then 33 years old, was intrigued by Kokoschka, who was seven years her junior. He was considered a revolutionary, eccentric, provocateur, and at the same time a brilliant painter. On 12 April 1912, Kokoschka received an invitation to the Molls' home on the Hohe Warte to paint Carl Moll, and Alma was present. Kokoschka later reflected on this evening in Döbling, noting that for Alma, her connection to Mahler was perhaps less about profound love and more about a shared musicality. 'In the wake of Gustav Mahler's funeral, she had distanced herself from society for a time, but now this young widow sought companionship again.'[3]

When Alma played the piano for Kokoschka, he was immediately captivated by her: 'I was fascinated by her appearance – young, moving through her grief, beautiful and so lonely.'[4]

When she proposed that he paint her in her apartment, he felt both delighted and melancholic. By April of that same year, Kokoschka was writing her passionate letters, oscillating between formal and familiar tones: 'If you, as a strengthening woman, help me out of my mental confusion, the beautiful, beyond our knowledge, which we adore, will bless you and me with happiness.'[5]

The ensuing relationship was unlike any Alma had previously experienced, and many of Alma's contemporaries, including her friends and biographers, claim that Kokoschka was the great love of her life. Their devotion to each other endured until their deaths. Alma, beautiful, wealthy, adventurous and well-travelled, sought the company of men who were geniuses. Oskar, on the other side, was handsome, sophisticated, sensual, articulate and deeply fascinated by women. But in reality, he also sought financial support, social status, coupled with love. What now began between the two can certainly be described as a euphoric, but also a stressful *amour fou*. Alma was rarely swayed by anyone as profoundly as she was by Kokoschka.

Yet, lingering in her thoughts were the two figures who had instilled in her a sense of fear and anxiety: Gustav and her first-born daughter, Maria Anna (Putzi), who had died in childbirth. With Oskar, she established a unique boundary; she rarely spent the night with him. When he visited her in Vienna, they would sleep together, but she expected him to depart the following day. This pattern reflected her need for independence and her desire to maintain clarity in her life. Meanwhile, she enrolled her daughter Anna Justine in a school for gifted children, but Anna soon struggled with the stringent teaching methods and left. Life continued its course. Alma revisited her old compositions, ventured out, and sought new acquaintances. Oskar, however, persistently sought affirmation of Alma's love, bombarding her with letters asking for reassurance.

Around 27 April 1912, when she went to Paris with her friend Henriette Amalie 'Lilly' Lieser, a patron of the Vienna art scene with a beautiful villa in the 13th district in Hietzing and a city palace at Argentinierstraße 20 in the 4th district, he penned:

> Alma, do you still love me? You have been gone for so long. I would be so grateful if this terrible impatience I constantly battle could be alleviated by you, my love. I often and loudly call your beautiful name, Alma, and in those moments, I feel a fleeting sense of joy.[6]

Alma admitted in her letters that her stay in Paris was very tiring for her. Lilly was one of the few friends she had. This wealthy socialite had a much more extravagant lifestyle than Alma's. Lilly openly shared her lesbian tendencies with Alma during their trip to Paris, but Alma made it clear, that she was not interested in such relationships. Despite this, the two remained friends, though their relationship was not always easy for Alma.

Oskar's affection for Alma soon took on intense, even frightening forms; he viewed her as the ideal woman, embodying Johann Wolfgang von Goethe's concept of the 'eternal feminine' and personification of the Viennese salon lady 'the powerful sensual presence of an incarnation of everything feminine'.[7]

He also admired her loyalty and valued the religious principles they shared: both were Roman Catholics, though neither was a regular churchgoer. In early July 1912, Alma travelled to Scheveningen in the Netherlands for a few weeks with her daughter Anna, and her friend Lilly Lieser. Just before she left, Oskar and Alma had quarrelled, yet his letters continued to reflect only the best he saw in her, as he deeply admired her loyalty. Oskar's letters show how deeply he disliked her departure, but Alma was undeterred. She and Lilly had a lot in common: they were both wealthy, enjoyed sophisticated lifestyles, loved to travel, and relished meeting new people. In Scheveningen, Alma also reconnected with her old friend Dr Joseph Fraenkel, who continued to court her.

In his letters to Alma from that time, Oskar Kokoschka revealed a proclivity for unusual sadomasochistic tendencies, occasionally asking Alma to be harsh with him. He wrote: 'I would like you to at least be dissatisfied with me, but still hit me with your lovely little hand.'[8]

Even as a child, Kokoschka apparently derived a certain pleasure from physical punishment: 'I often did something wrong on purpose,'[9] he recalled in his memoirs. Occasionally, he would even refer to himself as 'a boy who wanted to be mistreated by his strict mistress'.

That summer, their relationship experienced its first real crisis, fuelled by Kokoschka's jealousy, which Alma was increasingly unable to tolerate. Yet another factor complicated matters: Alma feared she was pregnant, a worry that surfaced in one of Kokoschka's letters from 27 July 1912:

> If you have a lovely child from me, then great – good nature is merciful and will erase all the terrible things and will never tear us apart again, since we rest and are supported by each other. You will now get well with me, and I have found my peace in you, my love.[10]

Alma soon confirmed she was indeed pregnant. After much discussion, Kokoschka reluctantly agreed to an abortion, which was carried out in mid-October 1912. Kokoschka, however, never forgave Alma for this decision and expressed his resentment:

> The reason my relationship ended before the war was because of this operation in the clinic in Vienna, which I did not want to forgive Alma Mahler for. One cannot intentionally prevent the development of a living being out of greed. It was an intervention in my development too, that is obvious.[11]

Oskar Kokoschka was convinced that he had to marry Alma, despite his lingering feelings about the abortion. In October 1912, he even spoke to Carl Moll about his intentions, and Moll gave his consent. Towards the end of the year, Kokoschka wrote to Alma: 'I am really looking forward to the beautiful, cheerful world when you will be my wife and will no longer be separated from me.'

Considered one of the greatest Expressionist artists of the twentieth century, Kokoschka created his most famous works with Alma as his model. The years of their relationship marked the most prodigious period of his life. During the last weeks of the year 1912, he was working on a double portrait of himself and Alma. He often portrayed her in various settings, painting landscapes, wall frescoes and everyday objects for her. In this particular portrait, she is depicted wearing a red dressing gown, gently touching his hands, holding hands as one would do during an engagement, both gazing calmly at the painter.

This picture also came to the attention of the architect Walter Gropius in the spring of 1913. Alma had been seeing Gropius again for about a year, a relationship that coincided with her growing involvement with Kokoschka, and continued to write letters to him, but in them, she remained silent about her acquaintance with Kokoschka. Gropius' feelings for Alma had cooled, and his letters to her also became less frequent.

Kokoschka, on the other hand, believed he was on solid ground and persisted in his efforts to compel Alma to marry him. He even ordered the banns, which Alma chose to ignore. However, when he ambushed her unannounced in Franzensbad (also known as Františkovy Lázně) during her summer vacation in mid-July 1913, it led to a scandal, and tensions between the two continued to escalate in the following weeks. Alma increasingly suffered from her partner's jealousy. After returning to Vienna, she stayed briefly in her apartment before heading to Tre Croci in Tyrol, deliberately avoiding a potential encounter with the infatuated Kokoschka.

Hesitant and apprehensive, Kokoschka nevertheless followed Alma to the Dolomites shortly afterwards. Despite the emotional tensions that had strained their relationship in the spring, the late summer weeks spent in the Italian mountains appear to have been marked by a rare harmony. While Kokoschka devoted himself to painting, Alma took long walks through the dense forests and delighted in watching young horses grazing in the alpine meadows. Outwardly, she appeared calm, even content – but inwardly, Alma remained cautious. The tranquil surroundings offered her a brief respite, yet the intensity of Kokoschka's love and the weight of his expectations lingered like a distant thunderstorm. For a fleeting moment, their passions seemed to settle into something almost serene – an interlude of peace before the inevitable storm.

In 1913 Kokoschka wrote a poem titled 'Allos Makar', an anagrammatic rearrangement of the names Alma and Oskar, which translates from Greek to 'different is happy'. He illustrated this poem with a graphic cycle of twenty drawings on Zinc lithographic plates for nine motifs in 1915. In it, he expressed:

> How wonderfully I was twisted, since a white bird called me from a misty world to look for her, ALLOS, ALLOS, which I never met. Because in an instant, she quickly turns into my being, like a back door. Ears suffer. Eyes seek to see her! I am the poor summer night that disappeared and cries from a crack in the earth.[12]

It was the artist's first attempt to break free from his relationship with Alma, which had mutated into an irrational and impossible dependency. Kokoschka's mother Maria Romana had long been worried about her beloved son's relationship with the woman seven years his senior. Later that summer, increasingly concerned by her son's obsessive behaviour, she wrote a threatening letter to Alma, stating that if his promising future were to be ruined, it would be Alma's doing. Maria Romana Kokoschka demanded that Alma release her son by a certain date, warning that otherwise, Alma would face dire consequences.

On the day in question, Kokoschka followed his mother to Alma's residence, anxious about the situation. He believed she was holding a gun, but he soon realised it was merely her fingers. Ultimately, Kokoschka reconciled with his mother and prevented her from pursuing Alma any further. However, the incident deepened his love for Alma, intertwining it with a sense of urgency and desperation.

The young artist's embraces became increasingly frequent, and Kokoschka envisioned himself as the future son-in-law of Anna and Carl Moll, dreaming of the house on the Semmering as his residence. Yet, storm clouds continued to gather in their domestic sphere. On 14 May 1914, Alma wrote in her diary: 'So – that too is over. I have lost Oskar. I can no longer find him in me. It is quiet around me; he has isolated me completely … We rubbed up against each other; now he can live peacefully and undisturbed.'

Amid this new crisis, the assassination of the Austrian heir to the throne, Archduke Franz Ferdinand and his wife, Sophie Chotek, Duchess of Hohenberg, on 28 June 1914, shook the nation. Alma was on the Semmering at the time. When she received the news of the declaration of war, she wrote: 'I sometimes imagine that I have caused all this upheaval in order to bring about some kind of awakening or reconciliation – and this could also mean death.'

This reflection showcases her complex feelings about the turbulent events surrounding her, as well as the personal turmoil she experienced in her relationships. In the first month of the war, Alma and Oskar repeatedly went to the Semmering. In Vienna, they continued to have separate addresses. In keeping with a new fashion, Oskar painted fans and gave Alma seven of them for her new house. These fans not only served as decorative pieces but also symbolised the delicate nature of their relationship, as they navigated the tumultuous landscape of their lives amid the chaos of war.

On 31 August 1914, Alma turned 35. However, the war was still raging, and she suffered deeply because of it, as she expressed in her diary: 'The terrible war is still ongoing. The earth is fertilised with the blood of the best men.'

She then quoted Kokoschka's words, which had impressed her very much: 'People cannot win – only lose … They will banish art from their lives, rub their eyes, and realise that Germans are always German and French always French. Romantics will always travel around the globe and talk about internationalism.'

A little further on, she reflected on her diminishing connection with Kokoschka: 'I want to get away from Oskar. He no longer fits into my life. He takes away all my drive.' She recounted how, just a few weeks ago, she played a piece from *Die Meistersinger* on the piano and enjoyed it. Alma concluded with a candid remark that she would give up any man for music.

On 6 October, Alma simply ran away from Oskar Kokoschka after one of their romantic encounters. She had not been feeling well all day and had asked Oskar not to come. However, she decided to 'get some fresh air', and at around half past ten in the evening, she and a friend went to the salon of the industrialist and art collector Carl Konrad von Reininghaus. There, she unexpectedly met Gustav Klimt and another acquaintance, Hofrat Josef Strzygowski, an art historian and founder of comparative art research and Coptic studies as an independent field. She engaged in conversation with them until three in the morning and returned home happy. She had escaped from Kokoschka's clutches and resolved never to let him remove her from her circle of friends again.

In the winter of 1914, the composer Hans Pfitzner came to Vienna to continue working on his opera *Palästrina* and wanted to stay overnight in Alma's apartment. However, she promptly put him up in a hotel. Pfitzner found the hotel too noisy and stood outside her door at night. Alma eventually took him in, leading to a flirtation with the composer. Chief conductor Siegfried Ochs also visited and brought her many rare musical scores as gifts. He expressed a desire to visit Alma's villa on the Semmering and stay with her. In response, Alma immediately shortened the tour and moved it to the Prater.

When Kokoschka begged her to visit him again, hoping to further his pursuit of becoming her husband, Alma found this very unpleasant. She marched to the popular *Salonnière* Berta Zuckerkandl, confident in Berta's match making abilities, especially since she had previously demonstrated a good understanding of Alma's wishes and needs in her relationship with Mahler. Berta had only one sentence ready for Alma: she reminded her of the young, handsome architect Walter Gropius, who had already courted Alma.

Alma immediately set out to find Walter, discovering that he had joined the military early and had been wounded in the war. One day before Christmas, she wrote him a letter: 'I am seldom alone – I have too many guests. I know that I could survive on my own, but I would like to be grateful for someone.'[13]

Nevertheless, she spent New Year's Eve with Kokoschka again, who, of course, got his hopes up once more. Alma thought she had been firm enough with him after that night, but on 2 January 1915, he wrote her an exuberant love letter. In it, he openly declared that 'the night she had taken him into her bed was unforgettably beautiful and incomparable', and that he wanted to be 'a good husband to her so that she would forget her dissatisfaction'. He concluded his letter with the anxious remark: 'My angel, I look nervously to the future until we are married and all your hopes rest on me.'

On 15 January, Alma noted in her diary that she had learned Walter Gropius was lying wounded in a field hospital. She felt this would have a significant impact on her life and decided to visit him there. Meanwhile, Kokoschka continued to send her love letters, though his desperation grew. In a final attempt to find a solution to his emotional turmoil, he chose to enlist in the military. Despondent, he believed the only way forward was to commit himself to the battlefields of the First World War. With the help of his friend, Austrian-Czechoslovak architect Adolf Loos, Kokoschka secured a place in the 15th Dragoon Regiment, the most distinguished cavalry regiment in the monarchy.

Alma travelled to Berlin with her friend Henriette Amalie 'Lilly' Lieser, to rekindle her relationship with Walter Gropius. Though he was still recovering from his injuries, Alma felt it was important to see him again. During their time together, she told him about her relationship with Kokoschka, but Gropius struggled to accept it. Alma, however, was resolute – she wanted to be loved on her own terms. To her, it was no mere coincidence that Gropius' birthday, 18 May, coincided with the death of Mahler.

They shared a brilliant evening together at a restaurant, enjoying the atmosphere, and she even stayed overnight with him once – 'without a nightgown or anything else', as she later confessed, 'Almost by force, I became this man's prey. I must say, I liked it very much.'

Before Alma and Lilly departed, Gropius returned to Berlin from a visit to his mother in Hanover, preparing for his imminent return to the front.

After his departure, Alma and Lilly drove to Berlin-Zehlendorf to visit Arnold Schönberg, who was living with his family in an apartment that had once been the studio of German sculptor Ferdinand Lepcke. Alma proposed organising a concert in Vienna and took charge of the planning, while Lilly managed the finances. Upon her return home, Alma invited many friends over, finding comfort in their company. Meanwhile, Kokoschka continued to send her letters from the front – though she rarely replied, doing her best to avoid him altogether.

As time passed, Alma became increasingly dissatisfied with her life, feeling that she wasn't living up to her own expectations. She even consulted a psychologist, though he could not make the decision for her. She found herself questioning again whether she should devote her life to Kokoschka, despite all the efforts she had made to win back Gropius. Seeking solace in music, Alma composed and dedicated four songs for piano and mezzo-soprano, which were published by Mahler's publisher, Universal.

At the same time, she organised a concert in the red salon of her apartment to celebrate the awarding of the 'Mahler Foundation Prize' to Austrian composer Julius Bittner. Afterwards, she retreated to the Semmering with Anna, conveniently avoiding the potential disaster of the Arnold Schönberg concert. Schönberg's music, still highly controversial at the time, was known for provoking strong reactions among conservative Viennese audiences. Just the year before, his 1913 concert at the Musikverein – later dubbed the '*Skandalkonzert*' – had ended in a near riot. Alma, ever conscious of her social standing and public image, may have sensed that attending another of Schönberg's avant-garde evenings, might involve too much unpredictability and too little elegance.

In his letters to Alma during this period, Walter Gropius expressed jealousy over her connection to Oskar Kokoschka. Upon returning to Vienna,

Alma found a letter from Gropius that made her reconsider everything. She realised finally that he loved her deeply, and she loved him more than she did Kokoschka. She longed to live in peace with a man who made her feel valued.

On 18 August 1915, Alma Mahler married Walter Gropius in a civil ceremony in Berlin at the registry office III in the Parochialstraße. Gropius was granted just two days of leave for the wedding before having to return to the front. The witnesses at the ceremony were seemingly taken straight from the street: Richard Manzke, a 28-year-old bricklayer, and Erich Subke, a 21-year-old military-technical pioneer from the special forces. A lavish honeymoon was out of the question: She wrote in her diary:

> On 18 August, 1915, I married Walter Gropius. Nothing should throw me off course from now on. My desire is clear … I want nothing more than to make this person happy. I am safe, calm, excited, happy, like never before. May God preserve my love for me.[14]

After the wedding, Alma returned to Vienna alone and had to navigate married life without her husband. She believed that she loved Walter Gropius, but in truth, the two had very little time to truly get to know each other. No one could have predicted how their relationship would evolve after the war. However, Gropius genuinely loved Alma and hoped to rebuild his life, upended by the war, with her by his side. He remained hopeful that the war would not drag on for too long. Alma and he were fully aware that their marriage would initially be long-distance, dictated by the circumstances of the war.

Alma desired an elegant husband and a child, and Gropius was so handsome that a child from him would undoubtedly be something special. Moreover, this marriage would likely free her from concerns such as Mahler's Jewishness and the entanglements of dependence on Kokoschka. She began referring to herself as Alma Gropius-Mahler or Alma Mahler-Gropius. She even entertained the idea of moving to America with her husband once the war ended, as she had friends there. However, Gropius, who came from the German middle class – a world quite foreign to Alma – showed little interest in her plans.

Gropius was granted only rare leave to return to Austria from the war, and for this reason, Alma decided to visit him herself from time to time. She felt comfortable in the role of wife. It was clear to Alma: with Walter, she would find fulfilment on one hand and her inner balance on the other. In her diary, she wrote:

> I have been married for over a month. It is the strangest marriage imaginable – so unmarried, so free, and yet tied down. I don't like anyone. I almost prefer women today because at least they are not aggressive. But I would like to finally enter a harbour. Our marriage is kept secret for the time being.[15]

During a visit to Berlin in October 1915, Alma accompanied her husband to a military equipment store on a very hot day in the midst of the war. She had to wait for him as he carefully selected the leather for his riding boots. Gropius had a great appreciation for quality and took his time choosing the right materials. Alma waited outside, but the heat was unbearable. As she stood there, she passed a book cart and decided to buy the monthly magazine *Die weißen Blätter*, one of the most important German monthly magazines of literary Expressionism. Flipping through it, her eyes fell on a poem by a certain Franz Werfel. The poem struck her and she was instantly captivated by Werfel's words. She felt it was the most beautiful poem she had ever read. Without hesitation, she went straight to her house on the Semmering and began to compose a piece, pouring her emotions into the music based on the profound feelings evoked by the poem.

Alma's complex past with Oskar Kokoschka seemed to haunt her even in her new marriage. News of his supposed death in August 1915 came as a shock, yet her reaction was unexpectedly detached. The harrowing account of Kokoschka's near-fatal injuries, relayed by his friend Adolf Loos, painted a dramatic scene: a bullet wound to the temple, entrapment under dead horses, and a Cossack's lance through his chest. The rumours of his death, however, proved to be false. Yet for Alma, the emotional impact was faint, her focus shifting instead to retrieving his love letters and sketches from his studio – an act that she later justified but which Kokoschka found difficult to forgive. Her letter to Gropius conveyed her growing indifference, doubting the severity of Kokoschka's wounds and his honesty altogether.

This episode marked a pivotal point in Alma's life, distancing her further from Kokoschka and solidifying her commitment to Gropius, despite her inner conflicts and past entanglements.

However, as soon as Kokoschka could be transported, he was sent to a hospital in Vienna to receive more professional treatment. In Vienna, he learned of Alma's marriage to Walter Gropius. Longing to see her again, he sent Hans Loos to intercede on his behalf – but Alma refused to meet him. She was convinced she did not want to waste her time on his emotional instability. Alma had no interest in men who needed to be rescued; she wanted to start a family. Although Gropius desired a traditional marriage and insisted that husband and wife could not be friends, Alma continued to seek stimulating company and intellectual exchange with other men – including the German choir director and composer Siegfried Ochs and the writer Albert von Trentini. If one of these men fell in love with her, she claimed, it was not her fault. Gropius was understandably unsettled by these friendships, but Alma now felt confident that she had tangible proof of genuine love – she was pregnant with Gropius' child.

Kokoschka, upon hearing about Alma's pregnancy, was deeply wounded. In the meantime, he recovered more quickly than his doctors had expected and requested to be sent to the Italian front as a negotiating officer. While on duty there, a saddle bridge he was on exploded and he was taken to the hospital once again. Alma refused his request to visit him. After his recovery, Kokoschka travelled to Dresden and then to Berlin, feeling he had had enough of Vienna for a while.

Meanwhile, Alma relished her pregnancy at her house on the Semmering, where she invited several women, including the two countesses Margarethe Gretl Maria Anna Coudenhove-Kalergi and Nora Drašković von Lützow. Alma thought a lot about herself and her evolution: after Gustav Mahler, she was now married to Walter Gropius, and both men gave her the great joy of having children. In her diary, she wrote:

> This strange pregnancy that I am in now. Now I long for the birth, which will give me new insights. It must bring another great new experience into my life. And the pain that women feel must disappear alongside it. It must be like this and not otherwise. Everything can only be thought of by God for joy.[16]

On 5 October 1916, Alma Manon Anna Justina Carolina Gropius, nicknamed 'Mutzi', was born. She was named after Walter's mother. Gropius had been given two weeks' special leave in September to be present for the birth and to support Alma, but Manon was born two weeks after he had already returned to the front.

It was only later, during a short leave in November, that he was finally able to hold his daughter in his arms for the first time. He was instantly enchanted, raving about her long, slender aristocratic fingers and her big eyes. Shortly thereafter, he had to return once again to the front. By this time, nearly two years of service had left him physically and emotionally down. What it meant to be confronted with the senseless slaughter of friend and foe every day remained a mystery to Alma. She repeatedly made scenes in her letters, especially when she had not heard from him for a while and suspected him of cheating on her. Alma now had a second, lovely little daughter, but no husband. She wrote in her diary:

> I am in love with this creature. Am I the same one who flew with Gustav Mahler, or is it someone else? Everything in my life is a mystery to me. Now I am feeding the child and do not understand the lust that I had once learned through life. Walter Gropius is at the front … we have been married for over a year … we do not have each other, and sometimes I am afraid we will become strangers to each other.[17]

Alma could have returned to Oskar Kokoschka at any time, but chose not to. She reflected: 'I am getting fed up with this makeshift life. Oskar Kokoschka has become a strange shadow to me … nothing about his life interests me anymore. And yet, I loved him once.'[18] Alma was relieved to find a sense of inner peace that allowed her to remain faithful to Gropius. She truly loved him and had no desire to leave him. As she assessed the men in her life, she made a revealing comparison: for her, Gustav Mahler emerged from the chaos of abstraction; Oskar Kokoschka, however, was the embodiment of genius. She viewed Walter Gropius as the improviser of desires and cultures, whereas Joseph Fraenkel was a master of brilliant improvisation.

Reflecting on the men in her life, she mused: 'I want children from Walter, artistic works from Oskar, and the triumph of spirit from Fraenkel, which he never offered me. I wish Fraenkel had moved into my house and spent the rest of his life with me.'

At times, Alma even considered devoting herself to the church, but knew it was neither feasible nor wise. When she looked at her daughters, her heart swelled with pride. Anna was now 13 and no longer needed her mother as much. Clearly Mahler's daughter, she possessed a unique spirit and was becoming increasingly like her mother. Having learned independence early, she maintained a certain distance, as if she belonged to another world entirely. She adored caring for her little sister Manon, and became almost a second mother to her. She admired her stepfather, even though she seldom saw him. When Gropius was home, he was the perfect gentleman, but his temper sometimes got the better of him – like the time he angrily threw a fan painted by Kokoschka into the fire, an outburst that baffled Alma.

After recovering from the birth of Manon, Alma re-engaged with social life, meeting friends such as Paul Kammerer, Alban and Helene Berg, Arnold Schönberg, and Gustav Klimt. She also took pleasure in literature, finding great joy in her acquaintance with Franz Blei. Meeting Blei in Vienna and on the Semmering, she even briefly considered him as a potential lover. Blei, a writer, translator, editor and literary critic, was renowned for his work *The Great Bestiary of German Literature*, in which he depicted contemporary writers as animal allegories. Among his most acclaimed translations were Oscar Wilde's fairy tales and *Dangerous Liaisons* by Pierre Choderlos de Laclos – still regarded as some of the finest to this day.

Walter Gropius was also enthusiastic about Franz Blei. When Blei left them again, he and Alma laughed and affectionately spoke of 'lead poisoning'. This was a playful wordplay on Blei's last name, Blei – which means 'lead' in German – and *Bleivergiftung* (lead poisoning), suggesting a light-hearted, affectionate teasing about Blei's somewhat overwhelming presence. Blei also offered to bring a dear long-time friend, Franz Werfel, to visit them one day. Having discovered Werfel's poem 'The Knower', in the October 1915 issue of *Die weißen Blätter*, Alma simply wanted to meet the famous poet.

As Alma moved forward, she found herself at another crossroads. Her past was both a heavy weight and a wellspring of insight, informing her as she entered yet another phase of her life. The deep love she had once felt for Gustav Mahler and the fiery passion that followed with Oskar Kokoschka were now tempered by the quietude of motherhood and the stability she sought in her marriage to Walter Gropius. And still, a new, unfamiliar horizon beckoned. With her curiosity and intellect, Alma was about to meet Franz Werfel, whose work she already admired. His arrival would open a further chapter in Alma's ever-evolving life, filled with fresh artistic, emotional, and intellectual exploration.

Chapter 5

The Complexity of Love – Alma's Relationships and Romances

In the autumn of 1917, Alma's marriage to Walter Gropius, strained by the pressures of war, had settled into a tolerable rhythm. Yet, as life continued with its uneasy calm, a small but powerful force was quietly approaching. Unbeknownst to Alma, her seemingly insignificant acquaintance with Franz Blei would soon lead her to someone who would forever alter her future. It was through Blei's introduction to his close friend that Alma would step into a destiny far grander than she could have ever imagined, making her future both thrilling and uncertain.

On 14 November 1917, Alma returned to her apartment in Elisabethstraße in Vienna's 1st district, still deeply moved by a conversation with the Saxon envoy Helene von Nostitz, who had just tragically lost her newborn son due to a medical accident – a carbolic enema that had burned the child's little body from the inside out. Distracted by the heavy news, Alma was surprised to find Franz Blei in her apartment, accompanied by the poet Franz Werfel, an Austrian writer of Jewish-German-Bohemian origin.

As Werfel had entered her home, he seemed at ease, as if the space were already familiar to him. Alma studied him with quiet interest. Werfel was a stocky man with sensual lips and beautiful big blue eyes beneath a Goethean forehead. The more he gave of himself, the more he won Alma's attention. His exaggerated love for humanity, and his familiar phrase 'How can I be happy when a creature on earth still suffers…',[1] struck a chord with her – though Alma could not help but recognise echoes of something she had once heard from Mahler. Werfel's true nature revealed itself later that evening when, in a moment of confession, he shared his own sins and his deep desire to 'live well'.

Franz Werfel was the son of Rudolf Werfel, an industrialist and glove manufacturer with international operations in cities such as Prague, Tuchkov, Paris, Berlin, London, Glasgow and Brussels. Drafted at the outbreak of the war, Franz spent most of his service in Italy, a country he grew to like, despite struggling with military discipline as a pampered only-son in his Jewish family. After injuring his foot during a mountain hike, he was transferred to the military press department in Vienna, where the work was not particularly demanding for him.

For this reason, he often frequented the Viennese coffee houses, for example the Café Central or the Café Herrenhof, whose other patrons included the writers Robert Musil, Egon Erwin Kisch, and Franz Blei, indulging in copious amounts of coffee and cigarettes. Alma had a deep aversion to these coffee-house circles. To her, they epitomised the less appealing side of Viennese society – too much smoke and endless cups of coffee. Moreover, these venues were often filled with cynical, predominantly Jewish intellectuals who snobbishly critiqued Austria's social order. Women were typically not welcome in such gatherings, and Alma found the idea of a male-only circle as distasteful as that of a ladies' coffee party.

When Franz Blei arrived at her apartment with Franz Werfel, Alma first saw in him the embodiment of a cliché she had always tried to avoid: a typical, plump, and rather short Jewish man with an air that made him seem much older than he was. But Blei, who was a well-known writer and critic, had introduced the young and talented Werfel to Alma, sensing a potential connection between the two. To her, he did not appear eleven years her junior. Although Werfel had begun his literary career, he had yet to reach the success that Mahler had when he met Alma. However, Werfel had a significant asset – his captivating voice, which quickly won over audiences during his readings. He was an intelligent man who did not need to monopolise attention.

The evening began with a political discussion, as Werfel passionately advocated for social democracy. However, as the conversation unfolded, he grew more relaxed, freer, and began to reveal more of himself. He shared his love for music, especially Mahler's compositions, which had drawn him to Alma. 'I thank my God on my knees that he allows me to interact closely with such spirits', Alma responded. 'The human experience is so magnificently wonderful that I always find it difficult to return from my delight to reality.'[2]

As the night deepened, Werfel confessed his sins to Alma, admitting his addiction to 'living well'. Unfazed, Alma answered, 'We don't always think about our deaths either.'[3]

Blei quickly suggested leaving, but he stayed on, unable to resist the magnetic pull of the evening. However, the snowstorm outside soon kept both – Blei and Werfel – from leaving Alma's apartment. As the night went on, Alma was swept up in the magical atmosphere of their conversation and music. Werfel spoke passionately about his admiration for the Slavic peoples, especially the Czechs, and he criticised the Viennese as too insular. He called the Austrian dramatist and writer Franz Grillparzer the archetype of the old Viennese, who could only live in Vienna. Later, however, Werfel's opinion on Grillparzer changed. Alma, deeply entranced, wrote in her diary: 'Many wonderful things happened … one night was … a lovely night … Werfel, Blei, Gropius. We cheered music … and committed adultery in front of the whole world. Franz Werfel is a wonderful miracle.'[4]

Shortly before Christmas, Walter Gropius returned home, and once again Blei and Werfel visited Alma. Alma played excerpts from *The Meistersingers of Nuremberg*, with Werfel singing along, followed by a recital of his poems. Alma felt a connection to him that she had never experienced with her husband. That night, Gropius announced he would stay in Vienna for Christmas, which disturbed Alma's plans to spend time with her daughters and friends. She found herself wanting nothing more than to spend her time with Werfel. As the new year approached and Gropius had to return to the field shortly before New Year's Day in 1918, Alma felt that it would likely be one of her last goodbyes to him, whom she no longer wished to accompany to the train, focusing instead on matters that seemed far more significant to her.

Alma and her daughter Anna planned to attend a concert at the Musikverein conducted by the popular Dutch maestro Willem Mengelberg. He was renowned as the finest interpreter of her late husband Gustav Mahler's music. That evening, Mengelberg was set to perform *Das Lied von der Erde*, Mahler's deeply personal work, showcasing a new compositional style and orchestration technique. However, just as they were about to leave Gropius unexpectedly appeared, having missed his train and needing to wait until the evening for the next one. Gropius expressed his desire to join the concert, but Alma was unwilling to give up one of her tickets. To avoid conflict, she instead invited Carl Moll and her mother for dinner at her home. The evening was sombre and quiet, and Gropius soon departed to catch his train.

The last days of the year were filled with concerts for Alma, passing by quickly. On 1 January 1918, New Year's Day, a concert featured Richard Strauss's *Ein Heldenleben* (*A Hero's Life*) and Gustav Mahler's *Fourth Symphony*. Alma had planned a dinner at her home afterward for Mengelberg, his orchestra, and seventy invited guests, including nobles and affluent Viennese, lasting in high spirits until three in the morning, with discussions about art and culture.

In her diary, Alma confessed meeting Franz Werfel at the concert:

> It was at the concert ... deeply connected by glances with Werfel. He came during the break, and we went home together. Our silent understanding brought us to the edge. It could only end with him taking my hand, kissing it, and our lips finding each other. He stammered words with no meaning or context.[5]

Alma was concerned about the age difference, much like Gustav Mahler had been when he started a relationship with her. 'This deep musical and spiritual bond with Franz Werfel felt almost fateful,' Alma confided. She expressed that their love was inevitable and sustained by music, which she believed shielded them. Alma mused, 'If I were twenty years younger, I would abandon everything and be with him.' Yet, her bourgeois life held her back, causing her sadness as she witnessed Werfel's path. He often urged her to visit him at Hotel Bristol, but she hesitated due to societal expectations. Despite her reservations, she eventually agreed to help him proofread his manuscript *Der Gerichtstag* (*The Court Day*). Those shared hours, though tinged with restrained affection, were profoundly meaningful to her.

After the holidays, life resumed its intensity, and Werfel returned to his duties at the Austrian War Press Headquarters. There, he collaborated with prominent Austrian writers such as Robert Musil, Stefan Zweig, and Hugo von Hofmannsthal, crafting articles on perseverance and sentimental soldier narratives for the press.

In January, Werfel was sent to Switzerland to deliver lectures on Austria's wartime efforts. By the time he boarded the train on 18 January, Alma was pregnant. He wrote to Alma during his journey, mentioning that he had listened to music they both cherished, specifically Hans Pfitzner's piano trio.

Amid the turbulence of early 1918, Alma suffered another emotional blow with the death of Gustav Klimt. Her former admirer, a symbol of her youth and artistic inspiration, who had been a lasting influence on her life, died on 6 February. He had suffered a stroke in his flat in the Wiener Westbahnstraße which had left him paralyzed on one side, followed by complications from influenza-like pneumonia in the General Hospital, in Vienna's 9th district, in Alser Straße 4. Alma, deeply affected by the news, was confronted with the reality of Vienna, losing one of its greatest modern artists. His passing not only symbolised a personal loss but also marked the end of an era, as the vibrant pre-war cultural world of Vienna was fading away.

His sudden death left Alma in a state of shock. She wrote in her diary:

> Gustav Klimt died on 6 February 1918. With him, a large part of my youth has gone from my life. I have never stopped loving him. How I once understood him! And I have never stopped loving him – albeit in a very different form. I was on the right path. I want to write down my many memories of him as they come to me.[6]

The loss pulled her back to memories of the vibrant, daring world they once shared. Despite the passing years and the complex web of relationships she navigated, she had never fully distanced herself from the emotional bond she felt with Klimt.

His works, particularly the grand university paintings that had been rejected, resonated deeply with her. 'He was an infinitely fine colourist. His large pictures for the university were rejected. They were too modern, too strange, in a word: too important. These gigantic pictures are the strongest thing he painted.'[7]

She felt an inner ache, a recognition of how ahead of his time he had been, and a sorrow for the cultural narrow-mindedness that stifled his genius. Klimt's death, in the midst of a devastating flu epidemic, left her with a sense of irretrievable loss. As she reflected, Alma noted, 'I still cannot understand that he should be dead.' It was as though a part of her, a piece of Vienna's once glorious artistic heart, had vanished forever. The acknowledgment of his respect for rising talents like Oskar Kokoschka highlighted the generational shift Alma was now witnessing, adding a sense of ageing and change to her grief.

Meanwhile Franz Werfel used his time in Switzerland until March 1918 to great personal advantage. He gave numerous lectures about Austria's wartime efforts, but he also read from his own works, such as *The Trojan Women by Euripides*, at the Zurich City Theatre, which quickly raised his profile in Switzerland. However, during a lecture in Davos, he launched a sharp critique of the bourgeoisie and militarism. This caused an uproar, and the Swiss authorities demanded his immediate suspension. Consequently, Werfel was ordered to leave Switzerland and return to Vienna without delay.

When he arrived in Vienna at the end of March, Alma was already three months pregnant. She fervently hoped that this child had been conceived with Franz Werfel after the Mahler concert in the new year, and not with her still-husband Walter Gropius at Christmastime. The situation became even more complicated when Gropius, seriously wounded, was transferred to a military hospital in Vienna – placing him unexpectedly close to his pregnant wife.

It was a strange situation for Alma, who wanted to give her husband the impression that the child was his and carefully concealed her ongoing relationship with Werfel. That summer, she moved with her two daughters into their house in Breitenstein am Semmering. However, they soon faced the bitter reality of war, with little food other than new potatoes, polenta, cheap meat substitutes, and mushrooms. At the end of July, Werfel joined them, eager to spend time alone with Alma. But then Emmy Redlich, the wife of Viennese sugar manufacturer Fritz Redlich, arrived with her 18-year-old daughter, disrupting their idyll. On the night of 27/28 July, a catastrophe unfolded. First, Anna and Alma played Mahler's *Eighth Symphony* on the harmonium for their guests, and Alma had to engage in a heated discussion with Emmy Redlich late into the night. After the two women went to bed, Franz Werfel sneaked into Alma's room, and the two made love with deep passion. Werfel forgot his moral, spiritual resolve – a gesture of warning – and later wrote in his diary: 'I had forgotten the sign and failed to control myself ... We made love. I did not spare her. At dawn, I went back to my room.'[8]

At daybreak, Alma woke up feeling unwell. She had started bleeding heavily, which was a result of the passionate encounter. At half past five in the morning Werfel was instructed by the English maid Maud Turner to fetch a doctor. It was raining heavily and he had to rush to a nearby sanatorium, returning with the on-call doctor, who himself had tuberculosis. At the same time, Anna ran down to the village to inform her stepfather, Walter Gropius, by telephone.

Meanwhile, the doctor was attending to Alma, who turned out to be a very stubborn patient. She looked at his rough hands in disgust and refused to be touched by him. Werfel, feeling guilty, blamed himself for the situation and decided to leave. At Breitenstein am Semmering station, he saw Gropius disembark from a military train, accompanied by a well-known gynaecologist. On 31 July, Alma was finally transported to Vienna, even having to be taken the last leg of the journey in a hearse to the Löw Sanatorium, where Mahler had died. It was an unusual situation, but the doctors there were excellent. The only way to save both mother and child was by inducing labour. During the night of 1/2 August 1918, Alma gave birth to a boy in great pain; Walter stayed by her side the entire time, believing he was the child's father. The baby was baptised Martin Carl Johannes Gropius. Meanwhile, Werfel received reassuring news about Alma and the newborn child, learning that the doctors had done all they could. 'An operation was not necessary. Everything is said to be very good. She is now in the sanatorium not far from here as I write this. Thank God. I am calm and happy. Allow myself to listen to music again.' After the good news, he went to the Herrenhof Cafe for dinner and met friends there.

Overcome with joy, he wrote a hymn-like letter to Alma. Once Alma recovered, the two exchanged daily letters, delivered by a messenger. In these letters, she addressed him as 'My beloved husband', and signed 'Alma Maria Werfel'. This game of secrecy from her still-husband, Walter Gropius, troubled her greatly. She confided in Franz Werfel daily, sharing her concerns: 'The hardest thing for me now is being with Walter.'

But Martin, Alma and Walter's son, was born frail and sickly. He had started having cramps on the third day after birth, as he seemed to be dehydrated due to his mother's prolonged bleeding and lack of nourishment. Alma, troubled by his delicate health, began to suspect that the child's condition was due to Werfel's genes rather than Gropius', whose lineage she believed was responsible for the striking beauty of their daughter, Manon. Tragically, Martin passed away after less than ten months, his short life marked by progeria, a rare condition causing premature ageing.

During the first few weeks after the birth, things generally seemed improve between Alma and Walter. Then, on 25 August, he received a devastating blow. He arrived at the sanatorium to visit Alma with a big bouquet of flowers and, by sheer coincidence, Alma was talking to Franz Werfel on the phone. Walter overheard her side of the conversation and her use of intimate first names made him suspicious. He confronted her and she confessed that she was talking to Werfel. In an instant, Walter understood the truth of the situation and collapsed as if struck by lightning. He had spent four years at war and carried the heavy burden of all his dead comrades; Alma knew he deserved better from her. Distraught, Gropius went to Werfel's home to confront him, but found no one there. He left a note: 'I am beginning to love you with all the strength I have. Spare Alma. Such misfortune can happen, especially if our (our!) child died.'[9] This seemingly paradoxical sentence reflects Gropius' emotional collapse – caught between grief, betrayal, and a desperate desire for some form of dignity or redemption.

When Werfel found this message, he initially saw it as nothing more than a noble gesture. Upon reflection, however, he was deeply moved, and began to have doubts: was his love for Alma truly right, or was it causing irreparable pain to those around them?

Werfel wrote a reply to Gropius, which he sent to the sanatorium; he also phoned Alma. In his response, Werfel expressed his remorse and acknowledged the pain caused by his relationship with Alma, but his emotions were still tied to her, and he struggled with the guilt of the situation. When he spoke to Alma, he conveyed his internal conflict, questioning whether their relationship was worth the suffering it was causing. Though he did not explicitly ask her to leave her husband, Werfel's words reflected his growing uncertainty about what the future would hold for them. Alma, in turn, was becoming increasingly worried about their son, Martin, and mentioned that he seemed exhausted, as though he had just returned from a long journey.

Faced with having to choose between two men, Alma acknowledged the deep bond between herself and Werfel. She agreed with Werfel's description that their attraction was profound and absolute, and felt that everything about him affected her in an all-encompassing, intense way. Unlike her previous relationships, Werfel did not rush her into anything. His calm, despite the turmoil, was like the sea – restless yet serene.

Alma did not know how to decide. Despite her feelings for Walter having subsided, it was still very difficult for her end her relationship with him. Confusingly, she also began to lose more and more interest in Werfel. Even the smallest things began to bother her. His apartment for example, where she described the furnishings as 'fake', and judged them to be cheap and tasteless. Walking into his apartment, she had the feeling of walking into the room of an art dealer's mistress. All these minor annoyances, coupled with the difficulty of the situation, built up, causing Alma to become more and more insecure and angry.

In early November 1918, with Alma back in Vienna and Walter Gropius still at the front, he wrote her a poignant letter. In it, he asked her to let him take their daughter, Manon, while suggesting she continue her life with Franz Werfel and their son, Martin. The letter left Alma deeply unsettled; she spent the entire day in tears. Later, when both Gropius and Werfel arrived, Alma made an emotional declaration: she would leave both men and choose a solitary path with her children. Gropius pleaded for her forgiveness for suggesting he take Manon, while Werfel tried to diffuse the tense situation.

A week later, just as the First World War was ending, an explosive argument broke out between Alma and Werfel. On 3 November, Austria-Hungary concluded an armistice with the Allies and on 9 November, Kaiser Wilhelm II abdicated, the Republic of Germany was proclaimed by Philipp Scheidemann from the Reichstag building, and two days later the war ended with the signing of the armistice treaty on 11 November between France, England and Germany, in a railway carriage in Compiègne in northern France. Charles I's written renunciation on 11 November 1918 of any part in the state affairs of the newly created state of German Austria marked the end of a process that had begun with the proclamation of the so-called 'Peoples' Manifesto' on 16 October that same year.

On Tuesday, 12 November 1918, the day after the official end of the war, Franz Werfel appeared at Alma's apartment, dressed in an older uniform and full of nervous energy and revolutionary fervour. He then headed to the parliamentary quarter in Vienna, where many Austrians had gathered to witness the birth of a new republic. His friends from the 'Red Guards' were striving for a Soviet dictatorship based on the Russian model. But before he left, Werfel asked Alma for her blessing and did not want to leave without a kiss from her. Although she did not fully understand what he was planning, she knew that it was a false revolution and in her heart she was against it; Werfel threw himself into the fray. When he returned to Alma's apartment that evening, she was horrified by his appearance. His eyes were bloodshot, his face bloated and his entire body was covered in grime – dirt clung to his hands, and his old military uniform was stained and dishevelled. The acrid smell of alcohol and tobacco clung on him. During the day, he had joined a group of radical young intellectuals and artists – some of them writers – who had loosely organised themselves into what they called the 'Red Guard', inspired by the revolutionary upheavals sweeping across Europe. These Red Guards were not yet a formal movement, but a makeshift group driven by revolutionary fervour, with some members advocating for a socialist or even authoritarian state structure in the new republic. Werfel, swept up in the moment, had gone with them to the parliamentary quarter, mingled with the crowds, and participated in the public demonstrations – shouting slogans, drinking, and, as Alma later surmised, possibly even getting involved in the more chaotic, disorganised elements of the uprising.

When Alma saw him in this state – unkempt, intoxicated, politically inflamed – she felt deeply repelled. The poetic sensitivity and spiritual depth she had once admired in him seemed to have vanished in the fever of the street. She turned away and told him to leave her apartment. Before he went, she offered a biting remark, less a piece of advice than a judgement: 'If you had created something beautiful, you would be beautiful now.'[10] What she meant was clear: in abandoning art for intoxicated political spectacle, he had lost something essential – and in her eyes, he had ceased to be worthy of admiration.

This encounter at her apartment, as well as Werfel's involvement in the revolutionary tumult, would forever alter Alma's perception of him. Her love turned to disillusionment that day.

The balance of power between Alma and Franz Werfel was redefined in those November days. From then on, Alma took charge of when and how they saw one another. Werfel, still young and susceptible to influence, assumed a more passive role and let Alma guide him. One of the first things she wanted to put an end to was his coffee-house life. To this end, she withdrew to Breitenstein am Semmering, where she received a striking letter from him:

> If Walter loves you too, then we should both marry you, because anything else would be a fraud, and it would have to be recognised as such. What does he want? He's only making you sick. In contrast, we are making each other happy. He doesn't belong to you, and he should see his mistake. Even if I didn't exist, he doesn't belong to you. Tell him that. Don't be weak or compliant … If you lack the courage to change our lives, then I will.[11]

Alma did not have the courage. Deep down, something reminded her of the first child she had conceived outside the sanctity of marriage, and the repercussions it had on the father. The vows of marriage commanded respect, even if she could not bring herself to live by them. Furthermore, she did not want to hurt people – especially not Walter Gropius, who had behaved more decently than was expected of him under the circumstances. After all, she also knew that the different political and religious views between them could give rise to conflict.

Gropius, meanwhile, found himself in a deeply compromised position, responsible not only for his own actions but also for the wellbeing of his wife, their children – Manon, Alma's daughter Anna, and their infant son, Martin. The public watched closely, waiting for any misstep. Despite their personal turmoil, Gropius viewed Franz Werfel as a trusted family friend and valued his literary talents.

In a desperate attempt to maintain some semblance of harmony, Gropius continued to foster a cordial relationship with Werfel, sending him letters of support and inviting him for coffee. At the same time, he threw himself into a pivotal architectural project, one that could secure his professional future and potentially salvage his marriage. With aspirations to create a revolutionary school of design in Germany, Gropius envisioned a new movement that would rival the grandeur of the Austrian Secession and the Wiener Werkstätten. And he already had an idea what he wanted to call this ambitious project: Bauhaus.

While Walter Gropius continued to focus on his ambitious plans of his Bauhaus-project, Alma and Franz Werfel retreated to Breitenstein am

Semmering, seeking solace in their seclusion and trying to escape the chaos of the revolution. Alma envisioned a peaceful home there for herself and Werfel, where he could work away from distractions. However, as Christmas approached, Alma's thoughts turned once again to Gustav Mahler. She began to feel emotionally estranged from Werfel, doubting his reverence for the Catholic holidays and questioning whether their connection could match the spiritual and cultural depth she associated with Mahler. Increasingly uneasy, Alma secretly hoped that Werfel would extend his stay in Prague, where he had gone to visit his family for the holidays. In an apparent attempt to divert her growing discomfort – both with her own ambivalence and with Werfel's absence – Alma picked a quarrel with his unmarried sister, Marianne Amalie Werfel, known as 'Mizzi'. She accused Mizzi of interfering in their relationship and blamed her for creating distance between herself and Werfel. But Werfel remained calm and resolute, explaining that the trip was a necessary familial duty: as the only son, he had to support Mizzi, who was now effectively managing the household in his absence.

In early 1919, Alma turned her thoughts back to religion and politics, reflecting in her diary on the concept of Bolshevism as the 'religion of the future'. She compared it to the early days of Christianity, seeing parallels with the Jewish anticipation of a Messiah. This period also saw Alma wrestling with her own Catholic identity and the turbulent political climate.

At the same time, her family struggles deepened. Manon, at 2½ years old, frequently asked for her father, and 'Uncle' Franz Werfel could not fill the gap. Anna, who helped care for the children, was unsurprised by Alma's inability to cook even a simple meal. Meanwhile, little Martin's health worsened, requiring a hospital visit for a procedure related to hydrocephalus, though it provided little relief.

Alma's emotional burden grew heavier. She poured her heart into Mahler's *Second Symphony*, feeling overwhelmed and even contemplating suicide. In a desperate moment, she wrote in her diary, reflecting on her anguish:

> Yesterday I was shaken by Gustav Mahler's Second Symphony like never before. Stung to the heart, I came home with the firm intention of killing myself. And I couldn't. God must help me. Everything would

> be so easy. Anna is free and easy. Manon consoles Walter Gropius … Franz Werfel is beyond barriers. If only I can find the tremendous courage to end my life and that of my boy, because this child is my whole concern and, despite little hope, my greatest happiness. Last night my greedy fingers hovered on the edge of death at the open window.[12]

To distract herself, Alma decided to resume her Sunday gatherings, which she had neglected during her time with Werfel and her pregnancy. She craved the company of friends again and invited Arnold Schönberg and his family for lunch. Afterward, some of Schönberg's students, pianists, played Mahler's *Sixth Symphony*. Alma felt an overwhelming sense of guilt, as though she was more fortunate and more beautiful than everyone else. In her guilt, she gave Schönberg's daughter a platinum bracelet with diamonds. Yet, in her gold dress in the red salon, she was Alma Mahler, not Walter Gropius' wife, who had fallen in love with Franz Werfel. On 2 February, she wrote in her diary that she 'loved Gustav Mahler and always would', and that she would continue searching for him, even beyond death, but would never find him.

Alma continued to reflect on her relationships, stating, 'Everyone who comes near me is immature and irrelevant – Kokoschka, Werfel, important artists – they are nothing compared to him. There's always something missing, which leaves me dissatisfied. I was so foolish to even look.'

Meanwhile, Martin's condition worsened, and the doctor gave no hope for his survival. As a result, Alma come to deeply resent Franz Werfel. She realised, 'Werfel must disappear from my life. He is the cause of all my misery, and my desire to love has overridden my own well-being.'

Werfel, perplexed by Alma's erratic emotions, chose to keep his distance, yet he longed for her commitment and hoped she would eventually decide in his favour. At this time, Alma's social reputation was suffering due to Oskar Kokoschka's notorious and scandalous antics. In summer of 1918, Kokoschka had commissioned a life-sized doll of Alma from the well-known Munich doll maker, Hermine Moos. The doll, a bizarre symbol of his obsession, became Kokoschka's constant companion in Dresden. He showcased it everywhere – at the opera, concerts, and gatherings, much to the amusement and gossip of the public. Even Hans Posse, a notable art historian and future curator of the infamous *Führermuseum*, who let Kokoschka live in his house, got involved, assigning a maid to care for the doll as if it were Alma herself.

Kokoschka lavished the doll with fine Parisian clothes, personally dressing it for social occasions. He even hosted elaborate parties in her honour, treating the doll as if it were his beloved. The spectacle reached its peak when Kokoschka decided to stage a farewell party to sever his ties with the 'Alma' doll. Inviting friends, musicians, and with copious amounts of champagne, he bid a theatrical goodbye. The next morning, the postmen reported a possible murder after spotting the doll, headless and drenched in fake blood, sprawled in the garden. The police arrived expecting a crime scene, only to find a mutilated doll. Amid laughter and embarrassment, the remnants were disposed of by garbage collectors, but the entire episode left a lasting stain on Alma's public image. It also cemented Kokoschka's status as a controversial and eccentric figure in the art world, showcasing his unhinged fixation on Alma and further complicating her already tumultuous personal life.

Oskar Kokoschka's reputation for bizarre antics continued. Once, he invited twelve women he had previously loved to a performance of Mozart's *Don Giovanni*, followed by dinner at his home. The affair took a strange turn as his servant, wearing white gloves, deliberately dipped his finger in the soup with each serving. This eccentric revenge on women who had wronged him became widely talked about. Alma found this amusing rather than shocking, and it helped that not many people in Kokoschka's Dresden circle knew she had inspired the infamous doll.

Meanwhile, Alma reassured her husband that she would visit him more often in Weimar, where he was bringing his Bauhaus vision to life. Despite her emotional entanglements, something held her back from fully severing ties with him. In a diary entry from 15 March 1919, Alma wrote: 'Sometimes it seems to me that Franz Werfel is not the right man for my current stage in life. He is so young and dependent, but I love him as one loves a man.'[13]

The planned trip to Germany was delayed as little Martin's condition worsened. One afternoon, Werfel and Blei brought the Hungarian writer, nobleman, and art patron Victor von Dirzstay to Alma's apartment. After lengthy discussions, Dirzstay stayed behind to deliver a message from Oskar Kokoschka. Despite being with another woman, Kokoschka wanted to reconnect with Alma. She explained to the Hungarian baron why a reconciliation with the artist was impossible and asked him to relay this to Kokoschka.

Later, Bertha Zuckerkandl visited Alma and Werfel to discuss emigration plans to Switzerland, though Alma leaned towards the idea of going to America. However, in her typical impulsive fashion, Alma disrupted these plans and travelled instead to visit her husband in Weimar. It was during this emotionally charged and confusing period that Alma began to fantasise about an entirely different kind of future – not one with Werfel, nor with Gropius, but with Oskar Kokoschka. Despite having earlier told Victor von Dirzstay that a reconciliation with Kokoschka was impossible, Alma's sudden reimagining of her future may have reflected her growing despair and desire to start over somewhere entirely new – perhaps even as a form of escape. Overwhelmed by grief, emotional exhaustion, and disillusionment with both her current and past relationships, she clung to the idea of Kokoschka as a kind of ideal – a figure from a time when her passion had still felt uncompromised. Tragically, while she was still in Weimar, Alma and Gropius received devastating news: their infant son, Martin, had died at the Löw Sanatorium in Vienna on 15 May 1919. He was only 9½ months old. Gropius delivered the tragic news, and the heartbreaking atmosphere in Weimar deepened when he expressed that he would rather have died himself. Alma telegrammed Werfel, who was in Breitenstein am Semmering preparing for a trip to Prague. He planned to meet Alma in Berlin and return to Austria with her. Alma discussed a potential divorce with Gropius, suggesting that Manon stay with him. The subject was dropped, however, and Alma briefly left Manon with Gropius to search for Kokoschka in Berlin, but she could not find him. Regretfully, she returned to Weimar, realising how much she missed Werfel.

Alma spent the summer in Breitenstein am Semmering, where she was reminded of Kokoschka's presence. Her love affairs had left her deeply confused. Kokoschka wrote her a letter, returning all her previous ones, saying he could not believe she had ever wanted something from him, and hoped she had arranged her life to find happiness.

In early July, Alma and Werfel travelled to Vienna, hoping for a few quiet days together. One afternoon at the Wurstelparter, Alma returned to a shooting booth she had once visited with Kokoschka. Behind a barrier, life-sized figures with cynical expressions jerked back and forth as customers threw wooden balls at them – a macabre game. A small boy, the son of the stall owner, constantly retrieved the balls, all day silently watching the 'puppets being murdered'. Years earlier, Kokoschka had remarked, 'It would take a miracle if this boy didn't become a murderer.' When Alma came back that day, she was told the boy had just killed his father during the night – with a pickaxe – in front of the stall. News of the murder had drawn a crowd. The tragedy deeply disturbed Alma. Werfel later wrote to the public prosecutor, asking for clemency, using a phrase Alma herself had often quoted – though slightly altered: 'It is not the murderer, but the murdered who is guilty.' Alma had adopted a similar saying years earlier, after hearing it from an Albanian minister during a voyage to Corfu.[14] Alma had written it down and repeated it often – and so Werfel came to use it too.

Werfel soon began working on a new novel, inspired by the proverb. They returned to Breitenstein am Semmering, where Alma wrote in her diary how happy she was with Werfel, though still feeling the weight of Gropius' name on her. She wrote to Gropius, requesting his consent for a ivorce, with Werfel encouraging her. Gropius agreed, but he could not bear to lose Manon. Alma felt his letter was sincere, but she was torn. She longed to be with Werfel, but she could not bear the thought of losing her daughter, who was the only young child she had left after Martin's death.

Meanwhile, her daughter Anna had become engaged to Rupert Koller, a young conductor, and Alma supported their plans. However, the prospect of becoming a mother-in-law or a grandmother was difficult for her to accept. During this time, Alma received two love letters: one from conductor Siegfried Ochs and the other from writer Albert von Trentini. The letters strengthened Alma's belief that she was neither old nor unattractive. In mid-November, she returned to Vienna while Franz Werfel travelled to Prague to visit his family. The temporary separation drew them even closer. Alma had one of the first telephones installed in her apartment, and she and Werfel now spoke on the phone daily. While Werfel met with writer Franz Kafka and composer George Szell, Alma received a letter from Kokoschka that left her unsettled and confused. In it, he vacillated between affection and distance – expressing both deep longing and philosophical resignation. He neither asked her to return nor cut ties completely, but rather lingered in a grey area, full of contradiction. His words stirred unresolved feelings in Alma and reminded her that his emotional grip on her life was far from over.

In early 1920, Alma, Werfel, and her children travelled to Italy, but the trip became a nightmare due to heavy rain, poor hotels, and rising costs. After returning to Vienna, Alma visited Gropius in Weimar, only to be caught in a general strike in Germany. She and Manon had to move into Gropius' small apartment, where there was no electricity and chaos from street battles. Alma arranged for a quick return to Austria, with Werfel picking her up in Berlin. However, she insisted on driving alone to Vienna after he requested she visit him in Breitenstein am Semmering, which she denied.

In April 1920, Alma and Anna attended a Mahler festival in Amsterdam, where Alma was celebrated and introduced to the Dutch royal family. Though surrounded by grandeur, Alma found her greatest joy in spending time with Anna and the Arnold Schönberg family. She yearned to be the wife of a living genius rather than a widow.

Alma devoted herself to Werfel, overlooking his flaws, but was adamant that he avoid the coffee houses where he indulged in alcohol and tobacco. She was so focused on Werfel that she barely reacted to the death of Mahler's personal doctor, Joseph Fraenkel, in April. The divorce from Gropius was delayed but when it finally began, Alma was determined that Manon maintain a relationship with her father. She went again to Weimar with Manon in October.

Meanwhile, Werfel had risen to fame, and wrote numerous letters to Alma, complaining about her silence. Alma, living in Gropius' small apartment with Manon, felt a disconnect from Werfel. She received another letter from him inviting her to visit, and finally left Weimar to go to Prague, where she took further steps in securing citizenship for Anna and herself, allowing the possibility of emigration to America. This was to take place before Anna's marriage to Rupert Kollner.

After her return home to Austria, Alma's life became somewhat calmer. She had agreed on the terms of the divorce with her husband. The proceedings were scheduled for the beginning of October 1920 at the State Court III in Berlin. Gropius proved to be a gentleman and took all the blame. He even staged an incident with a prostitute with whom he was to be caught in a hotel room, all of which was discovered by several detectives. It was thus not Alma, but Walter who was accused of marital infidelity. Since the facts were clear, the marriage of Alma Gropius-Mahler and Walter Gropius, was dissolved on 11 October 1920 without any major complications. Alma received custody of Manon. The divorce from his wife of five years ultimately came as a relief to Walter Gropius.

Alma's journey through this turbulent period reveals the profound emotional struggles she faced. It was a whirlwind of emotions, complex relationships, and unexpected turns, all set against the backdrop of a world at war. The breakdown of her marriage to Walter Gropius, the passionate, yet complicated involvement with Franz Werfel, and the personal turmoil she endured, paints a picture of a woman grappling with love, loss and artistic ambition. Even Oskar Kokoschka, whose presence continued to cast a long shadow over Alma's life, added to the emotional complexity of these years. And as if that were not enough, other men continued to court her, hoping for her attention, yet none was truly able to win her heart. Each relationship, each choice, echoed with the weight of personal sacrifice, against the backdrop of a world teetering on the edge of chaos. Alma's heart, much like her art, was in constant flux – a woman caught between the demands of her time and the desires of her own soul. It was an intense time, when social norms, artistic passions and personal desires clashed. The stakes were high, both personally and politically, making it an almost surreal period in her life.

As Alma stepped deeper into her relationship with Franz Werfel, she found herself on the precipice of a new emotional journey – one that would promise both solace and strife. But as the lines between love and dependence blurred, Alma began to wonder if she was once again entangling herself in the shadow of her past, rather than breaking free from it.

Chapter 6

A Fight for Freedom – Alma's Artistic Vision and Support for Werfel

Alma's life, marked by whirlwind romances and turbulent relationships, was once again on the verge of a turning point. While married to Walter Gropius, she had begun a new chapter with Franz Werfel, eleven years her junior – a poet whose fame had risen as quickly as their passionate union. But as she entered into this relationship, the shadows of past loves and the burden of her own restless desires loomed. As Alma reflected on how each man had treated her, she wondered, now that she was 41, whether this union would be a refuge or just another storm on her ever-evolving journey.

Alma became more focused on her own future. She took a brief trip to Italy, a country she adored and where she dreamt of owning a house. Upon returning to Vienna, she resumed her salon activities and hosted two musical evenings in her apartment.

Famous musicians and composers were constant guests at the house – including Arnold Schönberg, Ottorino Respighi, Hans Pfitzner, Ernst Krenek, and Alban Berg. In the autumn of 1920, Maurice Ravel stayed with her for several weeks, marking a particularly significant moment in her life. Ravel's presence, coupled with her intense social calendar, solidified her place in the heart of European musical culture. Alma, however, was determined to carve out a space for herself, turning her home into a hub for intellectual and artistic exchange. One of her first new salon activities featured composers Hans Pfitzner, Maurice Ravel, and Alfredo Casella in her Red Music Salon.

Another event showcased two simultaneous performances of Arnold Schönberg's *Pierrot Lunaire* for voice and chamber orchestra. The work was performed twice in succession at Alma's house. First by *Kapellmeister* Franz Stein, a student of Arnold Schönberg, and then by Darius Milhaud. It was spoken by Erika Wagner and studied by Schönberg himself, sung by Maria Freund, rehearsed by Milhaud. The performance, as Alma later described, went very well in her Red Salon room and eighty guests applauded.

Darius Milhaud, who created an admiring monument to Alma in his biography, was one of the overnight guests during these events, as was Francis Poulenc. Although Poulenc attended this second salon of Alma, he showed little interest in the contemporary Viennese styles. These salon activities – combined with the hosting of conductors and musicians – kept Alma exceedingly busy for the rest of the year. She always had the feeling that there was more spirit than feeling and more ability than impetus. And she enjoyed the music and the discussions with her guests so much; it was in her genes.

Alma stayed busy till the end of the year, continuing to think about the next music salons and meeting with friends in Vienna. Meanwhile, Franz Werfel, now in Prague, inundated her with letters. He was determined to marry her and refused to take 'no' for an answer. Despite his persistence, Alma ignored his letters, too preoccupied with her own life and artistic pursuits to respond.

The year 1921 began with unsettling events for Alma. First, Manon, barely 5, underwent a tonsillectomy. Then, Alma faced the sudden breakup of her daughter Anna's brief marriage to Rupert Koller. Having married in November 1920, Anna had left her husband by the beginning of the new year. In a poignant diary entry from September, Alma finally lamented the loss and the feelings during the weeks she shared with her daughter:

> Anna's marriage to Rupert Koller fell apart after a short time. Today my Anna left after being with me for over a month. I feel strongly what has been lost. Now everything is empty. I love her passionately, and that is the only reason I was so hopeless last summer. She is unhappy … unfortunately. She is completely over with her husband. Oh … and it was her wish and never mine. If she left him and came back to me, I would be happy beyond words. My heart aches with love.[1]

With hindsight, this marriage did not last long primarily due to Anna's youth. At just 17, she was still too much of a child when she entered into this important marriage with a young man from a good family. After their wedding in November 1920, the couple settled in Elberfeld, today known as Wuppertal, in North Rhine-Westphalia, Germany. Rupert Koller had a secured position at the city's opera house, but Anna found herself alone for long stretches of time in an unfamiliar environment, far from her family and support system. Isolated and overwhelmed, she struggled with the emotional burden of domestic life. Though there is no record of major arguments, the daily solitude and her sense of disillusionment became unbearable. In truth, she had married primarily as a means of escaping the tight grip of her powerful mother, Alma – not out of love for Rupert. Within a few months, the weight of this rushed decision became clear, and the couple quietly separated. Alma's resentment, particularly her sometimes antisemitic views, seems to have fuelled tensions between mother and daughter. Alma wrote in her diary: 'She is a stranger to me. Cold, superior and Jewish.'[2] On top of that, Anna had a very complex relationship with her mother. Alma's behaviour, including her flirting and the overtly sexualised atmosphere within the family, likely contributed to Anna's personal disillusionment. According to one of her later husbands, the Austro-American composer Ernst Krenek, Anna was psychologically burdened by her upbringing, which contributed to emotional instability. From a tender age, she had been exposed to the complicated love affairs of her mother, and reportedly became emotionally entangled in these dynamics – sometimes developing intense attachments or idealisations toward the men who came and went. Krenek described how these early experiences had left her with a complex mixture of frustration, jealousy, and resentment, ultimately causing her to seize 'the first opportunity' 'to escape the hell of the house'.[3] This combination of youth, emotional confusion, and complex family relationships, played a significant role in the failure of her early marriage.

In 1919, Franz Werfel had begun to work on his drama *Mirror Man: A Magic Trilogy*. Following an invitation from Max Reinhardt, Werfel himself read excerpts of the work at the *Deutsches Theater* in Berlin. By October 1921, the play was performed at the Altes Theatre in Leipzig and the *Württembergisches Landestheater* in Stuttgart. Viennese audiences first saw *Mirror Man: A Magic Trilogy* at the Burgtheater on 22 April 1922, albeit in a version omitting Werfel's biting critiques of Karl Kraus.

Amid these professional successes, Alma sent Werfel to her house in Breitenstein am Semmering to focus on his next dramatic play. Despite the idyllic surroundings, Werfel missed Alma deeply, as well as the young Manon, to whom he was no longer an uncle but a stepfather. Manon enchanted everyone around her with her beauty and her refreshing sense of humour, which was not so evident in either of her parents. With this special gift, she also held her family together. While Anna went to Weimar to see her stepfather Walter Gropius, with whom she got on well, Alma hoped for a relaxing summer in her house on the Semmering. The location was really unique; on the Kreuzberg ridge – a gently curved hill between the Semmering Pass and the rocky Rax Mountains – from there there is a clear view of the Schneeberg, which is over 2,000 metres high. The holiday home was unusual: the builder in charge used the largest blocks from the mountains to form an oversized fireplace, which eventually filled the entire long side of the room with the stone wall. The structural proportions and the low-slung roof with a larch shingle covering gave the two-storey villa the chunky charm of an American farm, which one would have expected to find in Texas rather than in the cool heights of the Austrian Alps.

In Berlin, Anna immersed herself in the nightlife of the bustling metropolis. At the Charlottenburg art academy, she studied painting but, like her mother, leaned more towards social activities. At the end of February 1922, she attended a carnival ball hosted by the music academy, where she met 21-year-old composer Ernst Krenek. Fresh from his studies with Franz Schreker, Krenek had been persuaded by his best friends to attend the ball. Captivated by Anna, he later wrote to his parents, praising her: 'She is very musical and extremely intelligent, so we had a great time talking.'[4] Over the next few weeks, the two met more frequently, and Krenek began to seriously consider courting Anna, although Alma was initially hesitant about meeting Ernst Krenek, unsure of what to expect. However, she eventually decided to give it a chance and agreed to meet him. Despite her reservations, she was willing to see for herself whether this young man, of whom Anna had spoken so highly, was someone she could connect with. She decided that the next time she went to Walter Gropius' home in Weimar with Manon, she would come to Berlin and get to know this young man.

When Krenek finally met Alma, he was so nervous and shy that he appeared inhibited. Having heard much about Alma's beauty, he was now faced with a person who reminded him of a 'rigged-up battleship', as he later described her. Neither of them felt any immediate connection. 'Her style was that of Richard Wagner's *Brünhilde*, transported into the atmosphere of *Die Fledermaus*.'[5]

Alma took it upon herself to introduce Krenek and Anna to Berlin's finest culinary scene. They dined at top-tier restaurants, savouring innovative dishes and indulging in a wide variety of alcoholic beverages. Krenek later reflected: 'She beguiled and enchanted her guests and was at her best when the senses and minds of her entourage were simultaneously dazed and excited.'[6]

Later that year, Alma invited Krenek and Anna to join her and Franz at the Semmering for the summer. Krenek remembered the following about what the family now called the 'Villa Mahler': 'It had large verandas all around that invited people to bathe in the shade, but were hardly usable for this purpose. Their main effect was that they made the adjacent rooms dark and gloomy.'[7]

The 'Villa Mahler' was alive with visitors. Among them was an Italian named Balboni, whom Krenek described as a colourful character resembling a gangster, accompanied by a 'harem' of women. Balboni's presence might have been tied to Alma's ambitious plan to acquire a Venetian palazzo. According to Erica Tietze-Conrat's diary, Balboni may have been acting as a real estate agent for Carl Moll or as the property's owner.[8]

While Alma would found soon solace in the serene beauty of her Venetian retreat, her life in Austria, especially in Vienna, was a whirlwind of social interactions and emotional complexity, particularly in the early 1920s. In the winter of 1922, Krenek was invited to join her in her Red Salon in Vienna, where he had an up-close view of Alma's persona and her personal struggles.

At the time, Krenek and Anna were living at his parents' home, but they spent much of their time with Alma. Krenek observed for example, that Alma ate a lot, but would often retreat to vomit, concerned about her curves. He also noticed that Alma's conversations frequently revolved around the sexual habits of both friends and enemies. Franz Werfel would often add a political twist, discussing world revolution. One particular evening, Krenek was deeply unsettled by a conversation with Alma's half-sister Maria, whom he described as 'a not unattractive person with a strong business sense and rather vulgar behaviour'.[9] Maria casually offered to 'provide Alma with lovers willing to pay substantial sums for her company'. After this uncomfortable evening, Krenek returned home, furious, and smashed a cupboard in frustration.

Despite the chaos and intensity of her personal life, Alma's world remained deeply connected to the broader artistic and cultural movements of her time. Figures like her former lover Oskar Kokoschka, continued to thrive in the art world. Kokoschka's friendship with Hans Posse, director of the Dresden Picture Gallery, led to his works being included in the museum's collection and culminated in his prominent participation at the German Pavilion during the 13th Venice Biennale in 1922, and Alma was deeply impressed by the exhibition when she visited and by the attention Kokoschka received in Italy.

Alma would certainly have seen him more often, if Franz Werfel had not come from Vienna completely broken by the failure of his play *Silent One* (*Schweiger*, 1922), which was not well received by fellow writers such as Franz Kafka and Arthur Schnitzler; the play premiered in 1923 at the New German Theatre in Prague, and became a popular success in Germany. Werfel and Alma spent a few days together in Venice, where they discussed his latest idea of writing a novel about the life of Italian composer Giuseppe Verdi.

During the summer of 1923, as Werfel was immersed in the creative tension of writing this first major novel at Alma's house in Breitenstein am Semmering, Ernst Krenek also came by for a visit to focus on his own musical compositions. The Austrian 'Villa Mahler' became a shared space of intense artistic energy, with Werfel's passion for Verdi, a figure he had long admired, finally taking shape in the form of the novel.

In a fervour, Franz Werfel dedicated up to twelve hours a day to writing about his beloved composer. Alma played a crucial role in supporting him, constantly advising that the book needed to be of the same calibre as literary classics, while also being accessible enough for mass appeal – suitable for sale at newspaper stands in train stations. Alma had grown frustrated with the modest income from Werfel's literary works, realising that a popular novel could yield much higher earnings than his previous expressionist poems and stories. However, a new approach was necessary to ensure the novel's success.

A financially strong publishing partner needed to be found, because Kurt Wolff, Werfel's publisher from Leipzig, Germany, could not satisfy Alma's ambitions. The opportunity for a new publishing house arose by chance in the autumn of 1923 during an evening at the home of the Hungarian noble Zsolnay family. Paul von Zsolnay,[10] a man whose life seemed as multifaceted as a labyrinth, hailed from a family of Jewish descent with roots in tobacco merchandising and industry. But his journey was anything but conventional. Despite his upbringing, he made a name for himself as a trained gardener, even running the largest gardening business in Czechoslovakia – a far cry from the world of literature. His entrance into publishing seemed almost accidental: after German-Austrian-Jewish actress Ida Roland suggested he start a publishing house and Alma offered him Werfel's Verdi novel, he decided to establish a literary press in Vienna with his mother's support.

The first publication of the newly founded Paul Zsolnay publishing house was Franz Werfel's *Verdi: Roman einer Oper* in 1924, which became the cornerstone of the publisher's legacy. Zsolnay exclusively published Werfel's works until 1938, with the novel's initial print run of 20,000 copies marking a significant milestone. The story is set in Venice, where Alma was contemplating purchasing a palazzo, a project she and Werfel had carefully developed together, intertwining their lives with the narrative of this monumental work.

Alma's forceful energy and ability to recognise talent were legendary. As the Austrian author Friedrich Torberg described her in his book *The Heirs of Aunt Jolesch*, she was a 'woman of tremendous artistic understanding and instinct. When she was convinced of someone's talent, she left the owner no other path open than that of fulfilment – with an energy that often bordered on brutality.'[11] This description captures her relentless drive to push those around her towards greatness, regardless of the personal cost.

Between Christmas 1923 and New Year, Paul Zsolnay approached Alma with a new request: to prepare Gustav Mahler's letters for publication in book form. This added significantly to her already substantial workload. On one hand, she was supervising Werfel's progress on his book about Verdi, while on the other, she had to carefully organise and edit her late husband's letters. The task was particularly challenging, as Mahler had rarely dated his correspondence, making it difficult to arrange them chronologically.

Meanwhile, the young composer Ernst Krenek married Alma's beloved daughter Anna on 15 January 1924 in Vienna, while she was still 19 years old. In between, Alma asked Krenek to complete two movements of her husband's

Tenth Symphony. Despite the generally positive events of early 1924, Alma remained restless and dissatisfied with her own life.

In April of that year, Alma finalised the purchase of a property near the Canale Grande, marking yet another bold chapter in her life. The 'Villa Mahler', as the Italian palazzo was then also called, was a two-storey building. Belonging to the Soranzo family, it was located in one of the most beautiful squares in the city, situated near the Basilica dei Frari and had a small garden. The Mahler family had this third residence in Italy until 1935. Although Alma had to renovate the whole house with new bathrooms and enlarged new rooms, Venice would become a new refuge for her and her family:

> I dream of living completely separated from the rest of the world, in my little house in Venice, all alone, protected by the wall of bricks – and to die there. But I do not still know whether I could bear that last great solitude … In my house![12]

And years later, in February 1928, Alma wrote in her diaries:

> I arrived yesterday. Venice! I live in my house. My house built from nothing, a sum of money that never worried me … if I sold it now I would gain a hundred thousand lira, a sum with five zeros. In exchange though, my universe would disappear and I would only have a few zeros more.[13]

The 'Villa Mahler', once Alma Mahler's Venetian sanctuary, continues its legacy as a haven of elegance and tranquillity, now transformed into the boutique hotel *Oltre il Giardino*. Nestled near the Basilica dei Frari, this historic residence maintains the intimate charm Alma so cherished. The building's preservation as a hotel ensures that visitors today can experience the serenity and beauty that once inspired Alma's reflections on life, art and solitude, creating a living connection to her remarkable story.

During one month in Venice with Werfel in June 1924, Alma finally found herself alone with him in the intimate solitude of her newly acquired home. The city's melancholic beauty mirrored her own inner world – a place of both

Alma sitting on her grandmother Maria Anna Schindler's lap. Her father, Emil Jakob Schindler, came from a family of manufacturing owners, who had been based in Lower Austria since the late seventeenth century. ©University of Pennsylvania

lma with her sister Margarethe Julie (c. 8–9 years old). Their mother, Anna Sofie Schindler, d an affair with her husband's artist colleague Julius Victor Berger, and it was rumoured that argarethe Julie was actually Berger's daughter. ©University of Pennsylvania

Alma photographed by Helene Karoline Berg in her Viennese apartment in 1915, dressed in a negligée. Berg was rumoured to be a daughter of Emperor Franz Joseph I, with whom her mother, Anna Nahowski, had a long-standing affair. In 1906, she met Alban Berg and married him. She maintained a close friendship with Alma Mahler-Werfel until her death in New York in 1964.
©Alban Berg Stiftung Wien

Mother Alma and daughter Anna Justine 'Gucki' share an intimate pose (c. 1912), following the death of Anna Justine's father, Gustav Mahler. Anna was their second child and was expected to have a musical career, but instead she studied art and painting, becoming an established sculptor and producing bronze heads of many of the musical giants of the twentieth century.
©University of Pennsylvania

he Vienna Musikverein played a significant role in Gustav Mahler's life and career. Admitted . a student in 1875, he received a thorough education in piano, harmony, and composition. He so conducted some of his own works, including the *Sixth Symphony*, at the Musikverein on 4 nuary 1906. ©Judith Grohmann

ne baroque Karlskirche was the venue for Gustav Mahler and Alma Schindler's wedding on March 1902. Their witnesses were Arnold Rosé, a Romanian-born Austrian Jewish violinist, ho was the leader of the Vienna Philharmonic for over half a century (and who also married ie very next day), and Alma's stepfather Karl Moll. ©Judith Grohmann

Alma came from a family of artists and was immersed in the cultural scene of the Vienna Secession, a revolutionary artistic movement in Vienna. Closely related to Art Nouveau, the movement was formed in 1897 by a group of Austrian painters, graphic artists, sculptors and architects. As a socialite, Alma connected with many Secession artists, including Gustav Klimt, who became the first man to kiss her.
©Judith Grohmann

After Franz Werfel's death, Alma became a widow for the second time and continued to hold court in the USA. She died on 11 December 1964, aged 85, in her New York apartment. She was buried in Grinzing cemetery, Vienna, in February 1965, alongside her daughter Manon.
©Judith Grohmann

The family buried Gustav Mahler in Vienna's Grinzing cemetery on 22 May, with Arnold Schoenberg and Gustav Klimt among the funeral guests. The grave itself possesses a profound simplicity: according to his wishes, only Mahler's name is on the tombstone: 'He who seeks me, knows who I was. The others do not have to know.'
©Judith Grohmann

Austrian artist Edmund Hellmer unveiled a marble statue of Emil Jakob Schindler on 14 October 1895, in the presence of Alma Mahler, at the Wiener Stadtpark. In this monument, Hellmer pursued genre-like naturalism to its utmost, depicting the painter sitting thoughtfully on a boulder, a small bouquet of flowers in his hand. ©Judith Grohmann

he ‘Haus Ast’, later called ‘Haus Hochstätter’ or ‘Mahler-Werfel Villa’, was built by Josef offmann from 1909 to 1911 for the building contractor Eduard Ast. The painter Carl Moll cquired the villa for his stepdaughter Alma. ©Judith Grohmann

Alma Mahler lived at 'Haus Ast' with Franz Werfel until 1938. The Art Nouveau villa was an intellectual and cultural hub of Vienna at the time, a meeting place for many artists, politicians and intellectuals. ©Judith Grohmann

The 'Haus Moll' at Wollergasse 10 was built in 1906/1907 by Josef Hoffmann for the painter Carl Moll, in an artists' colony created by Hoffmann on the Hohe Warte hill. ©Nadège Labrousse

Portrait of Alma Mahler, photographed in 1916 by Dora Kallmus, known as Madame d'Ora. A pioneering photographer of the early twentieth century, Madame d'Ora opened her Vienna studio, d'Ora, in 1907, attracting prominent figures from aristocracy, art, and society, including Alma Mahler. Her work established her as a leading name in artistic portrait photography. ©Bauhaus Archiv

The apartment building in the Auenbruggergasse, built in 1890 in Vienna's third district, is the work of the Austrian architect, furniture designer and urban planner Otto Wagner, who was a member of the Vienna Secession movement. ©Judith Grohmann

Gustav Mahler lived in the building for eleven years – from 1898 to 1909 – as commemorated by a plaque on the right side of the entrance gate. ©Judith Grohmann

Gustav Mahler had a close connection to the Vienna Konzerthaus. It was an important venue for the Vienna music scene, where Mahler's works were often performed. ©Judith Grohmann

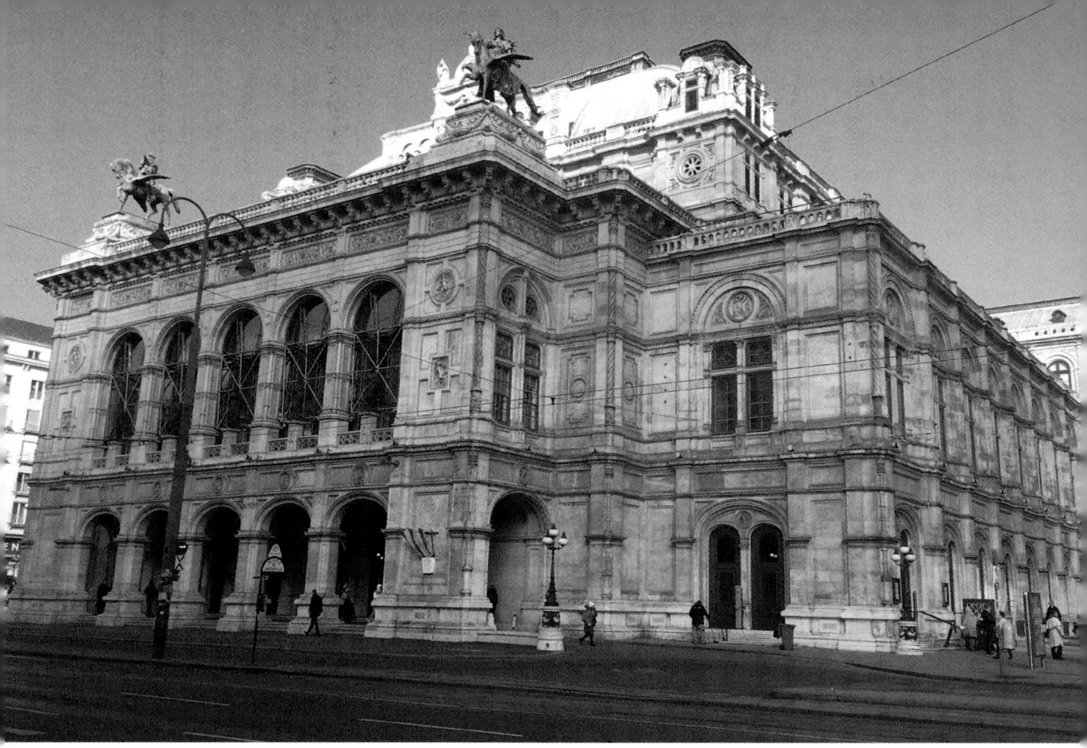

Gustav Mahler directed the Vienna Court Opera, now known as the Vienna State Opera, fron 1901 to 1907. He was one of the city's most important music directors and held one of the mos powerful positions in the world of music. Today, the Vienna State Opera houses the Gusta Mahler Hall, where chamber music matinees and other events take place. ©Judith Grohmann

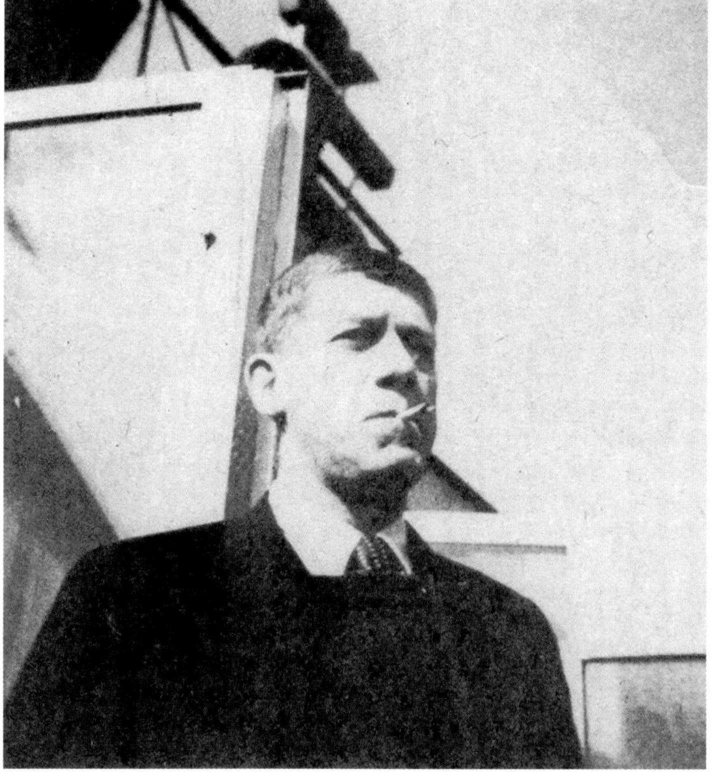

Oskar Kokoschka was considered the *enfant terrible* of the Viennese art scene. Violent and unbridled, he met Alma in 1912 and they began love affair that lasted fo many years. ©University of Pennsylvania

e summer villa built in 1901 by Gustav Mahler on Lake Wörthersee, in the Austrian village
Maiernigg. Its architect was Friedrich Theuer. Mahler spent the summer months there with
ma and their children. ©University of Pennsylvania

The brilliant composer Gustav Mahler needed the tranquility of nature for his inspiration. He found the ideal location in Klagenfurt-Maiernigg on Lake Wörthersee and also built his own little composer-condominium there. ©Mag. Peter Rosei

It was in this little composing cottage that Gustav Mahler created his major works during the summer months until the year 1907. ©Mag. Peter Rosei

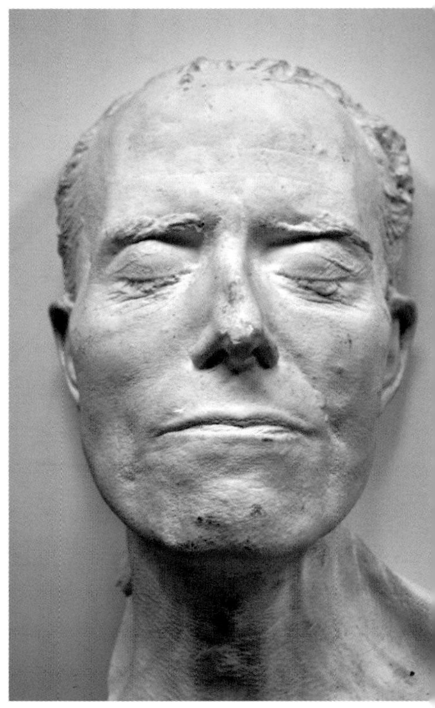

Death mask of Gustav Mahler, who diec on 18 May 1911 in the Loew Sanatoriun Vienna, from the consequences of bacte endocarditis. ©Peter Mahler, DSC 0887

On 5 October 1916, Alma gave birth to a girl named Manon, born to her husband, the German Bauhaus architect Walter Gropius, who captivated everyone from the very first moment. 'His spirit, my body! Our mutual perfection must create a demigod!' ©University of Pennsylvania

ma in 1926, dressed in fashionable attire Santa Margherita della Ligure, a comune the Italian city of Genoa. Alma often avelled alone from Austria to meet her sband, Franz Werfel, when he spent his ne in seclusion in Italy working on his xt novels. ©Alban Berg Stiftung Wien

Alma sitting and talking with Klara Amanda 'Andy' Zsolnay-Wallerstein and her son, the publisher Paul von Zsolnay, on a terrace of the Imperial Palace Hotel in Santa Margherita della Ligure. Paul von Zsolnay edited Alma's personal memoires to her former husband Gustav Mahler and the facsimile of the *Tenth Symphony*. ©University of Pennsylvania

1906, at the age of 21, Helene Nahowski met the up-and-coming composer Alban Berg, who s the same age as her, at the Vienna State Opera. They married in 1911. Alban Berg dedicated s opera *Wozzeck* to Alma Mahler-Werfel, who supported him financially in its realisation. e two had a relationship – despite Alma's friendship with Helene. Together with her husband, anz Werfel, she visited them in Trahütten, Styria, several times. ©University of Pennsylvania

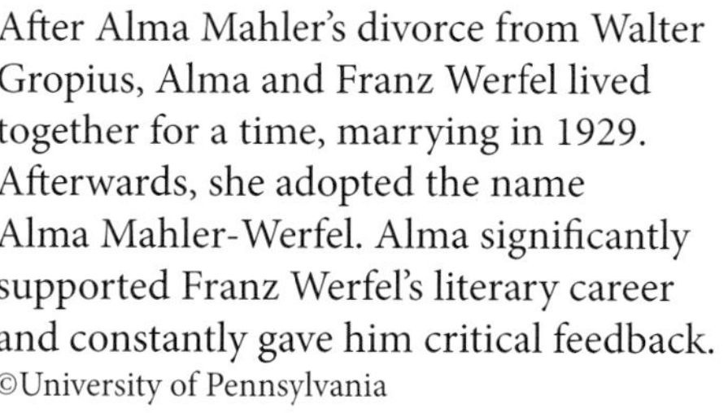

After Alma Mahler's divorce from Walter Gropius, Alma and Franz Werfel lived together for a time, marrying in 1929. Afterwards, she adopted the name Alma Mahler-Werfel. Alma significantly supported Franz Werfel's literary career and constantly gave him critical feedback. ©University of Pennsylvania

Alma Mahler, her daughter Manon Gropius, and Franz Werfel frequently spent time together in Venice at the 'Casa Mahler' near t
Church of San Toma. They lived there betwee
1922 and 1934. Sadly, Manon contracted poli
in Venice in 1934, and Alma and Franz Werfe
finally sold their house with bitter hearts in 1935. ©University of Pennsylvania

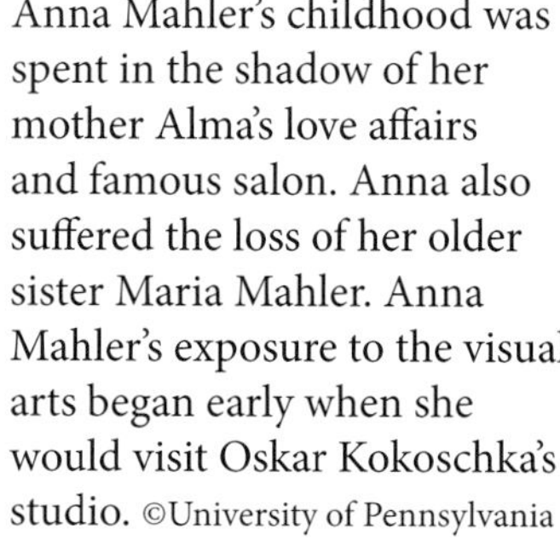

Anna Mahler's childhood was spent in the shadow of her mother Alma's love affairs and famous salon. Anna also suffered the loss of her older sister Maria Mahler. Anna Mahler's exposure to the visual arts began early when she would visit Oskar Kokoschka's studio. ©University of Pennsylvania

ma with her friends Thomas d Katia Mann, Lotte Walter ıdt, and Eugene Ormandy, er the latter conducted the s Angeles Philharmonic in uccessful performance of ahler's *Eighth Symphony* at the ıllywood Bowl in July 1948. e performance was notable for success and the attendance 18,000 people. ©University of ınsylvania

the age of 50 and at the ginning of the Second World ar, after her third marriage to e writer Franz Werfel, Alma ıigrated to the United States irst to Los Angeles, then to w York. It was the beginning a long exile. In her later years, e associated with Leonard rnstein, who influenced r popularisation of her first sband Gustav Mahler's works. niversity of Pennsylvania

During her time in exile in the USA, Alma Mahler-Werfel visited her former hometown of Vienna only briefly in 1947, with her nurse and companion Agnes Ida Gebauer, known as 'Schulli'. Her visit was primarily concerned with settling property issues.
©University of Pennsylvania

Alma Mahler with a guest and her chauffeur a valet August Hess at a party in her flat in New Yo
©University of Pennsylvania

Alma Mahler and the composer Igor Stravinsky had a close intellectual relationship, both being part of the émigré community in Los Angeles in the 1940s. Alma often hosted celebrities such as Igor Stravinsky, Arnold Schoenberg, and Thomas Mann at her home. To this day, there is no evidence of a romantic connection between the two.
©University of Pennsylvania

1952, Alma Mahler retired to New York and moved into two apartments at 120 East 73rd eet, Manhattan, where she spent the last years of her life. There she exhibited all the books, ılptures, and paintings she had collected throughout her life. ©University of Pennsylvania

e Vienna Court Opera was pinnacle of Gustav Mahler's nducting career. He made his out there as Kapellmeister 11 May 1897, conducting chard Wagner's *Lohengrin*. months later, he became ector of the Vienna Court era, a position he held til 1907. These years were ong the most productive in hler's artistic career: in the t four seasons, he conducted re than 300 performances, luding 25 premieres. Ioritz Nahr ©University of nsylvania

Alma had two daughters with her husband, the composer Gustav Mahler: Maria Anna (nicknamed 'Putzi') and Anna Justine (nicknamed 'Gucki'). Fate struck a heavy blow for the couple when Maria Anna tragically died of diphtheria at the age of 5.
©University of Pennsylvania

Alma Mahler's house in Venice, Fondamenta Contarini San Polo 2542, is now known as th small, luxurious Hotel Oltre il Giardino. Alm Mahler lived there until 1934 with her daugh Manon Gropius and her third husband, Fran Werfel, enjoying the Italian way of life.
©Oltre il Giardino-Hotel, Venice

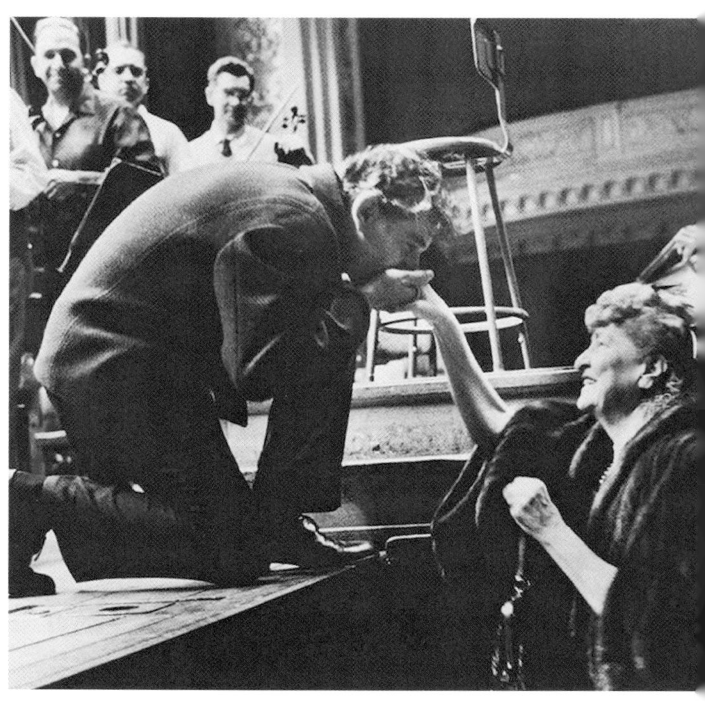

In 1960, Alma Mahler attended rehearsals of Gustav Mahler's *Second Symphony* by Leonard Bernstein and the New York Philharmonic at Carnegie Hall. Bernstein and the orchestra performed the symphony as part of a Mahler festival celebrating the composer's 100th birthday. In this photograph by Alfred Eisenstaedt, Bernstein kisses Alma's hand after a rehearsal.

©University of Pennsylvania

fulfilment and yearning. In her diary, Alma confessed the complexity of her emotions:

> I am now finally completely alone with him. We were very happy – without longing for anything else, without wanting anything else. And yet, it feels like a crime when I sometimes find myself longing. In those moments, I feel disconnected from Franz Werfel – to my own misfortune.[14]

These words reveal the paradox of Alma's life with Werfel. While she deeply cherished their shared moments, she could not escape the restlessness that had defined her relationships. Venice, with its labyrinthine canals and fading grandeur, became the perfect backdrop for her introspection – a space where love and guilt, contentment and longing, coexisted uneasily.

Amid the beauty of Venice and the solitude she shared with Werfel, Alma's mind often drifted to darker, more painful memories. 'As always, I am suddenly overcome by sadness and longing for my little boy. This child was what I wanted – and it had to leave us in this terrible way. God punishes severely.'[15]

The loss of her son haunted Alma throughout her life. Despite her outward composure, there were moments when the weight of this tragedy overwhelmed her. In the quiet of her new home, in Werfel's presence, she could not escape the rawness of her grief. The child she had longed for, the child who should have completed her family, was now a memory – a symbol of both her unfulfilled desires and the cruelty of fate.

Equally painful had been the loss of her first daughter, Maria Anna Mahler, known as 'Putzi', who had died of scarlet fever at the tender age of 2. Putzi's death added to the layers of grief that Alma carried with her throughout her life. Alma's heart, already scarred by the death of Putzi, was further broken by the death of Martin, leaving her with a deep sense of mourning that coloured her relationships and her artistic expression for years to come.

At the end of July, Alma stated:

> It's strange … I still please … and could seduce … But I'm terrified of sin. I would never want to be unfaithful to Franz Werfel. It's touching.

> After writing his great Verdi novel last year, he has finished a powerful drama in the last three weeks: *Juarez and Maximilian*.[16]

It revealed Alma's ongoing internal conflict: while aware of her own attractiveness, she was constrained by a deep sense of loyalty to Werfel. Her fear of betrayal, despite her own desires, underscored the strength of their emotional connection, even as she grappled with the complexity of her own feelings. As a backdrop to this, Werfel's creative output – his dedication to writing – also served as a counterpoint to Alma's emotional turmoil, illustrating how their artistic worlds intertwined.

At the end of August, Alma revealed: 'The voices of all my loved ones flow together into one organ tone … and that is my life.'[17] This evocative image reflected the complex symphony of relationships and emotions that defined Alma's existence – each voice, each memory, blending into one overwhelming, harmonious yet often tumultuous whole.

The relationship between Ernst Krenek and Anna Mahler soured quickly. By September 1924, Anna informed her mother of her decision to leave Krenek and pursue painting in Rome under Giorgio de Chirico. By November, Anna had definitively separated from Krenek. Around this time, Krenek was engrossed in composing his *Violin Concerto No. 1, Op. 29*, with support from Australian violinist Alma Moodie, and her Swiss patron Werner Reinhart. In gratitude, Krenek dedicated the concerto to Moodie, who premiered it on 5 January 1925, in Dessau. Krenek, however, did not attend the performance, as his brief but intense affair with Moodie had already begun.

Although Anna and Krenek had separated in 1924, their divorce was not finalised until 28 August 1926. In court documents, Anna cited her husband's excessive sexual demands, while Krenek alleged Anna's frigidity. However, their separation was ultimately driven by Anna's growing desire to assert her independence from her mother, despite still being influenced by Alma's behaviours and expectations.

In the autumn of 1924, Werfel and Alma travelled to Egypt for the first time. On the train from Alexandria to Cairo, Werfel enjoyed the hors d'oeuvres on offer, as a result he was extremely unwell when the couple arrived at the Hotel Continental. Despite this, the two ventured out to explore the el-Muski district, taking in its rich array of churches, monasteries, synagogues, and museums, alongside the bustling shopping streets. They purchased rose oil, a small, but meaningful souvenir.

Their days in Cairo included nightly visits to the Cairo Opera, where they were fortunate enough to see *Aida* – the opera originally composed for the opening of the Suez Canal. Yet, despite the exotic surroundings, neither of them enjoyed the local Egyptian cuisine. One night, in a moment of shared longing, they fantasised for hours about typical Austrian specialties: roast pork with sauerkraut, dumplings, saddle of venison with cranberries, and beef with mushroom sauce. The fantasy meal, though purely imagined, left them both feeling content, their appetites sated and their spirits lifted.

After their time in Egypt, Alma and Werfel travelled to Palestine for the first time. They left Cairo in the evening, arriving in El Kantara late at night, where they were subjected to strict passport controls and forced to disembark from the train. The coldness of the night seemed a harsh contrast to the warmth of their previous journey.

Upon arriving in Jerusalem, they were greeted by the wife of the dean of the university, but Alma, ever independent, went straight to the Allenby Hotel to unpack alone. Meanwhile, Werfel attended a children's event where 500 Jewish children planted trees – a vivid and symbolic scene that Alma later described.

In the afternoon, they visited the Czech settlements in the Emek Jezreel Valley. Not wanting to spend the night in a tent, they opted for a more comfortable stay and had someone drive them to Nazareth, where they found shelter in an English hotel. The following day, they made their way to the Sea of Galilee, then back to Jerusalem, where they met the German consul Karl Kapp and his wife. Since 1917 the German Empire had transferred the representation of German citizens and interests in Jerusalem to the Spanish consulate, so Kapp was working there. Together with the Kapp family, Werfel and Alma spent the day at the Dead Sea, experiencing yet another layer of the region's unique history and landscape.

At the end of March 1925, Alma and Franz began their journey home. On the way back, they made a stop in Sicily, where Alma's daughter Anna joined them, and the three of them enjoyed several sightseeing tours together. Alma, relieved to no longer have to hide her relationship with Werfel, felt a sense of freedom and contentment in being open about their connection.

Upon returning to Austria, Franz retreated to Breitenstein, where he intended to begin the next phase of his writing career. However, he soon found himself in a deep artistic and literary crisis, questioning the worth of his previous work. He described it as 'ponderous slush', the kind of writing the Austrians often disparaged as *Schmonzetten*.

Alma also remained active: she wanted to turn three of her songs into a symphony and spoke to Werfel about it again and again. Although she was encouraged by him, unfortunately, this project could never be realised despite good intentions. This idea reflected her enduring passion for music and composition, even in later years when other priorities often took precedence. Alma's ambitions to expand her songs into a symphonic form underscore her deep understanding of orchestration and her unfulfilled potential as a composer.

Parallel to the publication of the Mahler letters, Alma also published her own compositions. The Austrian publisher Weinberger released five of her previously unpublished songs, and Universal Edition produced a second, albeit limited, edition of *Four Songs* – a collection originally published in 1915 with Gustav Mahler's support.

Throughout this period, Alma and Werfel often spent time apart, agreeing to reunite after Werfel had made substantial progress on his writing. Alma remained in her house in Venice, while Werfel immersed himself in his next works at the 'Villa Mahler' in Breitenstein am Semmering.

After a visit to the Italian Riviera, Werfel continued his journey to Genoa and Santa Margherita. Meanwhile, Alma stayed in Nervi, Genoa, where she thoroughly enjoyed the company of the ever-changing groups of German artists and writers, engaging in stimulating conversations with them.

The summer in Breitenstein am Semmering brought both peace and a great deal of tension. Werfel found the courage to address a new, more significant subject: the drama *Paul Among the Jews*. In this work, he explored the separation of Christianity from Judaism, a theme that had clearly been influenced by his travels through Egypt and Palestine with Alma, and the profound experiences they had shared there. Werfel immersed himself in researching and writing for his next work. He spent hours each day and night discussing the topic with Alma, deepening their connection through their shared intellectual exchange. As time passed, Werfel grew increasingly wiser and more serious in his approach to life and work. Alma often remarked on his personal growth, noting that he was entirely self-reliant, though she humorously acknowledged that he had once been 'a scoundrel in his youth'.

In the autumn of that year, Werfel once again toured Germany. Although the tour proved exhausting, it also helped to increase his popularity. When the premiere of Alban Berg's opera *Wozzeck* took place in Berlin on 14 December, Franz and Alma did not want to miss this event. They had made a financial commitment to the opera's production, and the performance was dedicated to Alma. Alban and Helene Berg were among Alma's closest friends. The tall, talented Alban Berg, often compared to Oscar Wilde in appearance, could be somewhat grumpy, while his wife Helene was a beautiful and sensitive person, deeply in love with Alma. Although Alma did not reciprocate this affection, she was close to both Alban and Helene and felt a sense of responsibility toward them. Alban was a student of Arnold Schönberg, with whom Alma had also shared a long friendship.

The success of *Wozzeck* laid the foundation for Alban Berg's international success. Alma had been a confidante of Helene, but in recent months the pendulum had swung towards Alban, with whom she had developed a closer relationship. One reason for this was evidently the intimacy and passion of his affair with Werfel's sister Hanna von Fuchs-Robettin. Helene and Alban Berg had spent a few days in Prague at Hanna's house before preparing for the premiere in Berlin.

In the following period, both Alma and the author Theodor W. Adorno acted as messengers for Alban Berg's love letters to Hanna von Fuchs-Robettin. Adorno later reflected that 'the affair was doomed from the start, burdened by overwhelming pathos, as neither Berg nor Hanna Fuchs-Robetti – referred to as 'Mopinka' – were willing to leave their spouses and families.'[18] Despite the barriers, thirteen letters exchanged over the next ten years (until Berg's death) have survived. Helene Berg also noted the strong influence of 'Mopinka's' charm after Alban's first stay with the von Fuchs-Robettin family.

Werfel's receipt of the prestigious Grillparzer Prize in 1926 marked a key turning point in his career, particularly in terms of public recognition and financial success. The Grillparzer Prize, awarded every three years for 'the relatively best German dramatic work' performed on a notable stage, was a significant honour in the literary world. Werfel received it for his play

Juarez and Maximilian (1924), which was first performed at the Theatre in der Josefstadt in Vienna in May 1925 and was later staged in Berlin.

This recognition helped cement Werfel's status as a leading dramatist of his time. Not only did his work gain widespread acclaim, but his financial prospects also improved dramatically. The Zsolnay publishing house entered into a lucrative contract with Werfel, guaranteeing him a 22 per cent share of the retail price of his works, along with advanced payments upon publication. This partnership provided a solid foundation for Werfel's future endeavours in literature and further fuelled his rise to prominence during the 1920s and 1930s.

Such milestones in Werfel's life reflect both his artistic success and the changing literary landscape of the time, setting the stage for his later works, including *The Forty Days of Musa Dagh* and *The Song of Bernadette*.

In addition, Zsolnay paid the fee based on Swiss francs in any currency Werfel wished. Alma often raved about her 'Franzl', whom she and her closest friends also affectionately called the 'man-child'. He was now well on his way to writing more epic works for the Burgtheater.

Over time, Franz Werfel's relationship with Alma became increasingly shaped by a sense of dependency. Alma, who was deeply invested in his career, took a hands-on approach to his personal life and work. She closely monitored his habits, his progress as a writer, and his social life, and as time passed, this led to a shift in his relationships with his old friends. Whereas Werfel had once been part of the vibrant intellectual circles of Vienna, engaging late into the night in the city's famed coffee houses with literary figures like Alfred Polgar and Ernst Musil, his social world began to shrink. Alma actively discouraged him from these bohemian gatherings, which had previously been a vital part of his life. Instead, she sent him away to more tranquil environments, such as Semmering and Italy, to help him focus and work uninterrupted.

Alma also assumed the role of a critic, offering feedback on his writing, which, while at times nurturing, also pointed Werfel in a particular direction. This influence shaped his work and contributed significantly to his literary success. Many biographers and historians describe Werfel as someone who was somewhat dependent on the structure and support that Alma provided, both personally and professionally. He had grown accustomed to the comforts of his bourgeois upbringing, and the fame and luxury that accompanied his awards were realities he enjoyed due only to Alma's influence and the new works she helped shape. Despite his literary success, this created a complicated dynamic in their relationship, as Alma's guidance and control often extended into his personal autonomy.

His closest friends observed this change in Werfel with great suspicion. One of them was Milan Dubrovic, a cultural journalist at the time who later became the editor-in-chief of the Viennese daily newspaper *Die Presse*. Dubrovic, a freemason in the Viennese lodge *Zur Bruderkette*,[19] found the situation untenable:

> We, in the coffee house, basically condemned the effect that Alma Mahler had on Werfel. We said he had become a different Werfel, a 'success boy'. But he seemed happy with it. One evening, we sat together and discussed what each of us would consider the greatest happiness on earth. And Werfel answered quite openly: 'Success. For me, success is largely identical with happiness, yes, I would have to admit that.'[20]

But something else shook the year 1926. Since the summer, there had been several heated arguments between Alma and Werfel. Alma wrote in her diary at the end of July:

> It is sad that the political differences between Franz Werfel and me, as well as with all our friends, are growing to the point of being irreconcilable – everything, but not every conversation, leads to this in a sure-fire way. Our differing attitudes towards life make me fear for the future. For example, I want to meet Gandhi, whose mission I am convinced is of great importance. And I already fear Werfel's scepticism. Nevertheless, I am preparing for a trip to India. Hopefully, I will be able to surprise him with this trip, just as I did with my trip to Palestine.[21]

The growing tension in Werfel and Alma's relationship during 1926 marks a shift in their dynamic. Alma's strong sense of independence and her firm convictions become evident, as she reflects on the impending challenges in their relationship. Her pursuit of personal growth and spiritual discovery, exemplified by her planned trip to India, signals her desire for something beyond the conventional. Meanwhile, Werfel's increasing focus on success and his commercialised literary career reveal the widening gap between their personal goals.

As their differences deepened in 1927, Alma started increasingly to use antisemitic remarks to humiliate Werfel. Despite his being increasingly hailed as one of the best in the German literary scene, Alma made harsh comments, such as asserting that 'Jews were not fully-fledged human beings'.

When the Vienna Palace of Justice was set on fire a year later in bloody clashes between thousands of workers and state authorities, Alma was quick to assign blame. She was adamant that the perpetrators should be 'put out of business'. Werfel, horrified by these remarks, tried to explain the complexities behind the massacre, but Alma remained convinced of her own version of events. The more she clashed with him, the closer she grew once again to Oskar Kokoschka, to whom she found herself emotionally attracted. This brief period of emotional closeness with Kokoschka soon passed, however.

In December 1927, Werfel and Alma spent Christmas together on the Italian Riviera, with Paul von Zsolnay in Santa Margherita. For New Year's Eve, they were guests at the villa of Gerhart Hauptmann and his wife Margarete ('Gretl') in nearby Rapallo. Alma, now 48, got along famously with the 65-year-old Hauptmann, praising his nobility and presence: 'Gerhart Hauptmann is so beautiful, so completely noble, that I am always moved when I get to sit next to him.'[22] When he left, Hauptmann kissed Alma on the mouth and said, 'Finally, we are alone for a moment', all while his secretary stood nearby. Alma then hugged the secretary as well, but found the gesture less pleasant.

For Margarete Hauptmann, Alma's love affairs had gone too far. When Gerhart announced his intention to have a child with Alma in his next life, Margarete firmly intervened, reminding him that Alma would be taken in the next life as well.

The glamorous lifestyle between Vienna, Semmering and Venice, however, masked the growing turmoil in Alma and Werfel's relationship. Alma increasingly distanced herself from Werfel, often avoiding him altogether. In February 1928 she decided to retreat to Rome for a few days just to escape his company. Their differences deepened, and Alma's growing admiration for fascist ideologies only intensified her need for strong emotions and convictions.

The couple's heated arguments became more frequent, often culminating in door-slamming and angry shouting. There was no longer any doubt that their relationship had reached a deadlock, triggering a personal crisis for Alma. During these turbulent times, she found comfort in her beloved Bénédictine liqueur, sometimes drinking up to a bottle a day. In this strange blend of alcohol and antisemitic sentiment, Alma sank deeper into her own world of disillusionment. It seemed clear that their separation was imminent – Alma would not have predicted that, just months later, she would marry Franz Werfel.

At the beginning of 1929, Werfel was already engrossed in a new project: his novel *Barbara oder Die Frömmigkeit* (*Barbara: The Pure of Heart*). The story follows the life of Ferdinand R., a ship's doctor who reflects on his troubled past, including his early orphanhood, his strained education, and his eventual decision to leave the seminary for a medical career. The novel's theme of self-discovery through adversity mirrors Werfel's own struggles, particularly during the collapse of the Austro-Hungarian Empire, which he captures with remarkable psychological and atmospheric depth. This work, dedicated to his childhood nanny, Barbara Simunkova, offers an intricate exploration of the disillusionment of the post-war era.

From February to May 1929, Werfel resided in Santa Margherita, Italy, at the Imperial Palace Hotel, where he continued his writing with fervour. Alma joined him with Manon after spending time in Paris with her eldest daughter, Anna. While Werfel immersed himself in his manuscript, Alma was captivated by his work, especially his portrayal of the war and the revolutionary unrest in Vienna. Late nights of writing were fuelled by coffee, cigarettes and an unwavering focus, as Werfel read sections of the novel to Alma, who praised his vivid depiction of the social and political upheaval.

However, the constant social engagements in Italy, combined with the impending visit of Werfel's parents, left Alma feeling exhausted and alienated. Despite maintaining a cordial relationship with the Werfels, she had not bonded deeply with them, and the oppressive atmosphere led her to retreat to her 'Villa Mahler' in Venice. She left on 4 March 1929, via Nice, seeking the solitude she desperately needed.

Yet, Werfel's persistence never wavered. He urged Alma to marry him, reminding her that they had been together for nearly ten years. Alma, torn between her past loves and the need for personal freedom, found herself at a crossroads. The haunting letters from Oskar Kokoschka, who reminded her of their spiritual connection, only added to her inner turmoil. Kokoschka had also made a trip to Cairo and it reminded her of the good old days:

> It is as if we were attached to each other by a spiritual umbilical cord. And it is certainly nothing physical … it never was ... Oskar Kokoschka had different life patterns spread out in front of him than Franz Werfel, but he can't live up to them any more than Werfel. It is the purity that Oskar Kokoschka strives for with a soul that knows something.[23]

Alma wrote in her diary that though she had distanced herself from Kokoschka's obsession, his intensity still lingered in Alma's thoughts. It was a pendulum that swung in all directions. His determination and single-mindedness fascinated her. Werfel could not keep up with that. What bothered her most about Werfel was – in her eyes – his 'strange' political views.

But in the summer of 1929, everything changed suddenly and Alma finally relented to Werfel's pleas. She placed one condition upon their marriage: that he formally renounce his Jewish faith. Werfel agreed to this request on 27 June, but rather than converting to Christianity, he chose a more ambiguous path, quietly abandoning his Jewish religious affiliation without formally adopting a new faith. Alma, in turn, justified her decision to marry him, noting in her diary that it was not for herself, but for her daughter Manon, that she sought the stability of marriage. Despite her internal conflict, she was now ready:

> Tomorrow we are going to get married … I can't sleep. I'm too restless. I don't know if I'm doing the right thing with my desire for freedom. I'm not doing it for the 'neighbour'. Certainly not for myself. Perhaps for Manon. She should grow up in orderly, western circumstances. My freedom, which I had preserved despite everything, is being hit. My love has given way to a very close, intimate friendship. I have read

> through Oskar Kokoschka's old cards from the old days again, but he is now sleeping peacefully inside me. I am ready.[24]

On Monday, 8 July 1929, Franz Werfel and Alma Mahler were married at the Vienna City Hall. A few months later, however, Werfel made an enigmatic decision. On 5 November, he quietly converted back to Judaism, without anyone noticing. This unspoken act was likely a form of protest – a subtle rebellion against Alma's pressure and a silent defiance of the compromises he had made in his personal life, but also a sign of inner opposition to his new wife Alma Mahler, now Mrs Werfel.

The tensions between Alma and Franz, particularly regarding their ideological differences and their approach to religion, foreshadowed the difficulties that would plague their marriage. Alma's desire for autonomy clashed with his need for recognition and success, yet his conversion back to Judaism suggests a deeper, unresolved conflict. His actions hint at the complexity of their union – a marriage that, on the surface, represented stability and compromise, but underneath, was laced with silent resistance and the inevitable tension of two powerful personalities.

As Alma embarked on her new marriage, her diary revealed a mix of resignation and hope, a woman torn between her cherished freedom and the practicalities of stability. This union, unlike the passionate entanglements of her past, appeared to be born of compromise rather than conviction. Yet Alma's story has never been one of quiet contentment or predictable outcomes. With her restless heart and insatiable drive, she knew that she had to face a special future in her life. Alma's future seemed destined to unfold in dramatic and unpredictable ways, her life ever a stage for triumphs and tumultuous passions.

Chapter 7

A Time of Crisis – Alma's Struggle during the Rise of Antisemitism

As the summer of 1929 drew to a close, Alma's marriage to Franz Werfel seemed to be on a more than fragile precipice. It was indeed a constant up-and-down. Beneath the public facade of stability lay a quiet storm of rebellion, unrest and unfulfilled desires. Alma's path forward was surrounded by uncertainty, her restless soul drawn to the unknown – new alliances, unforeseen triumphs and battles and yet to be won.

In 1929, Anna's restless nomadic existence came to a halt due to illness. Ever the orchestrator of her family's affairs, Alma sent Anna to the Semmering region of Lower Austria to recuperate, choosing the luxurious Kurhaus, a grand hotel that had been a beacon of elegance since its construction in between 1907 and 1909. To keep her company, Alma enlisted the family's trusted friend Paul von Zsolnay, who was now a successful publisher – and, at 34, an eligible bachelor. Neither Anna nor Zsolnay initially welcomed this arrangement, but amid the serene, opulent surroundings of the spa, an unexpected connection blossomed. For Zsolnay, it was the beginning of a profound love, while for Anna, it became yet another step in her tumultuous search for identity and stability. Their relationship quickly intensified, culminating in Anna's third marriage on Monday, 2 December 1929, in Paris – shortly after Alma's own union with Werfel.

The von Zsolnay couple established their home in Vienna in the Kaunitz Castle (*Kaunitz-Schlössl*) at Maxingstraße 24 in the 13th Vienna district of Hietzing, turning it into a vibrant cultural hub in Vienna. This network complemented Alma's own salon at Hohe Warte, forging two powerful centres of artistic and literary life in the city. On 5 November 1930, Anna gave birth to her first child, Alma Ottilie Leonore Germany, named in honour of her formidable grandmother.

However, once again Anna's restless spirit soon clashed with the confines of marriage. In 1931, she fled with Romanian writer René Fülöp-Miller, sparking scandal and despair that led the pair to a failed suicide pact. Despite this dramatic rupture, Zsolnay managed to reconcile with Anna, bringing her back into their marriage in 1932. During this period of intense emotional turmoil, Anna turned to sculpture as both an outlet and a calling, establishing herself as a burgeoning artist. Her husband supported her endeavour, helping her secure a studio on Operngasse in Vienna's 1st district, next to the Vienna State Opera, where her work began to flourish.

Meanwhile, Alma's marriage to Franz Werfel had begun with great disappointments, leading to repeated, distressing scenes:

> Already I began to feel constricted in my new marriage – more so than I had expected. I would have liked both to leave and to remain; it seemed sinful to me to spend fifteen years lingering in the same places that you knew inside out. I felt my life drawing to a close, and though I had devoured people aplenty. I had seen only a small part of the world.[1]

Werfel's ancestry became a central point of contention in their relationship. This conflict would intensify in the years to come.

After Franz Werfel completed his monumental novel (*Barbara: The Pure of Heart*) in the winter of 1929 – a work divided into four 'life fragments' and dedicated to his Czech nanny – the Werfels decided to embark on their long-delayed honeymoon. Alma had meticulously planned a remarkable journey to India, securing cruise tickets and booking hotels. However, Werfel was decidedly unenthusiastic about a weeks' long boat trip to India.

Instead, he advocated for a journey to Palestine, Syria, and Lebanon – which were destinations that he both found deeply intriguing. Alma, swayed by her husband's enthusiasm, ultimately agreed, and they set off together.

Their first stop was Cairo, where they stayed at the Grand Hotel Continental Savoy. During their time in Egypt, Werfel contracted a mild form of malaria, which caused him intermittent bouts of fever. Despite this, he persevered, determined not to let the illness derail their plans.

From Cairo, the couple travelled to Palestine, which had visibly transformed since their previous visit. The changes impressed them both. From there, their journey continued to Damascus, a city whose deteriorated and melancholic state left a lasting impression on Alma and her husband. While there, they encountered an Armenian weaver who employed destitute children, many of whom were orphans. These children had lost their families during the Armenian Genocide, victims of Turkish pogroms, deportations, and mass executions during the First World War. This encounter deeply affected Franz, preoccupying his thoughts for the remainder of the honeymoon. The tragic stories of the Armenian children in Damascus began to take root in his mind, ultimately inspiring, what he considered material for a future novel.

After the couple returned to Vienna, Franz dedicated himself to preparatory work for his next novel. From June onward, he frequented the Mechitarist Monastery in Vienna daily, delving into the extensive library to research eyewitness accounts, maps, and the intricate history of Armenia. This meticulous study laid the groundwork for his novel, though it would take another two years before he began to shape these impressions into a written narrative.

While Werfel immersed himself in his literary pursuits, Alma faced fresh challenges. This time, tensions arose with the Zsolnay family, who pressured her to relinquish her apartment on Elisabethstraße. Alma later confessed: 'The new family now pressured us to buy a large house. I wanted to reduce my standard, never increase it. I'm trembling, I don't see why I should fixate so much on material things.'[2]

The family tensions in Alma's life showed no signs of abating. This time, the spotlight was on Carl Moll, her stepfather, who had authored a book about her father, Jakob Emil Schindler. Almost forty years after Schindler's death, Moll published *Emil Jakob Schindler 1842–1892: A Portrait Study*[3] through the Austrian State Printing Office. Alma's relationship with Moll had always been fraught, and throughout her life she found him insufferable. Johannes von Trentini, the son of Albert von Trentini, even noted that Alma rarely spoke about the Moll family, often downplaying her connection to them.

For Alma, her father occupied an exalted position, while her mother lacked the same affection in Alma's eyes. This sentiment extended to her stepfather, whom she openly disliked, and whom she referred with the dismissive moniker '*Scheißerl*' (Shitty). Similarly, Alma's feelings toward her half-sister

Maria were ambivalent at best, leaving Alma in a complicated web of familial discord and unresolved emotions.

By the end of 1930, Alma's family dynamics remained intricate, and her newlywed life with Franz Werfel faced mounting challenges. The couple's relationship, months after their wedding, was far from harmonious. Alma lamented more and more:

> Franz Werfel would never express a word of gratitude for all my efforts, for my unyielding support over the past fifteen years. Everything is simply taken for granted. The complete devotion of my entire self is expected. Gustav Mahler was similarly demanding, though his appreciation came too late … but then deeply. Franz Werfel will not have this realisation even when I leave him … or die. Gustav Mahler felt grateful to me, especially in recent years.[4]

In January 1931, Werfel retreated to his cherished Santa Margherita Ligure in Italy, taking residence at the elegant Hotel Imperial Palace to begin work on his novel *The Brothers and Sisters of Naples*. Set in 1924, the story revolves around a stern patriarch and his six children – three sons and three daughters. Werfel structured this familial fairy tale with a disciplined precision, though the characters occasionally come across as somewhat archetypal.

Meanwhile, Alma and Franz resolved to exchange their central city apartment for a more distinguished home in Vienna's upscale Döbling district, on the Hohe Warte. They set their sights on a remarkable villa located on Steinfeldgasse, an architectural masterpiece designed by the renowned Josef Hoffmann in collaboration with master builder Eduard Ast. The villa, boasting nearly twenty rooms, was a testament to the Wiener Werkstätte movement – a trailblazing collective of architects, designers and craftsmen that redefined modern aesthetics and functionality. The movement's innovative spirit influenced later design schools, such as Bauhaus and Art Deco. This building, with its sand-coloured facade, exuded elegance. Its entrance hall, clad entirely in marble, extended the luxury throughout the home with variations of marble hues adorning different rooms. Fully furnished with pieces from the Wiener Werkstätte, the residence embodied Alma's vision for a prestigious space suitable for high-level social and cultural gatherings.

Financial struggles during the global economic crisis compelled Eduard Ast to sell the villa, and Alma, enchanted by its grandeur, took swift action. Franz, often preoccupied with his creative pursuits in Italy or at the Semmering, offered little resistance to Alma's wishes. On 17 February 1931, Alma signed the purchase agreement, securing one of Vienna's most coveted addresses. Ever resourceful, she managed the relocation from their city apartment to Döbling independently, spending her final night in their old residence on Sunday, 29 March 1931.

The new house was located not far from the family home of Carl Moll. Some of her friends referred to the elegant Art Nouveau villa as a mansion. Franz was assigned a study with dark green walls on the top floor, while Alma created her own music room on the lower floor, clad in grey-green Cipollino marble. The villa's luxurious furnishings and spacious, well-designed rooms were perfectly suited for the grand gatherings and cultural salons that Alma was already envisioning for the future. Despite its simplicity, the building exuded classicist charm, with understated decorative details on the windows and the characteristic fluting adorning its facade.

The purchase of the villa was financed largely through Franz Werfel's substantial royalties, with his father, Robert Werfel, contributing an additional 40,000 Austrian Schillings (equivalent to €178,250 / £154,230 / $206,260 today). Werfel supported his wife's vision, though he did not intend to spend the majority of his time in the city.

Alma had carefully transported Gustav Mahler's desk, his collection of scores – including the manuscript of Anton Bruckner's *Third Symphony* – as well as an array of books and artworks to her new home. Among these treasures, Klimt's painting *Danaë* graced the oval ladies' room, while *Three Graces* by the Art Nouveau painter Josef Maria Auchentaller adorned the dining room. Once the move was complete, Alma wasted no time in hosting a series of lavish parties. Johannes von Trentini was a frequent guest, and the villa became a magnet for visitors eager to admire its stunning Art Nouveau design. Alma welcomed her guests in her signature style: dark, ankle-length dresses, elegantly coiffed finger-wave hair, and an array of glittering jewellery that caught the light. Her soirées were extravagant, with an abundance of food and drink ensuring a cheerful atmosphere. Alma's reputation as an exceptional hostess made her gatherings unforgettable, leaving friends and visitors delighted with both her hospitality and the allure of the magnificent villa.

The Art Nouveau villa quickly established itself as a spiritual and cultural epicentre of Vienna, an exclusive gathering place for the city's most prominent artists and intellectuals. What set Alma's salons and soirées apart was the unique mingling of diverse personalities. Musicians, actors, writers, and visual artists mingled with politicians, clergymen, and even philosophers, engaging in spirited discussions and profound reflections on the world. Alma had a gift for creating an atmosphere of indulgence and camaraderie, orchestrating unforgettable evenings where individuals from vastly different spheres could connect. These encounters, far removed from the bustle of Vienna's city centre and the prying eyes of the public, offered a rare opportunity for genuine exchange and inspiration.

Although Carl Moll was involved in fraudulent art dealings, both he and his wife consistently supported Alma and Franz in managing life in their grand villa. On 18 May 1931, to mark the twentieth anniversary of Mahler's death, Alma sent the famous Rodin bust of Mahler to the Vienna State Opera.

Meanwhile, the Werfels spent their summer months at their second home in Breitenstein am Semmering. It was there that Werfel worked tirelessly to complete his novel *Die Geschwister von Neapel (The Siblings of Naples)*, fuelled by an endless supply of coffee and cigarettes.

One day, Arthur Schnitzler came to Semmering. Schnitzler was cheerful again, incredibly witty and intelligent. While walking with Werfel, he suddenly felt dizzy. 'Dizziness is in space what impatience is in time,' Schnitzler remarked and Alma later said:

> Arthur Schnitzler was one of our most beloved and revered friends. His extremely significant and beautiful head, his deep blue eyes, his kind smile, his genius forehead – his witty, free speech – he was a great, successful creation of God. No one could escape his importance and charm.[5]

Franz Werfel's new book, *The Siblings of Naples*, was set to be a great success that autumn. The first edition, released in October, quickly sold out. Werfel had received his advance of £11,200 (around £194,000 or $259,000 at today's values), and his publisher had organised a reader's tour across Germany to present his new work. But then, on 31 October, Arthur Schnitzler, passed away, and the reader's tour began with a heavy heart.

Alma and Franz, however, flourished in Berlin, a city known for its sophisticated flair. They were invited to countless receptions, and Alma enjoyed this time immensely. But one day she received a telephone message from Vienna saying that Anna was ill. A telegram followed, stating that Anna was physically healthy, but mentally unwell. Eventually, a phone call from Andreas von Zsolnay confirmed that Anna and her husband, Paul, were in the middle of a divorce.

Alma immediately realised that this was not just about her daughter's wellbeing but also about the business relationships between her and Franz, and the Zsolnay publishing house. Therefore, she packed her bags and left for Austria, while Franz continued his reading tour. When she arrived in Vienna, she learned the full details of Anna's marital crisis – that Anna had been having an affair with the Hungarian-American writer and sociologist René Fülöp-Miller, a pseudonym for Philipp René Maria Müller, who had signed a new general contract with Zsolnay in July 1931. As noted in the previous chapter, Anna and Fülöp-Miller were devastated about their affair and had even contemplated suicide. Alma intervened just in time, confronting the author. But then, Adolph von Zsolnay caused a huge scandal, openly stating that Anna, twice divorced at the age of 26, could no longer be trusted.

Anna returned to her mother's house at Hohe Warte and soon realised she was pregnant. Unsure of the father's identity, she had the child aborted.

The Werfels and the Zsolnays maintained their friendship despite the turmoil surrounding Anna's divorce. That Christmas, the Zsolnays gifted the Werfels a large radio, which became a staple in their home at Semmering, switched on daily to hear the latest news. Yet, the relationship was not without strain. Franz Werfel depended heavily on the goodwill of Paul Zsolnay, particularly after his latest play, *Reich Gottes in Böhmen* (*Kingdom of God in Bohemia*), received tepid reactions from critics and readers. This dry spell left Werfel without clear material for a new project, heightening his financial concerns.

Although the Werfels owned property, they resisted selling any of their homes, determined to maintain their accustomed standard of living. They began to cut back – especially on travel and entertainment – but their savings efforts often clashed with Franz's aversion to household management and his penchant for luxury. Gustav Mahler's royalties, once a reliable source of income for Alma, had also diminished significantly. Antisemitic sentiment was rising across Germany, Austria and Switzerland, with publishers and venues increasingly reluctant to host Werfel's lectures.

Alma developed friendships with prominent cultural figures such as the Strauss family of conductors and the Hauptmann family of writers, often inviting them and other acquaintances to gatherings at her home. These gatherings were lively, filled with spirited conversations about art, music, and politics. With Franz, she listened to a speech by Adolf Hitler, whose magnetic oratory she found fascinating, though she was wary of his ideas. Franz, however, remained silent, offering no comment. Alma, reflecting on her past conversations with Margherita Sarfatti – the Italian journalist, art critic, and staunch supporter of Benito Mussolini – concluded that Mussolini was preferable to Hitler, despite the troubling implications of both.

As National Socialism loomed ominously over Germany and Austria, many of Alma's closest friends, including Arnold Schönberg and Hans Pfitzner, were deeply unsettled. They foresaw the catastrophic consequences of Hitler's rise to power and began making plans to leave Europe. Alma, however, saw no immediate reason to flee. Life continued as usual in her world, despite the growing unrest.

Meanwhile, Werfel was deeply engrossed in his latest literary project at their home in Breitenstein am Semmering. For the pair, there seemed no urgency to disrupt their lives or change their circumstances. The stability of their routine felt untouched by the storm brewing across Europe, even as the warning signs became impossible to ignore.

When Engelbert Dollfuß, the former Minister of Agriculture, assumed the office of Austrian Chancellor on 20 May 1932, the country was on the brink of profound political transformation. Over the next two years, Dollfuß ruled dictatorially at the head of the Christian Social Party. In a dramatic consolidation of power, he eliminated parliament and the Constitutional Court by 4 March 1933, effectively ending democracy. By 1 May 1934, the newly published constitution formalised a corporate state based on Christian, corporate and authoritarian principles. This marked Austria's stark departure from democratic ideals and values. Political Catholicism, central to this regime, struggled to address the challenges of a modern industrial society, and its doctrines often alienated Jews, who were increasingly portrayed as symbols of individualism and liberalism.

For Alma, the political turbulence and growing tensions in the country left an indelible mark. Feeling unsettled by the strange and charged atmosphere, she sought refuge in the Catholic Church, which she had left in August 1910. Turning to the spiritual guidance of her trusted Father Engelbert Müller at St Stephen's Cathedral, she confessed and renewed her connection to the faith. This return offered Alma a sense of solace and belonging amid the chaos. Yet, in truth, Alma's flamboyant personality, free-spirited lifestyle, and artistic inclinations stood in stark contrast to the conservative ideals of Catholic doctrine. Her relationship with the Church, while deeply personal, remained complex and multifaceted, reflecting the contradictions of her character.

The mounting pressures of financial uncertainty and societal prejudice created an undercurrent of anxiety in their household. Coupled with the upheaval in Anna's life, these difficulties weighed heavily on Alma, darkening her mood. Amid her growing despondency, she sought solace in music, turning to her own compositions for comfort. She started first to play some of her songs for Johannes von Trentini, momentarily finding refuge in the harmonies that had long defined her artistic soul. Yet, the shadow of uncertainty loomed large, casting its influence over the once-vibrant gatherings at the villa and the broader ambitions of their intertwined lives.

The Werfels briefly contemplated renting out their house on the Hohe Warte in Vienna to alleviate their financial burdens. In the summer of 1932, Alma, Franz and Manon retreated once again to their serene escape in Breitenstein, nestled in the 'Villa Mahler' on the picturesque Semmering. Yet the idyllic setting seemed to stir unrest rather than peace in Franz. Struggling to ignite his creative spark, he found himself mired in frustration. Unable to conjure new ideas for a novel, he turned, reluctantly, to revisiting his earlier poetry – a pursuit that only deepened his melancholy.

Alma, ever pragmatic and concerned about their precarious finances following the costly purchase of the Villa Ast, was unyielding in her reprimands.

Franz, she insisted, could not afford idleness. Their life of comfort and artistry depended on his productivity.

It was amid this tension that Franz's thoughts returned to a poignant memory from his past – a haunting story he had once heard about the plight of Armenian children in Damascus during the First World War. The memory, vivid and unsettling, grew into an idea that gripped him with urgency. By July, he had found his next great subject: the harrowing resistance of the Armenians on Musa Dagh. The idea consumed him, and he poured his energy into crafting what would become his magnum opus. Over the next sixteen months, Franz wrote with fervour, weaving a narrative that would span more than 900 pages. By November 1933, the novel *Die vierzig Tage des Musa Dagh* (*The Forty Days of Musa Dagh*) was complete and published in two volumes.

Their situation shifted dramatically with the arrival of cheques from the unexpected success of the translation of *The Forty Days of Musa Dagh*. This meticulously researched novel depicted the heroic self-defence of a small Armenian community near Musa Dagh, Aleppo, against the backdrop of the Young Turk government's deportations, concentration camps and massacres targeting the empire's Armenian citizens. The novel was an instant triumph, receiving glowing praise from critics in Austria and Switzerland alike. Its depth, humanity and unflinching portrayal of survival resonated deeply, marking it as one of Franz Werfel's greatest literary achievements. For Alma, it was not only a vindication of her demands but also a reaffirmation of her husband's immense talent and resilience and she breathed a sigh of relief as this literary triumph restored their financial stability. For Franz, it meant the freedom to return to crafting novels rather than being constrained to short stories, poems, and plays.

With Franz deeply immersed in his work and Alma now productively engaged in her own pursuits, she found herself with more time for personal reflection. She opened the suitcase where she had stored her compositions, but what she found left her disheartened. The music of her youth struck her as naive and unpolished – a reflection of a less mature self. Convinced that revisiting these pieces would be a futile endeavour, she decided not to waste her energy on them.

Alma's thoughts often wandered to Oskar Kokoschka, the artist whose passionate love for her seemed undiminished by time. Even in the early 1930s, before he had been in a serious relationship with the Prague doctor Olda Palkovská in 1934 – whom he would eventually marry in London in 1941 – Kokoschka continued to write to Alma. His letters overflowed with longing and emotional intensity, reflecting how deeply he remained entangled in their past. Alma, however, stayed distant, unsure how to respond to a man who seemed unable to move on.

Amid the quieter moments of personal reflection, Alma always followed political changes very closely. In mid-September 1932, she had travelled to Velden, in Carinthia, with Manon for the idyllic location and the mild climate. It was here that she met Anton Rintelen, a lawyer and university professor who had become a rising political star in Austria. His ambition had already propelled him to the position of governor of Styria before becoming Minister of Education. Alma was struck by his cool-headedness and his power-hungry nature, finding these qualities both intriguing and exhilarating. Over the next two years, a personal and political friendship developed between them. However, unbeknownst to Alma, Rintelen's feelings for her went far beyond admiration for her intellect and charm; he was deeply in love with her. Alma, in contrast, found his advances more a source of amusement, and the relationship between them became a source of disapproval among those around her.

In the last weeks of September 1932, Franz and Alma embarked on the reader's tour of Germany organised by Franz's publisher, which took them to cities such as Berlin and Breslau. Along the way, they encountered many intriguing individuals. However, a certain tension arose between them: Alma constantly criticised Franz for what she saw as his lacklustre public speaking skills. In her view, his delivery had become overly theatrical, which she believed did not resonate with the audiences on his reading tours. Alma felt she needed to guide him more firmly, insisting that he should not be so lenient with himself.

In Berlin, they met the former Reich Chancellor Heinrich Brüning, who personally explained the intricacies of German domestic policy to Alma. On 10 December, the Werfels were in Breslau, where Alma learned that Adolf Hitler was scheduled to hold a large rally in the city that day. Intrigued, she was eager to see him, as, like many others at the time, she found this politician fascinating. However, when she finally saw him in person, she was struck by irritation, noting there was nothing impressive about him. Franz, returning from his reading, caught only a brief glimpse of Hitler. When Alma later asked for his opinion, Franz replied with a measured, 'Not so unpleasant'.

Upon their return to Vienna, Alma resumed hosting her influential salons at her villa at the Hohe Warte, where she brought together prominent politicians, artists and industrialists. Among her guests were Education Minister Anton Rintelen, Justice Minister Kurt von Schuschnigg, former Federal Chancellor Rudolf Ramek, and Edmund Glaise von Horstenau, the head of the Austrian War Archives. Over time, Alma transformed her salon into a prestigious and high-profile networking hub, attracting Vienna's elite and establishing it as a vibrant meeting place for the city's most influential figures.

Despite her obvious sympathies for Hitler, Alma paid little attention to the unfolding political developments, including his appointment as Chancellor on 30 January 1933, or the emergency decree of the President of the Reich for the protection of the people and state, which paved the way for the NSDAP to establish a totalitarian regime.

Alma was far more preoccupied with her own affairs.

She had fallen in love once again.

She had first met the man in question at the inauguration of Cardinal Theodor Innitzer as Archbishop in 1932, an event she had attended alongside Federal President Wilhelm Miklas, Federal Chancellor Engelbert Dollfuß, his entire cabinet, and a host of local celebrities. A few days later, she invited several well-known churchmen to lunch at her villa. Among them were the cathedral organist Karl Josef Walter, Professor Andreas Weißenbäck, the church music consultant for the Diocese of Vienna, and the religious priest and theology professor Johannes Hollnsteiner, who all made their way to the Hohe Warte that morning.

The 37-year-old university professor had truly captivated Alma. In a very short time, he had gained a considerable position of power. He was the right-hand man of Cardinal Innitzer and had excellent connections in Rome, even with the Pope. Many already saw him as a potential successor to the Cardinal. He was talented, young, and driven – qualities that few in the church possessed at the time. Hollnsteiner also had political ambitions. He was extremely close to the future Federal President Kurt von Schuschnigg, acting as his confessor and spiritual advisor. The two men also shared a connection from the well-known Viennese student fraternity 'Norica', which would later serve as a breeding ground for the political leadership of the corporate state in 1934.

Although Johannes von Trentini observed Hollnsteiner with great scepticism, Alma asked him repeatedly to meet Hollnsteiner, who would explain all the political matters to him. But von Trentini remained secretive, instead turning to other political informants. He later explained why Alma valued Hollnsteiner so much: it was likely not because of his strict Catholic priestly behaviour, but rather due to his personal feelings, which seemed to resonate with her.

Hollnsteiner had found an intellectual approach to religion, and this impressed Alma very much. His deep understanding of theology and his ability to engage in philosophical discussions captivated her. Unlike many of the other clerics in Vienna, he was not bound by dogmatic traditions, but instead offered a nuanced perspective that aligned with Alma's own intellectual curiosity. His views on faith and politics often blurred the lines between spirituality and pragmatism, making him an intriguing figure in Alma's eyes. His charm lay not only in his youth and ambition, but in the way he presented religion as a living, evolving discourse, something that could coexist with the ever-changing political landscape. This intellectual approach drew Alma closer to him, feeding her fascination and ultimately her affection.

In March 1933, the political developments in Germany marked the end of the Weimar Republic and the beginning of the Nazi dictatorship, a shift that had profound repercussions for the West. Intellectuals like the renowned German authors Heinrich Mann and Bertolt Brecht fled Germany, but Franz Werfel took a completely different path – one that continues to surprise many even today.

Following a suggestion from the author Gottfried Benn, the Prussian Academy of Arts in Berlin – of which Franz Werfel had been a member since 1926 – sent a circular to all its members asking whether they would be willing to make artistic contributions to the academy in light of the changing political landscape.

An affirmative response to this question required the author to loyally contribute to cultural tasks in line with the new political order. The document was presented to the members with a simple choice: yes or no. The academy's new leadership wanted a swift answer, seeking to identify who would align themselves with the regime and who would oppose it. Of the twenty-seven members, nine rejected this offer, including notable authors like Ricarda Huch, Alfred Döblin and Thomas Mann. However, the majority responded affirmatively. Among those who pledged their loyalty were Gottfried Benn, Gerhard Hauptmann and Franz Werfel, who, on 19 March 1933, declared his support for the new regime and its leaders. Werfel appeared to be politically naïve, misjudging the National Socialists and believing that the nightmare of the brown shirts would soon pass. When Gottfried Bermann-Fischer, one of the most successful German-language publishers of fiction at the time, met with Werfel in April 1933, he was struck by Werfel's unexpectedly optimistic view of the future. Werfel seemed unusually cheerful and relaxed, possibly underestimating the threat to his works and career, and perhaps hoping that political censorship would not touch him.

The novel *The Forty Days of Musa Dagh* was scheduled for publication in November. However, it is quite possible that Alma was the one who urged her husband to sign this declaration of loyalty – all due to her enthusiasm for Adolf Hitler and his political ideas.

But things turned out different to how Werfel had imagined. Alma wrote in her diaries:

> I am very afraid for Franz Werfel. He is going through a difficult time. He was a lucky child from birth until he was over forty. Nothing went wrong for him … and now, all of a sudden, the persecution of Jews in Germany. His books are being burned – he is no longer courted. He is suddenly a 'little cheeky Jew' with moderate talent, for the masses who now dictate success. Now I will stick by him even more.[6]

When he signed the declaration, it was already too late. On 5 May 1933, the President of the Prussian Academy of Arts, Max von Schilling, sent a letter to Franz Werfel informing him that, following the reorganisation of the cultural state institutes in Prussia, he would no longer be a member. Werfel was deeply shocked and affected. Five days later, the full extent of the Nazi terror became clear: on the orders of Reich Propaganda Minister Josef Goebbels, numerous books by authors who refused to conform to the new political stance were simply burned in various German universities. Around 20,000 books were set on fire at Berlin's Opernplatz, including the works of Stefan Zweig, Arthur Schnitzler, Sigmund Freud and many other writers. During this truly harrowing time for him, Werfel also discovered that Alma was not merely friends with the priest Johannes Hollnsteiner, and that there was much more to their relationship than he had imagined. Meanwhile, Hollnsteiner came to their villa at the Hohe Warte every day.

While all this was happening, Anna Mahler also had a new admirer: the 28-year-old Bulgarian-British poet Elias Canetti, who would go on to receive the Nobel Prize many years after Alma's death in 1981. In his autobiography *The Play of the Eyes*,[7] Canetti described Alma Mahler-Werfel as a 'mellow old woman on the sofa', but also as a 'boastful widow … who had gathered the trophies of her life around her'. Canetti was both fascinated and repelled by Alma's theatrical self-presentation. He felt she made a spectacle of her past, constantly displaying her connections to great men like trophies in her drawing room. He was irritated by her grandiosity and self-mythologising, and by the subtle power she still exerted over those around her.

In a typically cryptic tone, Canetti wrote that 'he had the right to say that he had been told things, and could never be told that he would not be offended, but he would indeed be offended once again' – a convoluted reflection on his own tendency to be wounded by the arrogance and posturing of others, especially Alma. Under the title Trophies (*Trophäen*), he described the atmosphere in Alma's villa: 'The score of Gustav Mahler's *Tenth Symphony* with all the compositions displayed in a showcase, and also a gem from Oskar Kokoschka where Alma is portrayed as Lucretia Borgia: Kokoschka had referred to Alma as the "murderess of the composer".' Elias Canetti recalled Alma's words about 'little Jews like Mahler' in his memoirs. Such malicious wordplay became more frequent as Alma's relationship with the priest Johannes Hollnsteiner deepened. It was as if she had not only adopted his worldview, but also his language.

Outbursts of this kind became increasingly frequent as Hollnsteiner's influence over Alma increased. However, Alma's burgeoning antisemitism did not come without consequences. Her Jewish friends began to feel increasingly alien to her, as if insurmountable barriers had risen between them. Werfel, too, felt the effects of his wife's hostility toward Jews, which created a palpable distance between them.

In the autumn of 1933, Alma's friend Anton Rintelen, an Austrian lawyer and politician from the Christian Social Party, announced his visit. The politician, who had resigned from his post in the spring at the urging of Chancellor Dollfuß, was on his way to Rome, where he was to assume the role of Austrian ambassador on 13 November. Dollfuß, who saw him as an unwelcome rival, believed he had effectively 'removed him from the game', but Rintelen would later play a significant role in a Nazi coup attempt. Alma organised a farewell party for him in Vienna, and she increasingly enjoyed flirting with him. Rintelen, for his part, had fallen head over heels in love with Manon. Alma, however, saw no issue with her younger daughter growing up almost exclusively among older people. Manon seemed to accept this arrangement – it did not appear to bother her. She even signed her mother's letters to friends – including Rintelen – sending 'adoring greetings'. It went so far that Alma constantly mentioned the physical beauty of her daughter. Alma saw a certain attractiveness and sexual charisma in her daughter that she no longer possessed at the age of 50.

In mid-November, Franz Werfel fled to his family in Prague to escape his wife's increasingly erratic behaviour. But the city where he had grown up suddenly felt completely different to him – many houses and billboards were defaced with racist slogans. He became afraid, and his father, Rudolf Werfel, grew more anxious, fearing that the Nazi terror would soon spread to Czechoslovakia. In a review of the year 1933 in her diary, Alma noted some troubling reflections: her time with Hollnsteiner had been the happiest of her life, but Alma was still not entirely content. 'I have become very deteriorated physically and healthwise and have aged considerably this year.'

By the beginning of 1934, the domestic political situation in Austria had reached a boiling point. After Chancellor Dollfuß dissolved parliament in March 1933, the relationship between the ruling Christian Social Party and the opposition Social Democrats became extremely tense. He had already banned both the Communist Party and the NSDAP in May and June of that year. An uprising was imminent. On 12 February, the paramilitary Heimwehr conducted a house search, but the Social Democrats and their armed subgroup, the Republican Protection League, resisted. These battles in Linz quickly spread to Vienna, where workers' homes and community buildings became the focal points of the bloody conflict. Engelbert Dollfuß and his Minister of Justice, Kurt von Schuschnigg, responded to the uprising with ruthless severity. Heavy artillery was even deployed. The Karl-Marx-Hof, not far from Alma's Villa Ast, was caught in the crossfire, and the usually peaceful Hohe Warte became the scene of fierce battles. Alma sided with Dollfuß and the Heimwehr. To her, the agitators were nothing but a rabble, and she believed they deserved nothing less than these violent confrontations. Austrian writer Hilde Spiel even reported that a howitzer shell struck the garden of Villa Ast. Franz Werfel was in Italy at the time, and, for this reason, Minister Schuschnigg offered to bring Alma and Manon to him and allow them to stay with him for the duration of the uprising. Alma, however, politely declined. After two days, the uprising was over. It had failed due to the planned general strike by the Social Democrats, which, in the end, did not take place. Social Democratic officials were arrested in droves, including Vienna's mayor, Karl Seitz, and his city councillors. Some of the leaders of the uprising were even executed. Overall, it was a dreadful situation. The February riots led to the banning of the unions, the Social Democratic Party, and their associated clubs and organisations. Dollfuß expanded his influence and solidified his power through the establishment of his authoritarian corporate state.

Meanwhile, Alma travelled to Venice, where some repairs were needed at the 'Villa Mahler'. Franz came from Santa Margherita so that the two could spend a few weeks together. Though he was deeply concerned about the unrest affecting Manon and Alma, everything turned out fine, and he was reassured.

On 28 March 1934, Anton Rintelen arrived in Venice by plane. Alma was there to meet him at the airport, accompanied by Manon. Alma regarded him as 'a great statesman with far-seeing eyes'. However, Rintelen had brought along a guest: the 28-year-old young politician Erich Cyhlar, who quickly fell head over heels for Manon. While Manon stayed in Venice with her governess, Alma and Rintelen travelled on to Milan to meet with the Italian publisher Ricordi.

Upon their return from the short trip, Manon began feeling unwell. She had a headache and a loss of appetite – early signs of what seemed to be a mild flu. At the same time, Alma noticed that she had misplaced her crucifix, a gift from Johannes Hollnsteiner, and began to feel increasingly worried.

On 14 April, Alma and Franz travelled back to Vienna, leaving Manon behind with plans for her to join them in a few days. In Vienna, they were treated to a concert of Mahler's *Song of the Earth*, followed by a dinner at the Grand Hotel organised by Kurt von Schuschnigg. After the evening, Schuschnigg took them home, where Alma learned that Manon was unwell.

Alma immediately arranged a flight back to Venice with the nurse Agnes Ida Gebauer, known by the nickname 'Schulli'. Upon arriving at the 'Villa Mahler', they were shocked by Manon's diagnosis: she had contracted polio. A polio epidemic was sweeping through Venice, though the media had kept it under wraps. The doctors were gravely concerned about Manon's condition, and a spinal puncture was quickly performed. Within two days, her entire body became paralyzed, making her unable to be moved.

After several days, her condition stabilised enough for her to be transported back to Vienna. A special train, named the Emperor Franz Joseph train, and coordinated by Kurt von Schuschnigg, was prepared to bring her home.

A year of suffering began in Vienna, marked by the various fluctuations of Manon's illness. She was often in pain, but the doctors remained confident they could manage both the symptoms and the disease itself. When Manon was able to sit, stand, move her upper body, and even hold a pen again, she wrote to her father, Walter Gropius, reassuring him not to worry – her recovery was progressing. The summer passed with some stability, though her condition plateaued during the winter of 1934. Alma was growing desperate. Yet, paradoxically, within the family's social circle, Manon's illness seemed to draw a strange reverence. The image of the beautiful, suffering young woman elicited admiration and pity in equal measure. Visitors were brought to see her almost as if she were a sacred relic – a kind of living martyrdom that stirred awe and emotion. Manon had once dreamed of becoming an actress, but with the onset of this debilitating disease, that hope had, of course, vanished. Despite this, she was engaged to 28-year-old Erich Cyhlar, who had courted her. However, Alma became increasingly convinced that an evil curse lay over her family.

The illness took its toll on Alma. She had naturally hoped that her beloved young daughter would overcome the polio, but the disease slowly took hold of her child's entire body. On Easter Sunday 1935, Manon finally requested Johannes Hollnsteiner, likely sensing that she was nearing the end of her life. When Hollnsteiner arrived at the Hohe Warte, he found a team of seven doctors attending to the ailing Manon. When the doctors left the house at 10.00 pm, she still had hope. A doctor and a nurse stayed with her. But during the night of Easter Monday, her condition worsened. Manon Gropius died at 3.45 pm on 22 April 1935 from gastrointestinal paralysis; she was 18 years old. Before her passing, she whispered to her mother, 'You'll get over it, just like you get over everything.'

Manon's father was living in London at the time and received telegrams from Vienna. However, he received little information from Alma about the details, as she could hardly believe it herself. Walter Gropius was devastated by Manon's death, and while he was stuck in London, all the media reported on the death of his child.

Manon's funeral took place on Wednesday, 24 April 1935, and became a major social event, attracting Vienna's entire cultural elite to the small Grinzing cemetery. Artists, intellectuals, and dignitaries gathered to pay their respects to Alma's beloved daughter. Johannes Hollnsteiner, in his eulogy, described Manon as having 'gone home with an open gaze, her eyes free of sorrow and pain, and with a smile on her lips'. He painted a picture of her as no longer an ordinary girl but an angel on earth, a sentiment Alma publicly embraced. Alma declared Manon to be 'the only child', effectively erasing Maria, Anna and Martin from her narrative entirely, a statement that shocked even her closest friends.

The funeral solidified Manon's place as a symbol of tragic beauty not only in Alma's heart, but also in the public imagination. Alma meticulously arranged every detail, ensuring that Manon's image – both literally and figuratively – would remain untouched by time. Yet, beneath the surface of this public adoration, Alma's grief began to fester into a profound bitterness that would influence her relationships and decisions in the years to come.

Meanwhile, the Spanish Civil War was tearing Europe apart ideologically, and Vienna's intellectual circles were no exception. Franz Werfel supported the democratic government, while Alma sided fervently with General Franco and his Nationalists, largely influenced by Johannes Hollnsteiner and her conservative Catholic leanings. Their ideological rift led to frequent disputes, and their once close bond frayed under the weight of opposing beliefs.

In March 1937, Franz Werfel was awarded the Austrian Cross of Merit for Art and Science, First Class, on the initiative of Kurt von Schuschnigg. This honour, though prestigious, highlighted the tension between Jewish artists like Werfel and Austria's authoritarian state. Despite the accolade, Alma's admiration for her husband had diminished, and their emotional distance grew. Werfel increasingly sought refuge in solitude, writing in hotel rooms outside Vienna, while Alma, consumed by her grief and the weight of ageing, turned to alcohol, particularly the Bénédictine liqueur, to numb her pain.

At 58, Alma found herself in one of the darkest crises of her life. She viewed Villa Ast on the Hohe Warte as an 'unlucky house', filled with memories of loss and disappointment. Determined to leave behind its oppressive atmosphere, she decided to rent it out. Franz, who had always felt uneasy in the grand villa, supported the decision. On 12 June 1937, the couple hosted a farewell party at their Villa Ast, inviting an eclectic mix of nobility, industrialists, politicians, and artists. It was a dazzling affair, though its gaiety could not mask the couple's increasing estrangement.

After leaving Vienna, the Werfels made their home in their 'Villa Mahler' at Breitenstein am Semmering. Alma, unable to bear the city that had witnessed so much of her sorrow, sought distraction in travel. In October 1937, she and her daughter Anna visited Berlin for a few days. But even in her wanderings, Alma could not escape the growing shadow of political unrest and the inexorable approach of war.

The Werfels had planned to spend the Christmas holidays in Milan again, but Franz Werfel suffered a serious bout of bronchitis, so they decided to stay in Vienna. After Franz recovered, they flew to Italy on 29 December and stayed at the Grand Hotel. A few days later, they continued to Naples and Capri. The wonderful climate and lush vegetation inspired Franz, who began composing new poems. However, their idyllic trip was abruptly interrupted by political developments.

On 12 February 1938, Kurt von Schuschnigg was unexpectedly summoned to Berchtesgaden to negotiate with Adolf Hitler. Under immense pressure and threats, Schuschnigg reluctantly acceded to Hitler's demands, hoping to preserve Austria's autonomy. Alma and Franz, deeply alarmed by these events, found themselves uncertain about their next steps. They decided to stay in Italy, but Alma eventually resolved to return to Vienna alone at the end of February.

On 9 March, Schuschnigg announced a referendum on Austrian sovereignty, rallying support from intellectuals and left-wing circles, including Alma's friends. However, their efforts were in vain. Under the threat of German invasion, Schuschnigg resigned on 11 March 1938. Two days later, Adolf Hitler and Arthur Seyss-Inquart sealed Austria's annexation into the German Reich. Vienna's Heldenplatz was filled with a jubilant crowd celebrating the *Anschluss*.

Amid the chaos, Alma suddenly recalled an earlier prediction from her palmist and decided she had to leave Austria immediately to reunite with Franz in Italy. Spending one last night in Vienna, she stayed at a hotel with Johannes Hollnsteiner and her daughter Anna, engaged in fervent political discussions. The next morning, Alma and Anna departed via Prague, Budapest, Zagreb and Trieste, eventually arriving in Milan.

Reunited, Alma and Franz travelled to Rüschlikon, near Zurich, at the invitation of Franz's sister. However, the tension between the two women made the arrangement short-lived. Alma quickly began arranging passport and visa matters for their next journey. Along with Anna, she and Franz travelled to Paris and then to Amsterdam, where they were warmly hosted by the Dutch conductor Willem Mengelberg during a Gustav Mahler festival. The festival's success temporarily lifted Alma's spirits and boosted her self-esteem.

On 9 May, the Werfels travelled to London. Franz tried to convince Alma to settle there, but she was determined to return to France. By 1 June, they had arrived in Paris, where their recurring disputes resumed. Alma accused Franz of prioritising his family over their shared concerns.

But the couple was soon shaken by news of Johannes Hollnsteiner's dire fate. Despite Alma's advice to destroy sensitive documents, Hollnsteiner had refused, believing himself safe. The Gestapo uncovered incriminating letters during a search and arrested him on 30 March at the Augustinian Canonry. After eight weeks of interrogation, he was deported to Dachau concentration camp, where he endured daily beatings and maltreatment for eleven months.

Franz, deeply distressed by Hollnsteiner's fate, realised their own precarious position. Together, the Werfels fled to France, carrying with them the memory of their loyal friend and the grim realisation of the peril faced by those left behind.

As the Werfels fled from the mounting shadows of Europe's unravelling, they carried with them more than just suitcases and papers; they bore the weight of lost homes, fractured friendships, and a deep uncertainty about what lay ahead. The war would scatter lives like leaves in a storm; yet the couple clung to each other, uneasy allies in a world that seemed to be slipping into chaos. Exile would offer them safety or simply a new kind of isolation. Their love – so often tested by ambition, grief, and discord – might find new strength in a foreign land, or the strain of displacement and war might drive them further apart. The answers would not come easily, for the road ahead promised both refuge and peril, solace and sacrifice. As their footsteps faded into the unknown, one thing was certain: they would have to rediscover a sense of belonging in a world so intent on taking it away.

Chapter 8

Fleeing to Safety – The Escape from Europe to the USA

The world Alma and Franz Werfel had known was gone, swept away by the horrors of the beginning of a barbaric war and the cruel tides of fate. In the summer of 1938, the Werfels found themselves in France, a land of refuge and uncertainty, where they could only begin to imagine the future. The peaceful streets of Paris, once a symbol of cultural promise, now seemed like a temporary haven – an in-between place, suspended between the collapse of their former life and the uncertain journey ahead. As their feet touched French soil, the weight of exile hung heavily upon them – but so did the strange hope that, amid the upheaval, new beginnings might still emerge.

In mid-June 1938, Franz Werfel moved alone to the Hotel Pavillon Henri Quatre in Saint-Germain-en-Laye, a peaceful town near Paris. After months of neglect, he could finally devote himself to his writing and new projects. He rented a spacious, quiet room for this purpose. Alma, meanwhile, stayed a few more days at the Hotel Royal Madeleine in Paris. She spent her time meeting friends, indulging in cultural activities like visiting museums, and attending a performance of *Tristan und Isolde*, conducted by Wilhelm Furtwängler. Though she found the orchestra's performance lacking compared to the Viennese Philharmonics, she appreciated the artistry.

Soon, Alma set off for the south of France, intending to make the Côte d'Azur her new home for the sake of her husband's health. After a brief search with her friend Annemarie Meier-Graefe, on 1 July Alma chose the simple yet charming watchtower *Le Moulin Gris*, an old Saracen tower, in the small fishing village of Sanary-sur-Mer. The tower had been lovingly renovated by its owner, a painter. By 1940, Sanary would become a refuge for many prominent German and Austrian artists, including Thomas and Heinrich Mann, Lion Feuchtwanger, Berthold Brecht, and Ludwig Marcuse.

For Alma and Franz, *Le Moulin Gris* would be their sanctuary. Alma and Annemarie celebrated the decision together for an entire afternoon, as they had now become neighbours. Annemarie, a painter herself, was the wife of the writer Hermann Broch.

On the second floor of the building stood a round room that would become Werfel's ideal writing studio. Twelve large windows opened out to the vast expanse of the sea – an awe-inspiring and breathtaking sight. But on 1 July 1938, everything changed. Alma received an urgent call: Franz, who was in Paris at the time, had fallen gravely ill, and she needed to come immediately. Upon arriving in Saint-Germain-en-Laye, Alma found Franz in a dire condition: he had suffered a heart attack. The prognosis was grim, and he faced a long, difficult recovery. A British doctor who examined Franz him warned that his life was at risk. Yet, Franz's fear was far worse than the reality of his illness: 'I feel sicker than ever before. It's as if there is water in my head, threatening to burst from internal pressure,'[1] he wrote in his diary. Alma acted swiftly, arranging for her husband to be transferred to Paris, where his condition gradually improved. After four weeks of recovery, they were finally able to move to Sanary-sur-Mer, to their new home by the sea that Alma had chosen for them.

When they finally moved into the tower, Franz was given the top round room, as planned, while Alma had to make do with a damp, musty room on the lower floor, where she spent much of her time playing Bach. Despite the grave diagnosis from the British doctor, Franz soon began working on a new book. However, emigration did not bring the Werfels closer together, as one might have hoped. Alma's frequent antisemitic outbursts only deepened the rifts between them, tensions that did not go unnoticed by their friends. The writer Lion Feuchtwanger and his wife Marta often visited the Werfels, although the two men frequently clashed over their differing political views. Despite Werfel accusing Feuchtwanger of sympathising with Soviet ideologies, the couples formed a bond and met regularly. One evening, when Feuchtwanger was in Paris for an appointment, his wife Marta was invited to dinner by the Werfels. At first, everything seemed harmonious, but as they sat down at the table, the mood suddenly shifted. According to Marta, Alma and Franz began arguing over something trivial, and Alma abruptly stated: 'Don't forget that I'm not Jewish, I'm not Jewish.'[2]

Despite his weakened health and ongoing tensions with his wife, Franz adapted to life in the south of France surprisingly quickly – much faster than Alma herself. He took great joy in speaking French and discovering his new surroundings. During this period, he made the acquaintance of a group of political journalists and began writing articles. However, the journalists all constantly advised him to stick to literature, recognising where his true talents lay.

On her 59th birthday in August 1938, Alma recorded her despair in her diary:

> It's another birthday that has to be endured. What have I lived through? Into what pits of hell have I stumbled, gotten up, and fallen again? Should the lines of catastrophe in my hand, which inspired such horror in the palmist, continue to deepen forever? I want to hibernate … forget all the pain that is firmly armoured in my chest. The misery.[3]

Once again, Alma was deeply depressed, despite having followed her husband into exile and ensuring they had a dignified place to stay. Her relationship with him weighed heavily on her; in Alma's eyes, it had irrevocably failed. Emigration to the south of France had not brought them closer together. Instead, each pursued their own path: Franz with his writing, Alma with her increasing despondency. At this time, Alma actively considered separating from her husband, though divorce proceedings were never formally initiated. Many in their immediate circle already knew that their marriage was, in reality, little more than a formality. Alma's brother-in-law, Richard Eberstaller, had known as early as the previous year about her intention to divorce Franz.

Yet, despite her frustrations, disappointments, and the deteriorating state of their relationship, Alma ultimately chose to remain at Franz's side. At nearly 60 years old, the prospect of finding a new partner seemed increasingly unlikely. Moreover, she was deeply troubled by the escalating political situation in Austria and across Europe. In her diary, she lamented:

> It's just the way it is in the world, and it's terrifying. For weeks, we've been stuck between war and peace. And here we are … homeless,

> ignorant of the language, and immersed in foreign alienation. I long for home … But where is that? Franz Werfel has become a political journalist. Hopefully, it won't harm him, here and there. He's doing very well, but I'd prefer him to write poetry. Although I can understand that you can't write poetry at a time like this.[4]

Meanwhile, Alma received news that her mother, Anna Moll, had fallen gravely ill in late autumn of 1938. Severe bronchitis, compounded by acute heart problems, left Anna bedridden. Alma's diary entry at the end of November reflects her anguish and the confusion surrounding her mother's final moments:

> My mother died, and I didn't see her again! I wanted to call her. They said she was still breathing … How terrible something like that sounds – and is. But everyone there has already buried her in their hearts. Moll has to be constantly held back because he wants to kill himself.[5]

At the time Alma wrote this, there seems to have been uncertainty about whether her mother had already passed or was near death – a reflection of the emotional turmoil and possibly delayed communication. A day later, Anna Moll did in fact pass away, and Alma was overcome with shock and grief: 'My mother is no more. And for the first time, I feel that I am flesh of her flesh.'[6]

During this difficult phase, Alma travelled from Sanary-sur-Mer to London. The loss of her mother had left her with an urgent desire to see her daughter, Anna. In London, she also met her former son-in-law, Paul von Zsolnay, who had managed to escape from Vienna at the last moment and emigrate to England.

Meanwhile, Franz travelled to Switzerland, where he reunited with his parents and his second sister, Hanna, at his sister's house. His father, Rudolf, strongly urged him to emigrate to America as soon as possible. However, Franz hesitated. Although he and Alma had already arranged visas, he was unwilling to leave Europe until there was no other choice. After returning from Switzerland, they decided to spend the winter months in Paris, as life in the south of France had become unbearably lonely for them.

During the following months, Werfel worked in Saint-Germain-en-Laye on a new manuscript, a novel trilogy titled *Cella or the Overcomers*, while Alma pursued her social interests. She invited friends and acquaintances to her suite at the Hotel Royal Madeleine in Paris, reviving her famous salons – albeit on a much smaller scale. Regular visitors included the Austro-Hungarian writer and politician Guido Zernatto, the German novelist Franz von Unruh, film director Erwin Piscator, the composer Franz Lehár, German conductor and composer Bruno Walter, and even an envoy of the French Foreign ministry. Yet, as soon as the last guest had departed, Alma often sank back into her recurring depression.

The Werfels spent the summer once more in the South of France. Alma took up revising her memoirs of Gustav Mahler for the Amsterdam publisher Allert de Lange. Unfortunately, *Memoirs and Letters*, published in 1940, received poor reviews. Alma had gone too far with the marginal notes to Mahler's *Tenth Symphony*, presenting them as love letters addressed to her – a claim that provoked considerable outrage. Of the Mahler letters included in the book, only thirty-seven were reproduced verbatim, further diminishing the work's reception.

After the start of the Second World War on 1 September 1939, German-speaking emigrants in France were regarded as undesirable foreigners and potential spies. Arbitrary house searches and interrogations became routine. The emigrants were suddenly seen with suspicion.

On 6 September, the Werfel family received a visit from five police officers, who once again checked the couple's travel documents. The following day, an official even stopped Franz Werfel on the street. The official asked what he was writing, to which Werfel replied, 'I write novels and poems'.

The atmosphere was becoming intolerable for an emigrant, because Germans, Austrians and even Czechs were considered suspect. Worse still, anyone who spoke German was assumed to be either a convinced Nazi or a communist.

Before the outbreak of the war, Franz Werfel's parents and his sister Hanna had decided to move from Switzerland to the city of Vichy, in the Allier department in the Auvergne-Rhône-Alpes region. While in Vichy, Rudolf Werfel suddenly suffered a stroke, and his son was asked to visit him. Travel visas now had to be obtained. From then on, the Werfels commuted daily from Sanary-sur-Mer to Toulon, and by the end of October, everything was finally in order. The papers were ready, and the Werfels could begin their journey. After a six-hour break in Toulon, Alma and Franz finally reached the city of Vichy. The sight of his seriously ill father shocked Franz deeply: Rudolf Werfel could no longer leave his bed, nor could he speak. When Franz left the hospital, he felt as though he would never see his father again. He returned to Sanary-sur-Mer, and life on the Côte d'Azur continued quietly and normally for a time. His father died on 31 July in 1941.

After the German Wehrmacht invaded small Western European countries such as Belgium, Norway, Denmark, Luxembourg and the Netherlands in May 1940, it became clear to Franz and Alma that it would not be long before the troops reached France. They went to Vichy once again to visit Rudolf Werfel. When they returned to Sanary-sur-Mer, they quickly packed the essentials and left their house on 2 June 1940, for Marseille, where they spent the next sixteen days at the consulates trying to obtain new US visas. Strangely enough, their efforts to get new travel documents were unsuccessful.

Paris was occupied by the German Wehrmacht on 14 June. When Alma and Franz heard the rumour on 18 June that the Germans were already in Avignon, they finally decided to pack up and flee France. They took a taxi for 8,000 francs and planned to drive to Bordeaux and then on to Spain. However, the journey turned into a nightmare. Although they intended to take a route along the coast to Montpellier and then to Perpignan, the taxi driver accidentally headed for Avignon, further north, where the Germans were suspected to be. The journey became even more adventurous after Béziers, when the taxi driver suddenly drove in circles twice around Narbonne, forcing them to stop and take a break because it was already dark. Since not a single hotel would accommodate migrants, they stayed in a former hospital. Alma was horrified by the primitive hygienic conditions. She was particularly disgusted by the standing toilets that were common in southern France at the time. Their journey continued the next day, but the driver got lost again and drove north towards Carcassonne instead of Perpignan. There, a roadblock prevented them from continuing. Franz bought two train tickets to Bordeaux, and the two finally reached the port city in southwestern France thirteen hours late. Their luggage had disappeared, and they were greeted by agitated station staff because a heavy bombardment by the German Air Force had fallen the night before.

The loss of the valuable Mahler and Bruckner scores deeply hurt Alma and Franz, as they had planned to use them to finance a fresh start in the USA. After failing to find a hotel room, they were forced to spend the night in a former brothel. The next day, they decided to continue their journey to Biarritz, a spa town on the Atlantic coast. There, they met a Czech couple, Viktor and Bettina von Kahler, who were also on the run. From that point on, Franz and Viktor drove almost daily from Biarritz to Bayonne, tirelessly applying for visas at various consulates, but their efforts were fruitless. In the meantime, Alma received a tip about a Portuguese consul in Saint-Jean-de-Luz who was said to issue visas freely. When they arrived, however, they discovered that the consul had disappeared and, in a fit of panic or despair, had thrown all the passports and visas into the sea. At that moment, Franz could no longer hold back. He had a nervous breakdown and wept bitterly. In a stroke of luck, Viktor von Kahler managed to secure a taxi at the last minute, which took both couples via Orthez to Pau and eventually down to Lourdes.

The small pilgrimage site of Lourdes became famous through the story of Bernadette Soubirous, the firstborn daughter of a miller from Lourdes. She is best known for experiencing apparitions of a young lady who asked for a chapel to be built at the nearby cave-grotto. These apparitions occurred between 11 February and 16 July 1858, and the young lady who appeared to her identified herself as the 'Immaculate Conception'. The sleepy little town then transformed into a world-famous pilgrimage destination.

Franz and Alma took a modest room in the Vatican Hotel in Lourdes and waited for the moment when they could leave France with a valid visa. However, it seemed their only chance was to return to Marseille, as that was the only place where they could obtain the exit papers they desperately needed. They then had to wait a full five weeks for permission to leave Lourdes for Marseille, known in technical terms as *sauf conduits*. This delay was completely unexpected. To pass the time, Alma read up on the story of Bernadette Soubirous and regularly attended services in the grand Rosary Basilica in Lourdes. Franz, too, was captivated by the story of Soubirous. On one of his last visits to the Massabiello Grotto, the writer made a vow: if he and Alma managed to escape to America, he would write a book about Bernadette Soubirous.

When the exit papers for the trip to Marseille were finally granted on 3 August 1940, the return journey began. It had been six weeks since the Werfels had hastily left the south of France, and now they were back at the starting point of their odyssey. They stayed at the Hotel Louvre et Paix and, thanks to a personal intervention by the American Secretary of State, Cordell Hull, they were granted transit permits for Spain and Portugal, as well as a visitors' visa for the USA. However, all these documents were ultimately useless, as the French authorities refused to issue exit permits, citing a new law and Article 19 of the Armistice Agreement of Campiègne signed on 22 June, which allowed for the extradition of German refugees upon request. The respected art historian Louis Gillet even came to Marseille at the end of August to assist Franz and Alma, but he could do nothing to change their situation.

However, something positive did occur: Alma received her lost luggage, including a suitcase containing the valuable scores by Mahler and Bruckner. The hotel manager had personally intervened on her behalf, using his connections to retrieve it.

At the end of August, Heinrich Mann arrived in Marseille with his wife Nelly and his nephew Golo from Nice to wait for eventual visas. But when a 32-year-old US journalist named Varian Mackey Fry suddenly appeared in Marseille, the situation of all the refugees changed in an instant. Fry was a member of a newly founded Emergency Rescue Committee in New York, which helped intellectuals escape from France. The US organisation's main tasks included obtaining visas and coordinating private aid organisations. For Alma and Franz, it was clear: the young man was the right person for them at the right time.

Varian Mackey Fry spoke German and French and, thanks to his work as a journalist, knew the political situation in France very well. He was also a clever tactician, quickly forging contacts with corrupt officials and the Mafia in Marseille, managing to obtain false passports and transit visas. He visited Alma and Franz in their hotel, but was surprised to learn that they had checked in under the name of Gustav Mahler – a deliberate choice to disguise Werfel's Jewish identity and avoid attracting attention from the authorities. Fry made the following suggestion: Alma and Franz should leave France for

Spain, together with the Feuchtwangers, as well as Heinrich, Nelly and Golo Mann. There was a good chance that this could be done without exit visas.

Everyone agreed, and the departure was set for 12 September. Annemarie Meier-Graefe travelled from Saint Cyr to help Alma pack and to accompany her and the Manns to the train station the following morning. The Feuchtwangers were brought to America via a different route because they were considered stateless and had to follow a different set of rules.

When Alma and Franz arrived at the station with their twelve suitcases, Varian Fry and his colleague Leon 'Dick' Ball – one of the first volunteers of the Emergency Rescue Committee (ERC) – were extremely surprised. They travelled with them via Narbonne to Perpignan, then continued via Banyuls to Cerbère. In Cerbère, the escape was halted temporarily when Fry noticed that those leaving for Spain were queuing in front of the border police office and had to show their papers. As only Fry had an exit visa, he was very worried for his group of refugees and tried to calm them down, while his colleague Ball approached the border police in confidence. The police explained to him that they were not allowed to let anyone leave without an exit visa, and suddenly, they took away their passports and detained them. The refugees spent one night in the hotel next to the train station. The next morning, Ball spoke again to the border guards, who made it clear to him that 'we should get them out while we still can, preferably today'.[7]

There was only one option left for the refugees: to cross the border through the mountains on foot. Fry and Ball were sceptical about whether Heinrich Mann, who was already 70 years old, and the heavily overweight Franz Werfel would be able to complete the hike or endure the hardships. However, it was clear to everyone that there was no other choice at this point. After a brief discussion and explanation of the dire situation, Alma, as well as Golo and Heinrich Mann, decided to attempt the crossing that very day. Franz, on the other hand, began to tremble and stammer, pointing out that it was Friday the 13th – a day traditionally associated with misfortune. Alma contradicted him firmly, and Franz fell into a heavy, brooding silence.

Once the decision to cross the border was made, Fry took charge of the luggage, as his American status allowed him to transport it across the border by train without difficulty. He also handed each of the refugees a dozen packs of cigarettes to bribe the border police. In the sweltering heat, Ball accompanied the group as they began their climb to the top of the mountain. The ascent was particularly gruelling for Franz Werfel and Heinrich Mann, the latter requiring repeated support from his wife, Nelly, to endure the exertion. Werfel, meanwhile, grew increasingly anxious about the *Guardias Móviles*, the Spanish mobile security guards who might catch them, while Alma managed the march with surprising ease. She carried her money, jewellery, and the scores by Mahler and Bruckner securely in her handbag.

Upon reaching the summit, Ball returned to Cerbère. Alma and Franz, having gained a considerable lead over the Mann family, decided to press on alone. It seemed safer to cross the border in pairs to avoid drawing too much attention. When they reached the border, Alma discreetly handed a few packets of cigarettes to the gendarmerie officers, who gradually warmed up to them.

The gendarmes smiled and motioned for them to follow. When Alma and Franz spotted the *Guardias Móviles*, their fear returned momentarily, but the head of the French border post waved them through, and the soldiers helpfully pointed out the correct path. Alma and Franz reunited with Golo, Heinrich and Nelly Mann just before the Spanish border, which they all crossed without further trouble. After an arduous descent into the Spanish border town of Port Bou, they once again had to show their travel documents. The wait was nerve-wracking, but in the end, their papers were stamped, and they made their way to the train station, where Varian Fry was already waiting for them.

A short night in a simple hotel followed before the group continued to Barcelona. After a gruelling journey of nearly three hours, they reached the Catalan port city. For the first time in months, they could breathe a sigh of relief and recover, however briefly, from the physical and emotional strain. The next leg of their escape was a fifteen-hour train ride to Madrid. There, Fry sprinted ahead, managing to secure plane tickets to Lisbon for everyone. When the plane touched down in Lisbon on 18 September 1940, the group had nearly made it.

In Estoril, Alma and Franz settled into the Grand Hotel d'Italia. Alma proudly signed the registration form as Alma Mahler-Werfel, a statement to the world that nothing could separate her from Franz. They spent two idyllic weeks in peaceful Estoril before finally leaving Europe on 4 October 1940, aboard the Greek passenger ship *Nea Hellas*.

The *Nea Hellas* – a 177-metre (531-foot) vessel – offered first, second (or tourist class), and third-class cabins, along with restaurants and lounges. In its final years of service, the ship became a beacon of hope, reuniting Greeks with their loved ones in the land of freedom. Alma later described their passage:

> We finally had cabins on the last Greek ship, the *Nea Hellas*. The ship was mediocre, the tickets expensive, the food disgustingly bad. Shortly before we left Marseille, our luggage had arrived from Bordeaux and was immediately transported to New York, where some of it was lost – this time for good. The sea was boring, as always, because only the coasts are interesting, especially those populated by people. Otherwise, the monotony of nature is great, and we cannot absorb its absolute vastness.[8]

Despite the disappointing conditions, the group was elated to have escaped Europe's looming catastrophe. Yet Heinrich Mann spent most of the voyage confined to his cabin. According to Alma, it was 'because he felt sick'. His frustration manifested in sketches of women with large breasts – sometimes just the breasts alone. Alma reflected on their oceanic escape:

> On this voyage, we truly lost ourselves in the world. Nothing from outside could touch us. The pressure of the last few months, the feeling – no, the certainty – of a long-awaited freedom was overwhelming. We hardly ventured on deck, spending most of our time in our cabins, reading and talking. We didn't even participate in the life jacket drills. We dragged ourselves wearily to the neglected dining room. The *Nea Hellas* was an old Greek ship, likely making its final voyage, as rumours of war grew stronger every day. The spoiled food was disgusting. War with Greece was proclaimed in the middle of the ocean. Brave and full of hope, we climbed ashore on 13 October, 1940. Unfortunately for us, the ominous number proved correct.[9]

As the *Nea Hellas* docked in New York on 13 October 1940, Alma and Franz Werfel stepped ashore into a world brimming with both uncertainty and promise. They had left behind the ashes of war-torn Europe and entered a land of new beginnings, where their voices and talents could once again find expression. For Franz, America held the potential for his works to reach new audiences and to leave a lasting mark on literature. For Alma, it was a chance to build a life of stability and significance, carrying with her the legacy of Gustav Mahler and the determination to protect and elevate Franz Werfel's genius. Their journey of survival had ended, but a new chapter – one of creativity, resilience, and reinvention – was just beginning.

Chapter 9

Hollywood and the War Years – Alma's Salon and Werfel's Success

The towering skyline of New York City greeted Alma and Franz Werfel like a vision from another world. The roar of this bustling metropolis stood in stark contrast to the hushed terror they had left behind in Europe. America was vast, unfamiliar, and untouched by war – a place where millions had come to seek refuge and opportunity. For Alma, the city's frenetic energy carried with it a promise of renewal. She knew New York already, from her time with Gustav Mahler when he conducted at the Metropolitan Opera and the Philharmonic. But now, she had returned with a writer at her side. Culture remained, unchanged in its essence – it was only a matter of direction.

Here, Alma envisioned herself not as a survivor but as a protector, a curator of genius. Franz's literary success would be her priority, because in America, his voice could transcend borders and find eager audiences. At the same time, she saw herself as a cultural bridge – bringing the grandeur of Europe's lost past to this new, fast-paced society. It was not a complete reinvention but rather a transformation: the same Alma Mahler-Werfel, now navigating a different stage.

As the couple settled into the rhythms of their new life, the weight of exile remained a quiet companion. Yet Alma was determined to shape this unfamiliar world to her liking, finding opportunities where others might see only obstacles. America was not just a refuge – it was a blank canvas.

Alma noted in her memoirs the sense of security and relief that overcame them both when they arrived in the USA:

> Finally – finally, we were standing on truly free ground again, and everything that had come before seemed to sink into the night of the transient. If I hadn't been so embarrassed in front of the others, I would have kissed the ground of America. Arriving in New York Harbour was,

> as always, a magnificent experience. A large crowd of friends awaited us on the pier. Everyone had tears in their eyes – and we no less.[1]

Alma was the first to be allowed off the ship. She had secretly arranged this with the captain and, as soon as she stepped onto the pier, she greeted her longtime friend, the German author Carl Zuckmayer, with the words: 'Come to my hotel room tomorrow afternoon, no later than six o'clock. There are a few important people here, very valuable connections, but don't tell all the Jews.' Zuckmayer, whose maternal grandparents were assimilated Jews who had converted to Lutheranism, was startled by the remark. Alma's offhand antisemitism was all the more striking given that she was married to a Jew, had many Jewish friends, and had just fled Nazi-occupied Europe in the company of Jewish refugees – including her own husband.

On the quay in New York, they were also welcomed by Frank Kingdon, the English-born American journalist, activist and academic administrator, who was the first chairman of the Emergency Rescue Committee, an organisation that would save around 2,000 people from the Holocaust. Reporters and journalists were gathered there as well, eager to hear the details of the daring escape and to write articles about the rescued refugees.

For two months, Alma and Franz Werfel lived in a suite at the New York Hotel St Moritz, at 50 Central Park South, on the east side of Sixth Avenue, in Midtown Manhattan. Their friends, including the Zuckmayers, Feuchtwangers, Alfred Döblin, and Otto von Habsburg with his family, visited them frequently.

However, Franz Werfel remained deeply concerned about his own parents. Rudolf and Albine Werfel had relocated from Vichy to Bergerac, in the region of Nouvelle-Aquitaine, not far away from the north-east of Bordeaux. They were still in danger, as always. As a result, Franz and his sister Marianne Amalie Werfel-Rieser, who had already settled in New York, made plans to get their parents out of France. Meanwhile, Franz's sister Hanna von Fuchs-Robettin and her family had managed to escape to London.

Many German-speaking artists and intellectuals chose Los Angeles as a refuge from the National Socialists. Among them were Bertolt Brecht, Marlene Dietrich, Lion Feuchtwanger, Otto Klemperer, Fritz Lang, Ernst Lubitsch, Heinrich Mann, Thomas Mann, Luise Rainer and Billy Wilder.

Artists from other European countries also found new homes there, such as Luis Buñuel, Jean Renoir, Igor Stravinsky, Arturo Toscanini and many others. The emigrants made Los Angeles a lively centre of European culture in the 1940s, where great works by poets, conductors, directors and painters were created.

It was the sense of not being alone in the USA and the recommendation by the Austrian writer Friedrich Torberg that encouraged Alma and Franz to leave New York and move to California around 18 December. The mild climate and natural beauty of the region were especially appealing to Franz. In a letter to him of 15 December 1941, Torberg later praised 'the certain celluloid-packaged unworldliness' of Hollywood, in comparison to the 'cauldron' that was New York.

Adolph Loewi, a German-Jewish antique dealer known for his textile collection, had fled Italy in 1939 and settled in Los Angeles, where he opened Adolph Loewi Inc. Loewi offered to help the Werfels find a new home, and quickly succeeded in locating a residence in the Hollywood Hills, a villa district called 'The Outpost'. This area, bordered by Mulholland Drive to the north, Franklin Avenue to the south, Runyon Canyon Park to the west, and Hollywood Heights and the Hollywood Bowl to the east, was historically significant. In the 1920s, a large neon 'Outpost' sign towered above the area, though it was dismantled during the Second World War, with its wreckage left buried in the weeds.

Below the mountain was the Hollywood Bowl, an amphitheatre and public park in the Hollywood Hills of Los Angeles with a grand open-air stage, a fitting venue for outdoor performances by the members of the newly formed Theatre Arts Alliance, led by Christine Wetherill Stevenson.

If the wind was right, Alma and Franz could also hear performances from their terrace. Their house on 6800 Los Tilos Road, however, was modest. The front door opened directly into the living room, with a small hallway leading to the kitchen and dining room. Franz's study and their two bedrooms were located in the basement. The living space was humble and could not compare with the grandeur of their house in Breitenstein am Semmering or the Villa Ast on the Hohe Warte in Vienna.

Adolph Loewi, however, managed to find them a butler to make their lives easier. August Hess, a slender, medium-sized man with curly grey-blond hair and watery eyes, was a 34-year-old German from Heidelberg. Known as 'handsome August' due to his good looks, he had worked as an operetta tenor in a provincial theatre. But after the theatre ensemble went bankrupt following a tour of the United States, he stayed in the country and made his living as a butler.

Alma was charmed by him. She relished having a fellow German in her home, and August Hess proved to be more than just a butler. He was loyal to Franz Werfel; he didn't understand much of what he wrote, but admired him nonetheless. Hess was a chauffeur, gardener, drinking partner for Alma, and valet to Werfel, all rolled into one. It was impossible to imagine the Werfels' daily lives without him. Hess drove them around Los Angeles in a Cadillac Series 60, a symbol of luxury and refinement, its sleek, imposing frame a fitting companion to the couple's new life in the glamorous city, making visits to German conductor and composer Otto Klemperer or Austrian-born theatre and film-director Max Reinhardt, and attending tea parties, cocktails, and dinner invitations.

The Werfels had quickly settled into their exile. On 3 January 1941, Alma noted in her diary that Franz had already begun working on a new manuscript. 'Franz Werfel started working today. Thank God. It is such a miracle that he can concentrate again. It is Bernadette who is rumbling around in his head.'[2]

Werfel was truly fulfilling the vow he had made in the grotto at the pilgrimage site of Lourdes. He wanted to write a book about Bernadette Soubirous. The subject had captured his attention since her escape through southern France, and he devoted himself to it with great intensity, working several hours a day on the manuscript. The German priest, travel writer, and editor-in-chief of the Catholic weekly *Allgemeine Rundschau*, Dr Georg Moenius, who had fled from Bavaria to the USA in 1938, supported Franz, providing him with theological advice for his manuscript. Then, after only four months of hard work, Franz had completed the 'Bernadette' manuscript. To finalise this version, he hired his own secretary, Albrecht Joseph, a man from Frankfurt am Main who had fled to the USA in 1939. In California, he worked as an anonymous scriptwriter and as a private secretary not only to Franz Werfel, but also to the German exiles Emil Ludwig and Thomas Mann.

Werfel usually asked Joseph to come to his house in the morning; Joseph would drive to the house and stay in his car for a few minutes to listen to Alma playing the piano before venturing into the house.

Then Werfel and Joseph would retire to the office in the basement for work and Franz would dictate from his notebooks for several hours. Alma usually asked Joseph to drink a glass of Bénédictine with her in the afternoon. He remembers in his own notes that this drink was too sweet for him and that he drank a glass of whiskey instead. When he did not want to drink anymore, Alma said: 'You can't drink with me because you're a Jew.' Although Joseph tried to refute Alma's prejudice by referring to well-known Jews who were also known to be alcoholics, Alma would not change her mind. Franz also suffered from Alma's antisemitic comments, which were just as incorrigible and extreme in America as they had been in Europe before their emigration.

Despite their shared exile, the ideological divide between Alma and Franz was glaring. Alma often expressed extreme views, shaped by her admiration for German culture and nationalism, even under Hitler. She infamously referred to the Germans as 'supermen' in comparison to the Allies, whom she considered weak and degenerate at that time. She was unrepentant in her elitism and prejudices.

Franz, however, stood in stark opposition to Alma's sentiments. As a Jewish writer who had fled Nazi persecution, he was horrified by Hitler's regime and the atrocities committed under it. Their arguments on these topics were frequent but futile, as Alma's opinions remained unshakable. Albrecht Joseph recalled Werfel's frustration vividly – how he would pause on the spiral staircase, shake his head, and lament: 'What can you do with a woman like that?' He shook his head. 'You must not forget that she is an old woman.'

Despite the emotional strain these disagreements caused, Werfel remained committed to his work. After the heated exchanges, which rarely lasted more than ten minutes, he would tap Joseph on the shoulder, signalling that it was time to return to the basement office. There, away from the tensions of the household, Werfel would refocus on dictating his manuscript and on channelling his energy into the creative process.

'I've finally found real friends here', Joseph heard Alma say one day when he arrived for work at the Werfels' home. Alma spoke of Gustav Otto Arlt and his wife Gusti, with whom she had become close after being invited together with them to Arnold Schönberg's home. Gustav Arlt was a Germanist who had worked at the University of California, Los Angeles, since 1935, later becoming dean. He was deeply committed to expanding the university library's German collections, a task facilitated by his connections with numerous German exiles. Arlt also translated several of Franz Werfel's works into English.

A very close friendship quickly developed between Alma and the Arlts. Albrecht Joseph, however, found the couple pushy busybodies, politically suspect, and unpleasant company. Gustav Otto Arlt had a reputation as a staunch anti-communist with alleged sympathies toward the Nazi regime in Germany. In Arlt's presence, Alma could freely rail against Marxists and Jews without hesitation. According to Joseph's recollections, from that point on, the Arlts were constantly present in the Werfel household, fuelling Alma's growing animosity toward Russians and democrats. Franz, by contrast, remained rather distant toward the couple. He found Gusti Arlt particularly difficult to endure, describing her as a 'caricature of the typical German housewife, someone puffed up with spite, ugly, and fat'. Yet, recognising how important this friendship was to Alma, Franz often withdrew to his basement study, putting on a brave face. The Werfels' butler, August Hess, however, was less diplomatic. Echoing what many around the couple thought, Hess bluntly accused the Arlts of opportunistic motives to their faces.

The Arlts became connected to a particularly telling marital episode that underscored the tensions in the Werfels' relationship during their American exile. On 31 July 1941, the day Franz Werfel received word that his father Rudolf had died in Marseille, the Arlts were once again at the Werfels' house. Rather insensitively, they proposed a sightseeing excursion and dinner together. Reluctantly, Franz agreed, choosing to avoid yet another argument with Alma. From then on, Franz's attention turned increasingly to his 70-year-old mother, now alone in France. But when he learned that she was en route to Portugal and would arrive in America at the end of September, he was greatly relieved.

In early autumn, the Werfels travelled to New York to welcome Albine Werfel and they prepared for a longer stay. Alma wasted no time establishing a salon in her hotel suite, reminiscent of her gatherings in Vienna. There she entertained politicians, remnants of the Austro-Hungarian monarchy's high nobility, and artists – among them was the painter Marc Chagall. Reflecting on Chagall, Alma confessed:

> In the winter of 1941, I met Marc Chagall. He has bright, water-blue eyes and an equally bright mind, even though he often creates absurd things. He is a real Jew in the best sense of the word. He is free of any charismatic pretence. He has illustrated the Old Testament in exemplary fashion and now wants to illustrate the New Testament. He could be beautiful … if only he could! His wife could be beautiful too … if she were beautiful. But she isn't … she, too, has the opportunity to be … but since there is no subjunctive in life, she simply isn't beautiful.[3]

One of the Werfels' closest friends in the USA was the Austrian writer, journalist, publicist, translator, screenwriter and editor Friedrich Kantor, who wrote under the Pen name 'Friedrich Torberg'. Torberg, who described himself as a Czech, an Austrian and a Jew, was an integral part of Prague's German literary scene. In California, an especially intense male friendship blossomed between him and Franz. Before long, Torberg felt almost at home in the Werfels' modest residence, and his presence seemed to compensate Franz for the sorely missed Vienna and its coffee-house atmosphere.

Alma, for her part, became something of a mentor to Torberg – praising, criticising, and offering guidance. And Torberg appreciated this dynamic and wrote to her with heartfelt sincerity:

> Dear Alma, your lovely lines just arrived in last Saturday's post, which means I'm guaranteed a pleasant weekend. You know that this is really the case – you know that every expression of your life makes me happy, especially one so clearly focused on me as a letter. You also sense the quiet rebellion that lies in this emphasis on 'concentration': it is directed against the unfortunately unmistakable fact that things are not always so concentrated, that suddenly some I don't say no comes in, which is also limited to not saying no.[4]

The correspondence between Alma and Torberg is, in many ways, reminiscent of her exchanges with composer and conductor Alexander von Zemlinsky, her husband Gustav Mahler, and her lover Oskar Kokoschka.

In his letters, Torberg frequently expressed frustration at Alma's inability to engage in genuine dialogue, while she, in turn, occasionally tormented him with jealousy and her characteristic self-satisfaction. Torberg failed to grasp that this unique mixture of self-centredness and an almost playful inclination to insult, allowed Alma to assert her dominance over him – a man whose relationship with his own Judaism was far less conflict-free than he liked to pretend. Alma's methods proved effective, however, as Torberg's subsequent letters revealed his growing admiration. He even wrote that he and his friends often spoke of her and how deeply they all loved her. Alma had succeeded in becoming his great role model.

When the Werfels were away from Los Angeles – now also spending time in New York – Friedrich Torberg wrote them long, heartfelt letters, often expressing how eagerly he awaited their return. Alma, however, replied in her characteristic manner:

> Dear friend,
>
> I have been silent for a long time. You write so often and so cheerfully to B. (Uschi) Meier-Graefe that I didn't want to waste your time too. But you don't have to tell her that … Werfel arrived here yesterday after missing several trains. We will be back in mid-January. Maybe just to pack up and leave again – maybe to stay. Circumstances will show this. We have already experienced enough blackouts in France. This fun is no longer fun for us. Please write again. And don't mention the 'fun' I wrote about at the beginning in your letter or to B.M.G.
>
> All the best, Alma Maria[5]

When Franz and Alma returned to their house in Los Angeles after nearly four months in New York, in February 1942, Alma complained about American culture for the first time:

> When we left Hollywood last September, we had the film contract in our pockets: fifty thousand dollars – and the expectation that the 'Book of the Month Club' would take Franz's new book, *Song of Bernadette*.

She began, initially quite pleased. But then came the plot twist:

> But everything went wrong. Producer Dieterle is broke, the 'Book of the Month Club' fears that Werfel's book is too Catholic, which is a misunderstanding, as Franz only wanted to portray the power and effectiveness of some faith. And now we're sitting here … we've arranged our lives on a grander scale … we have almost no money … no capital at all … we sold our old car and haven't bought a new one because everything is now sequestered … and if we get a new one, it will cost a fortune again – or rather, the fortune.[6]

She missed Europe, especially Italy and Austria. Alma wistfully thought back to the years spent in her house in Venice or the hotel in Santa Margarita Ligure, where Franz loved to work. 'Italy is our old home', she concluded.

On 1 April 1942, Thomas Mann began his day with coffee and his morning routine, and he also found a little time to write. Around midday, lunch was planned with the American art collector, diplomat, philanthropist, and one of the co-founders of the Dumbarton Oaks Research Library and Collection in Washington, D.C., Robert Woods Bliss. In the evening, there was one of those fantastic invitations from Alma and Franz Werfel in Hollywood. Despite the looming uncertainty over Franz's publishing prospects and their financial insecurity, Alma continued to perform her familiar social role with gusto, hosting artists and intellectuals in their Hollywood exile – a reminder of the world they had lost, and the cultural capital she still commanded. Alma had invited the Manns, Gustav Otto Arlt and his wife Gusti, as well as the Austrian-American composer, conductor and pianist Erich Wolfgang Korngold and his wife Luise 'Luzi' Sonnenthal-Korngold. Alma was in high spirits, enjoying the opportunity to serve her guests good food, champagne, and plenty of coffee. Her butler, August Hess, had his hands full, darting back and forth between the kitchen and the dining room while the guests enjoyed lively conversation and the evening festivities. Alma also drank her Bénédictine and encouraged August Hess to join her in toasting, though he loathed such displays. Yet, despite Alma's fears, Franz's fortunes were about to change. Thanks to the determined efforts of their publisher and growing interest in religious themes during wartime, *The Song of Bernadette* was accepted for publication in early 1942 – a turning point that would soon catapult him to national fame.

The Song of Bernadette became Franz Werfel's most successful book, soon ranking among the best-selling books in US publishing history. When it was released in US bookstores on 11 May, with an initial print run of 200,000 copies, its author had already become an icon and a national celebrity. Within two months, the novel had sold 400,000 copies, and Twentieth Century Fox acquired the film rights.

The story of Bernadette Soubirous moved the readers to tears. At the request of his American publisher Benjamin W. Huebsch, Franz and Alma travelled to New York in mid-June, as there were countless requests for interviews. Radio programs were broadcast nationwide, where Werfel read from his book and commented on it. All major media outlets published interviews, reports, and reviews of the book. New York's high society wanted to meet the bestselling author in person. Franz and Alma went from one New York party to the next, and Franz also spent time with his mother Albine and his sister.

When the Werfels returned to California at the beginning of July, the social activities of their New York days continued. On 11 July, conductor and composer Bruno Walter invited them, as well as the Korngolds and Thomas and Katia Mann, to dinner. A little later, their firstborn, the 37-year-old German actress, cabaret artist, writer and editor Erika Mann, who had been in a relationship with 66-year-old Bruno Walter for some time, arrived. The unlikely lovers were very cautious, as Bruno Walter was still officially married. While Bruno Walter played the *St Matthew Passion* on the piano, Erika Mann and Alma got drunk. Thomas Mann watched this drinking session with astonishment.

But the countless social obligations that Alma and Franz performed together could not hide the fact that there was tension between the couple. Again and again there were episodes between the two which left Alma in no doubt that she had only left her homeland to protect Franz:

> The Jews are now experiencing a test – another punishment! The younger ones have fled to America, and the older ones stayed behind, planning to end their lives in familiar surroundings. But Hitler is

> directing things differently. And now the young ones have to do everything to get the older Jews, who are far away in their inner lives, to come over, with enormous financial sacrifices. And now comes the great conflict. It is as if the shed skin is revived, and the first reproach is that the young and strong ones are being overlooked by even stronger old Jews. It is interesting to see how the young ones fear the old ones. When I look at old Mrs X., waving her countless hands around, screaming and always obsessed with herself, then you can imagine how everyone else is suffering.[7]

In the summer of 1942, Alma's frequent antisemitic outbursts, as recalled by Albrecht Joseph, deeply pained Franz. Unable to endure the tension, he sought refuge in the tranquil surroundings of Santa Barbara, about 80 miles south of Los Angeles. There, he moved into a bungalow at the luxurious Biltmore Hotel, hoping the serene environment would allow him to focus on his writing. This temporary separation from Alma proved to be a necessary reprieve, enabling the couple to reconcile and sustain a marriage that, despite its challenges, endured for over twenty-five years.

Their relationship seemed to be built on a mutual understanding of their distinct roles: Franz immersed himself in his literary endeavours, crafting a new play titled *Jakobowsky und der Oberst* (*Jacobovsky and the Colonel*). Meanwhile, Alma turned her attention to organising yet another move. By the end of summer 1942, the Werfels resolved to leave their home in the Hollywood Hills in favour of the more exclusive neighbourhood of Beverly Hills.

Not far from Santa Monica Boulevard, a beautiful bungalow with a large garden was listed for sale. The house at 610 North Bedford Drive had been designed and once inhabited by the American actress May Robson. It was a typical middle-class residence of the time: charming and elegant on the outside, but somewhat dark and lacking in taste inside. The Werfels decided to make it their new home, moving into a neighbourhood filled with friends and acquaintances. Among their neighbours were Friedrich Torberg, actor Ernst Deutsch and his wife Anuschka, as well as the Korngolds, Schönbergs and Feuchtwangers. Alma, ever the socialite, quickly struck up a rapport with the 44-year-old German-born novelist Erich Maria Remarque, whom she had met at a party. Tall and stately, Remarque exuded a captivating masculinity and had a special aura about him. The two delighted in spirited conversations over drinks, and after each night of revelry, Remarque would write Alma a letter – a gesture she greatly appreciated. On 11 October 1942, the Werfels hosted their first party in their new home. All their friends from the neighbourhood attended, and Alma once again demonstrated her remarkable talent as a hostess, creating an evening to remember. Alma was really in the mood to celebrate, as her daughter Anna was about to marry for the fourth time. Alma's fourth son-in-law was the Kyiv conductor Anatole Fistoulari, who came from a family of musicians. His father was also a well-known conductor, and so Alma was very happy for her daughter.

This time, the couple spent the New Year in New York, as Franz wanted to see his mother Albine again, who lived in a large apartment building; she was very isolated and rarely met friends because few of them lived in the USA. As soon as Alma entered her hotel St Moritz in New York, she invited everyone to a salon again and thus had the opportunity to meet old friends and acquaintances.

But in the first week Alma caught the flu, which kept her in bed for a whole month and meant that she was unable to enjoy her entire stay in New York. After three years in the USA, the two Werfels found that life was quite good in their Californian exile. On her 64th birthday, 31 August 1943, Alma said: 'We are in Santa Barbara. It is a paradise. Franz Werfel was wonderful that day; I will never forget it. He has had great battles over his play, and it is not over yet.'[8]

Two weeks later, on 12 September, Franz Werfel celebrated his 53rd birthday with his wife – and from then on something was about to change in their lives. Franz was just lighting a Havana cigar, his good friend, the author Friedrich Torberg, was sitting opposite him, when Alma carefully reminded her husband that the doctor had expressed concerns about his nicotine consumption. Franz immediately threw the cigar away and within a few minutes lit another, slightly smaller cigar. Cigarettes followed. It was late, and Alma decided to go to bed. A few minutes later, Franz followed her. And then the unthinkable happened: on the night of 13 September 1943, Franz Werfel suffered a serious heart attack. His German-American heart specialist, Dr Erich Wolff, strictly ordered Franz to give up smoking and also showed him where smoking would lead, if he did not give it up. But Franz just laughed. For as long as he could remember, he had smoked one cigarette after another. He once considered breaking this habit. However, Alma took the diagnosis very seriously and carefully monitored Wolff's orders. The deepening friendship between Friedrich Torberg and Franz Werfel is highlighted by Torberg's loyalty during the Werfel's recovery. Torberg spent nights at Franz's bedside, and when Alma was absent, he would light a cigarette and blow smoke in Franz's face, defying Alma's orders and offering a small act of comfort to his friend.

This moment underscores the tension between Alma's control and Franz's dependence on his habits. While Alma strictly enforced health regulations, Torberg's rebellious gesture reveals the complexities of their relationships – between care, addiction, and the bond of friendship. Despite the good care provided by his wife and the support of his friends, Franz Werfel's health remained seriously threatened for a long time. He suffered from choking attacks, sweating, shortness of breath and high fever. On the morning of 21 October, he had his second major heart attack. When the doctor finally arrived after a long wait, the crisis had passed and the patient had calmed down. A separate concern arose when the doctor observed a thickening of the intestine and ordered an X-ray. During this examination, Franz collapsed. He was ordered to stay in bed, and his weak condition improved only very slowly. At the beginning of December, Alma wrote to her friends Lion Feuchtwanger and his wife Marta, that a visit would soon be possible. But on 14 December, her husband suffered another severe heart attack with choking attacks. Due to the seriousness of his condition, Franz missed the premiere of the *Bernadette Soubirous* film adaptation. The enthusiasm for his film adaptation of Lourdes was still great: he had sold more than a million copies of his book, and the premiere of the film was another high point. Alma and her husband sent all their friends to the Cartgy Circle Theater in Hollywood, and they themselves followed the spectacle on the radio. Franz was very weak, but Alma invited Gustav Otto Arlt and his wife Gusti to her house to celebrate New Year's Eve with them, while Franz Werfel listened to everything from his bed.

On New Year's Day, Anna sent a telegram from London with best wishes for a happy New Year 1944 and in the hope of a reunion with her mother and Franz. She had become a mother for the second time on 1 August 1943, to a little Marina Fistoulari-Mahler. When Alma thought of her daughter and her two little grandchildren, who lived in Europe and whom she had not seen for five years, she began to cry bitterly. She regularly sent money and food parcels to her daughter in London to support her and her family.

Alma was exhausted from caring for her husband around the clock. Franz's recovery took six months. At the beginning of July 1944, his condition had stabilised enough for him to move back to Santa Barbara. He wanted to finish a writing project that he had already started in 1943. Within a few days, he had written five chapters of his time travel novel under the working title *Brief Visit in the Distant Future*. The book would later be called *Star of the Unborn* and is about numerous personal experiences wrapped up in a science fiction story. Since Franz Werfel was still not completely healthy, Alma hired a personal doctor for him, Bernhard 'Benno' Spinak, who was born in Warsaw. His patients in Germany affectionately called him *Schwammerl* (little mushroom). He became Franz Werfel's constant companion.

Despite his poor health, Franz continued to work on his time travel novel with a certain amount of energy, only interrupted by short walks, rest breaks and phone calls with his wife. Sometimes he visited the Franciscan monastery where his friend Father Johann Cyrill Fischer worked. On weekends, he went back to Alma in Beverly Hills. Meanwhile, his friend Friedrich Torberg received an offer to move to the renowned *Time Magazine* in New York. Since he was constantly short of money, this was a wonderful promotion for him, and he accepted the job. The call from the East Coast to work with friends such as Willi Schlamm and Alfred Polgar seemed like a sign of fate for Torberg. Before his departure, he gifted Alma a photo by Oskar Kokoschka, which she considered thoughtfully for a long time. After Friedrich Torberg moved to New York, their lively correspondence continued.

Despite his health issues, Franz Werfel was exceptionally productive during the summer of 1944. Each day, he wrote four to five pages, which he sent to Albrecht Joseph to type up. Alma celebrated her 65th birthday on 31 August with the Arlts, marking the occasion with modest festivity. In the following months, the Werfels continued their routine of commuting between Los Angeles and Santa Barbara.

The severity of Franz's illness had drawn the couple closer, with Alma taking on the role of a devoted caretaker and allowing their marital disputes to fade into the background. However, despite her focus on his physical wellbeing, Alma could not help but notice Franz's attention wandering towards other women. She analysed this behaviour – was it his emotional impulses, his tendency to act on whims, rather than his years of smoking or overexertion, that had truly contributed to his failing health? While his physical habits clearly played a role, Alma began to suspect that his impulsive nature, perhaps manifesting in emotional distractions or flirtations, was a significant factor in the toll on his health.

In the spring of 1945, Europe lay in ruins. Millions of lives had been lost to the Second World War, leaving a legacy of relentless bombings, immense fear and the oppressive grip of totalitarianism. Alma's family viewed the collapse of the Thousand-Year Reich as a personal catastrophe. In April 1945, her stepfather Carl Moll took his own life in his villa, along with his daughter Maria and her husband, Dr Richard Eberstaller. Moll had penned a farewell letter dated 10 April 1945, stating: 'I fall asleep without regrets; I have had everything beautiful that life has to offer.' Their subtenants, Carl and Rosa Sieber, discovered the bodies and immediately alerted the authorities. Alma's reaction to this tragic news remains undocumented.

By early summer, Johannes Hollensteiner had reached out to the Werfels. Alma had learned that, following his release from the Dachau concentration camp, he had abandoned his priesthood and joined the NSDAP. According to Alma's informant, Siegfried Trabitsch's wife, Hollensteiner had even entered into marriage. In a letter from 1945, Hollensteiner attempted to justify his actions and provide an explanation for his decisions. A decade later, Alma met him in New York, where they had a long discussion. By the end of their conversation, Alma chose to forgive her old friend.

On Friday, 17 August 1945, Alma received an excited call from her husband in Santa Barbara, who was delighted to tell her that he had finished the script of his time travel novel, *Star of the Unborn*. He planned to return to Beverly Hills as soon as possible. Alma advised him to leave in the evening when it would be cooler, but Franz was adamant and set off in the blazing midday heat. When he arrived home, Alma noticed he was utterly exhausted. He walked the short distance from the car to the house with heavy steps. With their regular doctor, Bernhard 'Benno' Spinak, on leave, the heart specialist Dr Erich Wolff was called. He injected Franz with heart medication and prescribed a morphine injection for the evening. However, that night, from

Saturday into Sunday, he suffered another severe heart attack. The doctors ordered three days of bed rest. By the following week, Franz felt much better and began writing poetry from his bed.

Seven days later, he ventured out to Romanoff's Restaurant in Beverly Hills for dinner with the conductor and composer Bruno Walter and Walter's daughter, Lotte. Before setting out for the restaurant, Bruno Walter played a few bars of Smetana's opera *The Bartered Bride* on the Werfels' Steinway grand piano. Franz hummed along to the aria and even attempted a playful dance. The evening was filled with joy and laughter. The next morning, Franz awoke in good spirits and discussed a possible trip to Europe with Alma. Vienna, London, Rome and Prague were on their itinerary.

After lunch, Franz lay down for a rest while Alma waited for the Arlts, who she had invited for coffee. Shortly before their arrival she checked on her husband, who was sitting at his desk, deep in thought over the planned volume of poetry. Hours later, when she looked into his study again, she was met with a horrifying sight.

On Sunday, 26 August 1945, just two weeks before his 55th birthday, Franz Werfel suffered another heart attack and lay lifeless on the floor. Alma screamed for help, and August Hess came immediately and laid Franz on his bed. Together, they tried to administer heart massages, but to no avail. Franz could not be saved. The doctor who arrived later confirmed his death and arranged for the removal of his body. Devastated, Alma was given a sedative and spent the night in Franz's bed. The Arlts stayed with her, watching over her through the whole night.

The news of Franz Werfel's sudden death spread quickly through Los Angeles, and in the days that followed, friends came to support Alma. The memorial service was held on 29 August at the Pierce Brothers Mortuary. It was a dignified and moving event, attended by 114 mourners who signed the condolence book. Bruno Walter and Lotte Lehmann performed, and Albrecht Joseph organised the proceedings. However, Alma refused to be driven to the funeral. Instead, she remained at Franz's desk, working on Father Georg Moenius' eulogy for the service.

Years later, Friedrich Torberg recounted a surprising revelation from Alma: she admitted that she 'could have performed an emergency baptism when she found him – but she would never have dared'. The confession added a haunting dimension to the tragic scene of Franz Werfel's passing, a moment that would forever remain etched in Alma's memory.

The death of Franz Werfel marked the end of Alma's third great marriage, and with it, the close of a chapter defined by profound love, collaboration and loss. In the years that followed, Alma's life took on a more solitary yet determined character. She became the guardian of Werfel's legacy, ensuring his works continued to inspire audiences worldwide. This responsibility brought her a renewed sense of purpose, though it also underscored the loneliness that had become a recurring theme in her life. With her boundless energy and unyielding ambition, Alma would channel her grief into cultivating her own legacy, drawing strength from the memories of the men, who had shaped her world and the artistic vision she had long championed.

Chapter 10

A Widow's Final Chapter – Memoirs, Estates, and Legacy

Alma Mahler-Werfel now found herself at a crossroads. The death of her third husband, Franz Werfel, had left her with an unfillable void, but Alma refused to give in to despair. Despite her immense grief, she knew her life's work was far from over. Determined to honour the legacies of the men she had loved and lost, she envisioned a new chapter where her own voice could resonate just as powerfully. Alma's tireless energy and sharp wit remained undiminished, enabling her to face the challenges of widowhood with characteristic tenacity. As Europe began to recover from the turmoil of war, she searched for ways to reconnect with the continent that had shaped her formative years. The post-war years offered Alma opportunities to engage with emerging cultural movements, forge new alliances, and leave an indelible mark on the global stage. This new chapter promised not only reflection but also reinvention – a chance for Alma to shape her final act on her own terms.

In Beverly Hills, Alma initially found comfort in the companionship of her neighbour, conductor and composer Bruno Walter, and her dear friends Gustav Otto and Gusti Arlt. They were always just a phone call away when she needed their help or their company. Surrounded by memories of Franz Werfel, her home provided a semblance of security. Yet, at 66, Alma faced the stark reality of living alone in a foreign country – without a partner or husband, without children or parents, and, for the first time in her life, without a lover. Newspapers and radio stations had extensively reported Franz's death, and Alma busied herself reading the countless letters, telegrams, and condolences. The outpouring of sympathy exceeded even what she had received after Gustav Mahler's death.

But the fervent support of fans and friends could not fill the silence that enveloped her every night when no one was there to bid her goodnight.

Her loyal servant, August Hess, became her constant companion during this time.

By the autumn of 1945, Alma decided to spend most of the winter in New York, seeking solace and distraction in the bustling energy of the city. Before leaving Beverly Hills at the end of September, Alma wrote a letter to a dear friend in New York, who had eagerly been awaiting her arrival:

> Dear friend, I am sending the German Theologumena herewith. The German Bernadette should give the pig, Gottfried B(ermann) Fischer, who dropped the book under the table, to you – you can find the large edition of the volume of poetry at the public library. I have only a single copy and don't want to send it by post. Since we have to sit for fourteen hours, I'll be a bit far – but I urgently ask you to call me in St Moritz. I'm always sick – I'll just feel worse this way! Don't tell anyone that I'm coming – warn Mom too! I'm longing for you! Alma.[1]

On 4 October, Alma and August Hess arrived by train in New York City, where, as they had done several times before, they stayed at the Hotel St Moritz. However, after a brief period, Alma and Hess moved to the apartment hotel The Alrae, at 37 East 64th Street. This establishment was nestled between the prestigious Park Avenue and Madison Avenue, on Manhattan's Upper East Side. Alma had reserved a suite here for the end of February 1946. Opened in 1927, The Alrae was designed by architect George F. Pelham. It remained a prominent address until its sale to Louis Schleifer in July 1950, followed by a transfer to the Ira Fischer Syndicate in June 1951. It would not reopen until 1984 as the renowned Plaza Athénée Hotel.

It was in this elegant setting that Alma Mahler-Werfel found herself after arriving in New York in October, her grief over the loss of Franz consuming her. Despite her sorrow, she engaged in frequent meetings with Friedrich Torberg and his new girlfriend Mariette Bellak, a journalist. Their conversations offered Alma new perspectives and ideas as they discussed the handling of Franz's estate, for which she was now responsible. The Torbergs married in New York that winter, and Alma was pleased to serve as their maid of honour.

Alma also reconnected with several old acquaintances, including Erich Maria Remarque, actress Marlene Dietrich, Alfred Polgar, and Carl Zuckmayer. Together, they spent long nights discussing and celebrating life. Alma also attended concerts by the New York Philharmonic and performances at the opera, seeking inspiration to reignite her musical passion.

In early December 1945, she received a heartbreaking letter from her loyal nurse and later servant, Agnes Ida Gehbauer (Schulli), who lived in Vienna. The letter revealed that the top floor of the home she had shared with Franz had been destroyed in an air raid. There, among the rubble, were the letters and manuscripts of both Franz Werfel and Gustav Mahler.

'They were probably burned. I still can't believe that they have disappeared forever. In my confusion and haste, I had placed these most important documents on the top floor because I thought they would be safest there…'[2] Alma later recalled with sorrow.

After nearly five months on the East Coast, Alma made the decision to return to Beverly Hills at the end of February 1946. Although, Alma soon began to feel increasingly uncomfortable in the house she had shared with Franz. The memories of her time with him were too overwhelming, and August Hess was starting to become a burden. He had already proven to be a choleric man during Franz's lifetime, though Alma had found it easier to cope with his temper then. As a widow, however, she began to fear the outbursts of the 'handsome August'.

Her friends, Gustav and Gusti Arlt, who still held a grudge against him, strongly advised Alma to fire him, to be rid of her worries. When Alma travelled to San Francisco at the end of August to mark the anniversary of Franz's death, Gustav Arlt was tasked with informing Hess that his services were no longer needed. However, when Alma returned to Beverly Hills at the beginning of September, Hess was still living in her house. After a lengthy conversation, Alma ultimately decided to keep him on. Franz's assistant, Albrecht Joseph, later speculated that Hess might have known too much about Alma's financial situation to be easily dismissed. Hess was also a witness to the events of the hours leading up to Franz's death.

The relationship between Alma and Hess seemed suspicious to many. Some even speculated that the two were having an affair, despite the fact that the 'handsome August' was homosexual and made no attempt to hide it.

Nevertheless, in this case, Alma seemed determined to captivate the man with her feminine charm. In her diary, she wrote an analytical reflection: 'Homosexuals torture without knowing or wanting to. They let you lick a piece of sugar and then calmly put it in your pocket.'[3]

It was time for Alma to pay a visit to Vienna to check on her villa and clarify the ownership situation. Having obtained American citizenship on 14 June 1946, she was now officially considered a foreigner in Austria and required an entry permit to return, something she referred to in a letter to Friedrich Torberg on 11 September 1946:

> I'm waiting for my passport – because I have to get to Vienna as soon as possible! No fun either! Just an expense – and I have precious little of that kind right now. When I finish selling the house, I'll use the money for a house in New York that will need just as much of a down payment as I can manage. I want to get a tiny apartment there – two rooms – and spend a lot of time in New York, if I can make it financially possible … At the moment, I have no income at all, and the little money we had in the bank is now half sequestered. But I have ridden these waves so many times in my life – I'll just have to simplify things a lot, as I've always been able to do! I hug you both warmly.[4]

Alma's relationship with Franz Werfel's family had been strained since his death, as Franz had declared her his sole heir. His mother and sister, feeling excluded as close family members, raised objections and demanded proceeds from his European royalties. The dispute led Alma to enlist the help of Rudolf Monter, a New York lawyer who had worked with Franz on numerous occasions. The conflict reached a sudden conclusion when the Zsolnay publishing house confirmed it had transferred the rights to Alma of its own accord, leaving Hanna and Albine Werfel empty-handed. Despite the resolution, the family ties remained fractured for years. Alma's grief over Franz remained profound, and she often confided in friends and family: 'Just like on the first day – that's how I feel today – I can't live without him!'[5]

In her letters to friends, Alma repeatedly stressed that the Werfel family from Prague must have had a terrible jealousy complex. She also complained about still waiting for Austria's permission to enter the country:

> Unfortunately, it seems he was right to flee his parents' home as a young man. I don't want to discuss it – it's pointless! I'm still waiting for my entry permit. Whether I come to Vienna or not, it will be difficult in any case! I just want to save the spiritual values; everything else can come later![6]

She went on to explain in a letter from mid-September 1946 to Friedrich Torberg that she would find her villa in Vienna in a terrible state:

> I can't live like this in my house in Vienna. The Russians ripped out and burned all the parquet floors – it must look horrible, this Vienna! This poor Vienna! I'm coming to New York soon! I can't stand it here any longer! Franzerl's room is just as he left it, though there are always more flowers in it now than there were back then. If I can manage it financially, I want to keep everything as it is! But I don't know if I have enough money for that. I hug you.[7]

The year 1946 passed without any major incidents. However, while Alma was still waiting for her entry permit to Austria, she kept herself busy in Beverly Hills during the spring of 1947, working on the estate of her late husband. She dictated the novel fragment *Cella, or, The Survivors* and edited several of his short novellas and poems. She also planned to publish Franz's early prose at a later date, though not all at once.

Alma shared her mental state only with her closest friend in New York:

> As I'm not well, I'm only allowed to play the piano a little – which doesn't improve my mood! I have lots of friends, new ones too, but I can't find happiness in anything anymore. Except – I'd like to see you again! Hugs.[8]

At the end of the summer of 1947, Alma finally received her entry permit for Austria, and in September, she decided to fly home. The press release from the city of Vienna reported: 'Mrs Alma Mahler-Werfel, the widow of Gustav Mahler and Franz Werfel, arrived at the airfield in Tulln from America for a stay of several weeks in Vienna.'

However, the trip to her hometown was, as she later described, 'terribly strenuous, and the stay there was even worse'. Alma flew to Vienna via London, where she quickly visited her daughter Anna, whom she found in poor condition. Anna appeared visibly emaciated, had a pale complexion and looked much older than her 43 years, which greatly concerned Alma. It was clear that Anna was struggling, though the exact cause of her condition remains unclear. Alma later mentioned that Anna had been feeling unwell for some time, which intensified Alma's worry during their brief meeting.

On 12 September, Alma's plane landed at the airfield in Tulln, Lower Austria. Several reporters were waiting to capture the moment. The captain of the plane escorted her down the short gangway and into the visitors' area, where delegates awaited her with a huge bouquet of flowers. In the report, Alma is described as radiant, dressed in a black jacket, a light grey silk blouse, and a black skirt, with a very long pearl necklace. Her grey hair was carefully pinned up, with a curly head of hair framing her face. It was said that Alma visibly enjoyed the media attention and the respectful reception.

She moved into a room at the former Hotel Kranz-Ambassador, located at the corner of Neuer Markt and Kärntner Straße. The hotel, renovated after the war and a bombing raid, was renamed and reopened as the Hotel Ambassador in August 1947, shortly before Alma arrived.

As soon as Alma was in Vienna, she was devastated to find out that much of her family's legacy had been destroyed by bombs. Gustav Mahler's and Franz Werfel's desks, once filled with irreplaceable treasures of letters and manuscripts, had been obliterated. In stark contrast, the paintings of her father, Jakob Emil Schindler, had miraculously survived unscathed. They now hung in a modern gallery, having been 'unjustifiably donated', as Alma later recorded, by her stepfather Carl Moll. Retrieving these works proved an arduous task. Alma faced bureaucratic resistance, and one official even confronted her with thinly veiled hostility: 'How dare you, a daughter of our great Schindler, marry a Gustav Mahler and a Franz Werfel!'[9]

Alma had been dreading the reunion with her stepfamily, but this reunion never happened – for tragic reasons. Only now did she learn that Carl Moll, along with his daughter and son-in-law, had joined the ranks of many leading Nazis in Vienna by taking their own lives in April 1945, shortly before the arrival of the Russians.

During her time in Vienna, Alma attended court hearings almost every day. The focus of the complicated negotiations was the return of valuable paintings to her possession, such as Edward Munch's *Summer Night on the Beach*. Alma had received this painting as a gift for the birth of her daughter Manon, but had been forced to leave it behind, along with most of her belongings and her Art Nouveau villa, when she fled from the Nazis with Franz. According to Alma, her half-sister Maria Eberstaller, the daughter of Carl Moll, sold the painting in 1940 for 7,000 Reichsmarks to the Austrian Gallery Belvedere – without Alma's express permission. Alma was now suing for the return of the Munch painting.

In the weeks that Alma spent in Vienna, a battle over her rights ensued. She sought to reactivate old contacts who could help her prove in court that the Molls were guilty of selling the paintings behind her back for their own benefit. However, there were counter-statements from Alma's loyal nurse Schulli (Agnes Ida Gehbauer), as well as from Willi Legler, Margarethe Schindler's son and Alma's nephew, and from the publisher Paul von Zsolnay. All testified that the relationship between Alma and the Moll family had been amicable, and that they had consistently helped Alma during difficult times.

More than five years later, the court sided with these testimonies. However, a financial prosecutor lodged an objection, and the proceedings dragged on. Alma flew back to the USA on 23 September in 1947, very sad and without having achieved her goal. It would be the last time she visited Vienna. The reason she would remain in the USA – against her will, – was largely due to the Austrian court's refusal to return the Munch painting to her.

From March to April 1948, Alma's daughter Anna stayed for four weeks in California with her mother. They enjoyed their time together, talking extensively. On 22 March, Alma even organised a dinner party for Anna, inviting close friends such as the Arlts, as well as the author Thomas Mann and his wife Katia, and the Franciscan priest Father Georg Moenius. The evening was filled with champagne, good food and lively conversations about art and the post-war period.

However, for Alma, this time with Anna proved to be increasingly difficult, as she later confided to friends in her letters:

> I was not in a good state, so I had to give up my trip to Vienna. The visit of my daughter was extremely stressful for me. She is intelligent

> and warm, but I have become so accustomed to great loneliness that the change took a heavy toll on my nerves. Franzerl has drained everything that was left in me. And the most important thing – my will to live – has left me! But why am I telling you this – young, promising people?[10]

She repeatedly contemplated relocating to another country, but each time, she concluded: 'I long to leave this place, but the rest of the world seems so unpromising – so what do I do with the remainder of my wishes? Here, I just vegetate on like this.'[11]

In early 1909, Auguste Rodin had created a bust of Gustav Mahler, commissioned through the efforts of Alma's stepfather, Carl Moll (as described in Chapter 3). Moll retained one cast, while Alma donated the second to the Vienna State Opera in 1931. While Moll's bust survived the war unscathed, the one at the opera house suffered damage during the chaos of war. Determined to restore Mahler's legacy, Alma decided that the bust from Moll's estate should be returned to her late husband's former place of work. She planned a special ceremony for the spring of 1948 to mark the occasion.

At Alma's request, the Vienna Philharmonic invited her close friend, conductor and composer Bruno Walter, to participate. Walter agreed and made plans to travel from the USA for the event. However, on 14 April, just days before his departure, Walter learned that Alma had abruptly cancelled her trip to Vienna. Confused, he discovered that Alma had been misinformed by a mutual acquaintance, who claimed that Walter was boasting about inaugurating the renovated Vienna State Opera during the event.

This misunderstanding hit a sensitive nerve for Alma. The event was not about the opera house reopening – which had already occurred in 1945 – but a heartfelt tribute to Gustav Mahler. Deeply offended, Alma chose not to confront Walter directly but simply stayed away, withdrawing entirely. Walter's subsequent letters, filled with explanations and pleas to resolve the misunderstanding, fell on deaf ears. Alma's pride and sense of control over her late husband's legacy were immovable. As those who knew her often said: 'don't cross Alma'.

Alma's friends, particularly the successful author Friedrich Torberg, who was now working as a translator, freelance journalist, and theatre critic in New

York, grew increasingly worried about her and expressed their concerns in writing.

> Alma, I don't have to tell you how well I understand the roots of your condition or how deeply familiar I am with the difficulties of dealing with them. And I don't need to assure you that it is not out of frivolity, but from this very understanding, that I tell you: you must leave Hollywood – radically and permanently. Not because the memories of a happier and more meaningful past are so vivid and close to you there (they will remain so, no matter where you are, and you neither can nor should rid yourself of them). But as long as you stay in Hollywood, those memories are futile – they serve no purpose. They don't compete with your life, they neither suppress it nor inspire it. The fact that your life is being neglected is not the fault of those memories, but of Hollywood itself.[12]

Torberg, with his keen psychological insight and persuasive rhetoric, tried to encourage Alma to follow through with her plan to return to New York, where he also lived and was happily settled with his beloved wife:

> You were in excellent shape during your last visit here. You were doing so much better than at any time since 1945, and you lived so clearly from the pent-up reservoir of your own life force that reading a letter like your last one makes one want to grab their head in disbelief – or, in fact, drag you by the hair to the nearest train or plane. And the fact that there is no one in all of Hollywood who would do that, well, that really says it all.[13]

Torberg was right, as in California, Alma found herself with fewer and fewer opportunities for variety. She did meet with friends from time to time, including the Arlts, the Feuchtwangers, and Bruno and Lotte Walter. However, beyond these gatherings, nothing remarkable was happening in California. There were no evening events, no spectacular concerts, no dinner parties. But in the summer of 1948, that was about to change.

Alma was contacted by the chief conductor of the Philadelphia Orchestra, who was planning a performance of Mahler's *Eighth Symphony* at the Hollywood Bowl. He invited Alma to the rehearsals and concert, which would turn into a rare, positive experience in her life. Suddenly, all the attention was on Alma once again. She arrived at the general rehearsal in grand evening wear, accompanied by Bruno Walter and his wife, and Thomas Mann, as guests of honour. Right from the start, Alma was honoured and greeted with a standing ovation from the applauding guests.

In his speech, Dr Karl Wecker, the general manager of the Hollywood Bowl Association (whose salary was linked to Bowl profits), pointed out to the 18,000 guests that Alma had even composed her own pieces. This recognition seemed to do Alma good, as that evening, she embraced her role as the grande dame everyone had come to expect of her.

In the spring of 1949, Alma received a package from Vienna sent by her servant Schulli. Inside the package were all the letters that Franz had written before 1938. Alma was overjoyed. She read each letter over and over, savouring the words, before setting to work typing them up to ensure they were safely preserved.

Then, she decided to write from her house in Beverly Hills a letter to her friend Friedrich Torberg:

> I have a lot of work ahead of me, and some of it is already behind me. I've now received all of Franzerl's letters from the burned house in Vienna, here in New York, and I'm typing them all up. Today, there are already 100 letters – though it's only the beginning! You will be enraptured when you read them! Such a sweet soul – he was, and still is, that to me! I am reliving these twenty-seven years as if it were today![14]

At the time, Alma even considered publishing Franz's letters. At the beginning of summer 1949, Alma wrote a foreword for the proposed collection, meant to honour the beloved poet. In this foreword, she played the role of an objective observer, describing her relationship with Franz in great detail, from their first meeting to his death. Franz was portrayed as the 'wooing youth', while Alma described herself as a 'beautiful blonde woman', perhaps reflecting how she saw herself in their early years together, consistent with the detached tone she sought to adopt in recounting their relationship.

In the summer of 1949, Alma received a remarkable letter from Oskar Kokoschka, who wrote to congratulate her – in his uniquely poetic and dramatic way – on her upcoming milestone birthday:

> My dear Alma! You are still a wild creature, just as you were when you were first entranced by *Tristan und Isolde* and used a quill to scribble your remarks about Nietzsche in your diary, in the same flying, illegible handwriting that I can only decipher because I know your rhythm. Ask your friends who are preparing your birthday party not to tie you to a stupid, random, fleeting calendar year. Tell them to erect a living, imperishable monument to you instead, that is, to find a truly American poet with a sixth sense for language, interpretation, rhythm, and tone – one who knows the emotional scale from tenderness to the most depraved sensuality, can learn it from my *Orpheus and Eurydice*, and translate it into American – so that we can tell the world what we have both done with and against ourselves and can pass on the living message of our love to posterity.[15]

On 31 August 1949, Alma celebrated her 70th birthday, receiving numerous honours and warm tributes. Eager helpers transformed her house and garden in Beverly Hills into a festive venue. A lavish buffet with a variety of delicacies was set up in the dining room, and August Hess ensured that guests were served only the best: champagne, Bénédictine, and, of course, fine coffee. Alma greeted the many well-wishers with joy.

Among the many thoughtful gifts she received, one stood out as particularly special. Gustav and Gusti Arlt had, over weeks and months, contacted Alma's friends and acquaintances, asking each to design a page for a collective tribute. By the summer, seventy-seven personalised pages had been carefully compiled and bound in leather to create a unique gift book. Alma was overwhelmed upon receiving it, but it was only in the days that followed that she fully grasped how extraordinary it truly was. Contributors included luminaries such as the authors Carl Zuckmayer, Thomas and Heinrich Mann and Lion Feuchtwanger, conductor Ernst Krenek, Eugene

Ormandy, the French composer Darius Milhaud, Igor Stravinsky, former Austrian Chancellor Kurt von Schuschnigg, and even her former husband Walter Gropius. Each had written something special for her. The book was not only overwhelming but profoundly moving, a testament to the impact she had made on so many lives.

After the celebrations, life grew quiet again for Alma. Occasionally, she visited the Manns, though her visits became shorter, and her demeanour began to change. She often left earlier than she once had, and a slight unsteadiness in her gait was noticeable. The legendary drinking binges seemed to be a thing of the past. The truth was, Alma had been struggling with health problems for some time, including high blood pressure and persistent heart trouble. On 23 June of the same year, she had already written to Friedrich Torberg about her feelings about her country of birth and her health issues:

> I have the least desire to go to Austria – if anything, then Paris, Rome, and Jerusalem! I don't know how I am! I get little scares here and there – which I ignore – and, above all, I don't consult a doctor. I think that's the healthier tactic.[16]

Alma was also visited by her daughter Anna, who had recently separated from her fourth husband, British conductor Anatol Fistoulari, and was seeking to reconnect with her beloved mother in the United States. Anna's move to the US with her daughter Marina marked the beginning of a more artistically productive phase in her life. She first ran a studio in the home of Austrian-American novelist and screenwriter Gina Kaus, born Regina Wiener. In 1950, Anna held a teaching position in life modelling for sculpture at the University of California, Los Angeles. Initially, she lived on N Laurel Avenue in Central LA, but later relocated when her mother purchased a small house for her on Beverly Glen Boulevard, conveniently close to her workplace at the university. There, Anna also had a studio where she worked on her sculptures daily. After the move, Anna became acquainted with Albrecht Joseph, her stepfather's longtime assistant. Over time, a love affair blossomed between them, and they married in 1970. Albrecht Joseph became Anna's fifth husband, and their extraordinary relationship endured for thirty-eight years.

Alma, however, observed Anna's progress with great interest and pride:

> Anna, whose talent as an artist I had never doubted, had developed extraordinarily well. She had finally become a sculptor in her own right, creating a series of remarkable works. Her exhibition in London had been a resounding success, reaching far beyond England. In short, she had truly made her mark. The pieces that captivated me most were, of course, two particularly beautiful busts of Werfel and Schönberg. Anna has caused me a great deal of sorrow in my life, but she has never disappointed me.[17]

But the joy of the reunion became short-lived – living in the same city as her mother proved to be a true test for Anna.

Since the death of Franz, Alma had grappled with an ever-deepening sense of loneliness. Though she continued to visit friends and was frequently invited out, the absence of a life partner left a void she could not fill. In the evenings, she would retreat alone to her sprawling villa in California, where the solitude weighed heavily on her. To combat her growing ennui, Alma leaned increasingly on Anna and Marina.

However, Anna, now 46 years old, had her own life to manage. She was a thriving artist with obligations, a blossoming career, and a new partner – all of which demanded her time and attention. The close proximity in Los Angeles of the two women and their respective lives became a source of strain and friction. When Anna occasionally declined her mother's invitations, Alma's emotions flared – anger, jealousy, and a pang of abandonment swept over her.

In the summer of 1951, another tragic loss struck Alma: her beloved friend, the composer Arnold Schönberg, passed away. Schönberg was a deeply superstitious man. He suffered from triskaidekaphobia – a great fear of the number 13 – and, as Katia Mann once recounted, he dreaded the idea of dying in a year that was a multiple of 13. He frequently consulted astrologers to predict the year ahead. On his 76th birthday, an astrologer wrote him a note warning that it would be a critical year, pointing out ominously that 7 + 6 equals 13. This depressed Schönberg deeply, and as fate would have it, Friday, 13 July 1951, was not really his day.

On that day he was bedridden, ill, anxious and discouraged. His wife, Gertrud, later recounted to her sister-in-law, Ottilie, via telegram: 'At about a quarter to twelve, I looked at the clock and thought to myself: just fifteen more minutes, and the worst will be over. Then the doctor called me. Arnold's throat rattled twice, his heart beat strongly, and that was the end.' Schönberg passed away at 11.45 pm, just minutes before the day he so feared came to an end. In her diary, Alma described the scene:

> I went there with Anna. It was a tragic sight. For reasons unknown to me, the chin of the deceased had been tied up. Trude Schönberg sat there, utterly broken, stroking her dead husband. In the meantime, she had aged terribly. The children stared at the body, bewildered. The beautiful daughter, Nuria, had removed her shoes and stockings so as not to make a sound.[18]

Yet, Alma's restlessness had already set her mind on a change. For some time, she had been contemplating a move back to New York. There, in Manhattan, she had purchased a townhouse at 120 East 73rd Street, just two blocks from Central Park, shortly after Franz's death in 1945.

This four-storey building was a typical Upper East Side brick townhouse. Each floor contained two apartments, each with one bigger room, a kitchen, and a bathroom.

In 1952, Alma made the momentous decision to leave California, a place she found weighed down by difficult memories. Reflecting on this turning point, she wrote:

> In 1952 I finally decided to leave California, which was burdened with so many difficult memories for me. I bought a house in New York and tried to start a new life there. As I did almost everywhere, I soon gathered friends around me. Without further ado I was given the privilege of attending the rehearsals of the Philharmonic Orchestra, which became my favourite pastime.[19]

In 1952, Alma moved to the East Coast, though she initially kept her house in Beverly Hills. She was eager to embrace her new life in the bustling metropolis of New York, a city she had come to appreciate through Gustav Mahler, and where she had made many friends during her time with Franz Werfel. Here, she would spend the final years of her remarkable life.

In total, Alma reserved four adjoining apartments in a townhouse on the Upper East Side, eagerly anticipating a fresh start in the metropolis. At 73 years old, the streets of New York strongly reminded her of Europe. Everything was easily accessible on foot, and for longer journeys – such as visits to the Metropolitan Opera or concert evenings – she preferred to take a taxi.

Alma settled on the third floor, accompanied by August Hess, who had followed her from Los Angeles and now lived on the fourth floor. One of the adjacent apartments was reserved exclusively for her guests. Alma's living arrangement comprised two connected apartments: one served as her bedroom, while the other was a living room where she received her many visitors. The two spaces were linked only by a corridor in the stairwell.

Photographs from this period depict rooms brimming with family memorabilia: paintings by her longtime lover, Oskar Kokoschka; works by her beloved father, Emil Jakob Schindler; the scores of her first husband, Gustav Mahler; and the manuscripts of her last husband, Franz Werfel. A grand piano occupied a corner of one apartment, serving as the heart of a lively New York salon where Alma entertained artistic royalty and intellectuals from various disciplines.

The living room was a cozy and eclectic space. Bookshelves stretched to the ceiling, with a side table beneath them displaying several cherished photographs of Mahler. At the centre of the room stood a round coffee table, draped in a colourful tablecloth and surrounded by three wide leather armchairs. Additional seating was arranged at the back of the room for larger gatherings. Several paintings by Oskar Kokoschka adorned the walls between the shelves, and two of his drawings were even mounted on a door.

Alma's second apartment was entirely dedicated to music. Its focal point was a Blüthner grand piano, proudly positioned in a corner with a portrait of Mahler resting atop it. Opposite the piano, a wooden carving of a religious figure graced the wall. Nearby stood a baroque chest of drawers, covered with photographs of friends and family. The walls were further decorated with portraits of her beloved father and adorned with chandeliers. Immersed in this rich tapestry of art, culture and memories, Alma created a world that reflected her extraordinary life.

In the autumn of 1952, Alma embarked on a trip to Europe with her friend Gusti Arlt. While Gusti visited her family in Germany, Alma settled into the Hotel Royal Madeleine in Paris, a place that had once served as one of her cherished refuges during her exile with Franz Werfel. Alma had initially planned to stay in Paris for two months – November and December 1952 – before continuing on to Rome in January and February 1953, a city she noted had 'almost become her second home'. Afterward, Alma and Gusti began their journey back to the United States aboard a ship.

Notably, Alma did not visit Austria on this trip, despite repeated invitations from her good friend Friedrich Torberg, who encouraged her to reconsider. But Alma stood firm in her decision and would never return to Austria. She later reflected:

> But I did not come to Vienna again. I was invited to the pompous reopening of the State Opera, but I declined. The only thing that still interested me in this context was Rodin's bust of Mahler. The Nazis had melted down the bronze bust, but I still had a copy. I gave it to the opera, and it was placed in a suitable spot in the foyer.[20]

The journey across the Atlantic proved pleasant and restorative. Alma also made an unexpected and remarkable acquaintance. While sitting on the ship's deck, a man approached her and spoke kindly:

> On one of my trips, a handsome, tall man with an unusually wise face spoke to me on the ship. He introduced himself as Thornton Wilder. I had admired him for many years, even when his early work, *The Bridge of San Luis Rey*, was published. We began a conversation that actually lasted until we landed in New York. By the time I disembarked, we had become friends.[21]

Alma was captivated by the 53-year-old writer, and the friendship endured. 'It is a great pleasure to joke with Alma Mahler-Werfel,' he later admitted. Thornton Wilder called her the 'affirming embodiment of self-confidence and courage'. And she described him thus: 'The days passed like minutes. His every word was a joy – and so, later, was his every letter. Since Franz Werfel's passing I have treasured nothing more than Thornton Wilder's friendship.'[22]

The two corresponded frequently, and Wilder visited her whenever he was in New York. Perhaps, it was through his gentle encouragement and their conversations that Alma felt inspired to take the next step in her life, venturing further into her own personal journey.

Since 1944, Alma had spent a lot of time collecting her letters, notes and diaries. She wanted to use all of these documents to write her memoirs. By the end of 1947, she had managed to write around 200 pages, repeatedly starting with preliminary work and then stopping again due to other, external circumstances. There was so much material to sift through in order to write a perfect manuscript that she was looking for a ghostwriter. In 1945, Paul Frischauer, novelist, journalist and son of an Austrian publishing family, had moved to the USA and worked briefly as a ghostwriter on Alma's autobiography in 1947. However, when he discovered the antisemitic opinions in her first 200 pages, and other material she had given him, they fell out. He sharply criticised Alma's many antisemitic outbursts and was asked by her to hand the books and manuscripts to August Hess, as their work together was over. She paid him $800. In mid-December 1947, he wrote to his former client that he was sorry and asked her not to take the very harsh criticism in his critical notes seriously. They were merely a reflection of what could be said against her, if the book was published in this style. It was a friendly warning about what could be said about Alma. But Alma did not want to respond to it; for her, this author was not the right one for her book project.

Seeking assistance again in 1955, Alma turned to a potential ghostwriter recommended by her friend, Hertha Ernestine Pauli – an actress, author and journalist who had moved to New York. Hertha's husband, Ernst Bash, was a sought-after German-to-English translator and an experienced writer with excellent contacts to British and US publishers, and since Alma's memoirs were set to be published first in the USA, he seemed the right man for the job. Bash accepted the assignment and began to work on organising the vast collection of Alma's writings into chronological order. He worked under the pseudonym E.B. Ashton, and on 1 August 1956, the two signed a contract with Hutchinson Publishing for the English-language edition of the memoirs. It was understood that extensive passages would need to be censored, including her antisemitic outbursts and numerous attacks on living individuals. On Friedrich Torberg's advice, Bash was instructed to first focus on the individual periods of Alma's life, believing this approach would make it easier for Alma to recall and organise her memories. To construct a timeline, he began by asking Alma a series of questions, but found himself struggling to get answers. To further simplify the process, Bash sent Alma written questionnaires, hoping she would answer them in writing. This tactic, however, only served to infuriate her. Alma felt insulted by what she perceived as an overly systematic and impersonal approach, and the collaboration grew increasingly strained. Furthermore, deciphering her notes proved challenging.[23] Alma, by this point, was already suffering from heart problems, had experienced a mild stroke, and was still recovering from a broken hand.

Despite his efforts, when Ernst Bash personally approached Alma to clarify certain events in her life, their conversations often ended in tension. Alma was particularly dissatisfied with the way Bash rendered her monologues, feeling that his interpretations of her words were banal and unworthy of her. On these occasions, Alma would often say: 'The deep meaning of my expressed thoughts is missing.'[24]

And so, E.B. Ashton was eventually left to his own devices in revising Alma's memoirs. When her work finally appeared on the American book market in the spring of 1958 under the title *And the Bridge is Love – Memories of a Lifetime*, the reactions from her acquaintances and friends were varied. Paul von Zsolnay maintained his 'unchangingly strong and lasting' impression of her manuscript, while her ex-husband Walter Gropius was deeply upset by the two-page account of their love, marriage and bond. According to Gropius, Alma's depiction made it seem as if their meeting in Tobelbad and their passionate nights of love were nothing more than a fleeting flirtation. Their love letters were not mentioned, nor was her swift decision to marry him. Gropius, profoundly disappointed at being portrayed in such a poor light, wrote Alma a scathing letter. She attempted to soothe him by blaming her ghostwriter and the publisher, but Gropius saw through the excuse. In 1960, Alma felt compelled to justify herself to him once again, but her efforts to mend the relationship were unsuccessful. From that point on, her relationship with Gropius was irreparably damaged.

In 1960, Fischer Verlag planned a German translation of her memoirs. For this, Alma hired as her co-author Willy Haas, a 69-year-old Austro-

Hungarian publicist, film critic, screenwriter and childhood friend of Franz Werfel. Haas, who lived in Hamburg, ensured a collaboration that was both legendary and extremely pleasant. He regularly sent completed sections to New York and consulted Alma on unresolved questions, all while conducting a careful smoothing out of the original manuscript. This was precisely what Alma wanted, as she wished to avoid the rejection and criticism she had faced with the US version. However, when the German edition was published, speculation about the extent of the revisions immediately arose, a topic that remains debated to this day.

Countless congratulatory telegrams from all over the world arrived in New York on Monday, 31 August 1959, as Alma celebrated her 80th birthday. Many of her acquaintances and friends sent their good wishes on this milestone anniversary, but the lavish festivities in her honour were unfortunately cancelled. Her health was no longer stable – her heart problems and multiple mild to moderate strokes had taken their toll, and Alma was now nearly deaf in both ears.

Her daughter Anna flew from Los Angeles to New York to spend the special day with her mother. But to Anna, Alma seemed a little confused and she became convinced that Alma would need constant care moving forward. August Hess, who by this time had worked for the family for fifteen years, was already 55 years old and planning to retire soon. He intended to return to Los Angeles to spend his remaining years in peace. Tragically, Hess passed away in October 1960, unable to enjoy his retirement.

Left in need of care, Alma reached out to her long-time former Viennese loyal nurse and later servant Schulli, who had been living in Vienna after a divorce. Alma inundated her with letters and telegrams, pleading for her assistance. Schulli accepted the job and moved to New York, where she provided round-the-clock care for Alma.

In her final years, Alma suffered from insomnia. Late at night, she and Ida would reminisce about the past: Vienna, Breitenstein, Gustav Mahler, Walter Gropius, Franz Werfel, and Alma's much-loved father, Jakob Emil Schindler. The past seemed to become Alma's present. Occasionally, she left her apartment to visit her favourite restaurants for a small meal or drink, or attended a concert or opera. On Sunday afternoons, she invited friends over, though the number of guests dwindled as many had either passed away or returned to Europe. Over time, Alma lost interest in hosting these gatherings.

From 1964 onward, Anna became increasingly worried about her mother and visited her more frequently. Alma often reflected on Gustav Mahler, telling Anna, 'If Mahler came through the door, I would go with him.' In contrast, she spoke very little about Franz Werfel during that year. Alma also expressed unexpected sentiments to Anna: 'If I had known you as I know you now, I would not have treated you so badly.' These words astonished Anna, who found them difficult to reconcile with the mother she knew.

Despite a diagnosis of diabetes that required her to give up alcohol – especially her beloved Bénédictine – Alma stubbornly refused to comply, opting instead for a Martini, a drink she detested, describing it as tasting like turpentine. She continued to maintain her appearance, applying powder, makeup and lipstick daily. She would dress in a pink petticoat embroidered with colourful flowers, a black dress, and a jacket, but refused to wear traditional knickers.

In her final months, Alma's health deteriorated significantly. She became weaker, her legs swelled, and she required drainage shots. In December, Anna was called and asked to come to New York urgently. Things were looking very bad. Alma had developed pneumonia and was bedridden. During her bouts of fever, Alma claimed to have even met Crown Prince Rudolf of Austria on a mountaintop, where he expressed a desire to have a child with her. She also spoke of Plankenberg Castle, the historic site near Tulln in Lower Austria, where she had once lived with her family. Alma recalled how her father, Emil Jakob Schindler, had leased the property in the winter of 1884 to provide them with a retreat away from the busy life of Vienna. She remembered the quiet, green landscape where she had once sought solace – and thought back to a time when she had felt the weight of her pregnancy in the silence of the retreat.

'She didn't want to die,' her granddaughter Marina Fistoulari-Mahler later recalled. 'But she was already in a coma. My mother and I were staying in the small apartment next door. It was terrible. My mother wouldn't let me see her.'[25] And so Marina was unable to accompany her grandmother in her final hours and minutes. The wonderful memory of Plankenberg Castle seemed to give Alma a feeling of peace in her closing moments. But she absolutely refused to leave this world.

Then, as the morning of 11 December 1964 dawned, Alma's final phase arrived. In a last attempt at life, she spread her arms and called out to Ida Gehbauer: 'So help me, Schulli'.

At 6.35 am, Alma Mahler-Werfel passed away.

At the time, Marina waited for her mother Anna; she vividly remembered the moment: 'Then we heard Mama screaming,' Marina explained.

> After a few minutes, my mother came back from the other apartment and said that when Alma died, she had clung to her daughter. But Anna couldn't release her dead mother's grip from her hand. Anna had to sit down now. It felt like an eternity. It was terrible for her to see her mother die before her eyes.[26]

After her mother's passing, Anna Mahler informed friends and acquaintances without delay with a simple message: 'Mama has just died'.

Alma's body was prepared by the Frank E. Campbell funeral home in New York, a practice customary among America's upper circles. Schulli ensured that Alma's coffin contained everything she had wished for, including the sheet music for *Tristan und Isolde*. The Austrian-American photographer Trude Fleischmann was granted permission to take a photograph of Alma in her coffin. The funeral took place on 13 December 1964, at the Frank E. Campbell Funeral Church on Madison Avenue and 81st Street. Jewish writer Soma Morgenstern delivered the eulogy, recounting Alma's life, particularly her marriage to Gustav Mahler, and recalling their last meeting: 'I felt that was the last farewell. The time of mourning was near.' After Friedrich Torberg, Adolf Klarmann and Franz Theodor Csokor had strongly advocated for Alma's burial in Vienna; Alma's coffin, weighing 330 kilos and hermetically sealed with a metal casing, was transported to Austria under Schulli's supervision. Anna flew to Vienna on 30 January 1965, while Schulli made the journey by ship. On 31 January, she received Alma's coffin at Schwechat airport.

Though Alma's obituary listed 8 February as the burial date, she was interred on 4 February 1965, at the Döblinger cemetery beside her beloved daughter Manon and not far away from her first husband Gustav Mahler. Among the attendees were Anna Mahler, and US Ambassador to Austria

Clare Boothe Luce and her husband Henry. As the priest blessed the coffin, a singer performed a moving American song in tribute to Alma's years in exile, as noted by Erich Rietenauer,[27] a frequent guest in the home of Alma and her mother Anna Moll, who attended the funeral. This was followed by eight pallbearers carrying the heavy coffin on the extendable floor of the hearse. Brahms's *Waltz in A-flat major, Opus 39* – a piece Brahms had once played with 8-year-old Alma – accompanied the procession.

However, the grave had been dug too narrow, and the coffin remained on a frame above the open grave until the following day. On 5 February 1965, Alma Mahler-Werfel finally found her resting place. An adventurous, dramatic and extraordinary journey had come to its end.

Alma Mahler-Werfel, a woman of overwhelming intellect, ambition and contradictions – a muse, creator, celebrity, rebel, influencer, and yet a controversial figure who left an indelible mark on the cultural history of the twentieth century across two continents – had now returned to her home town Vienna. Resting in Döbling, the city's most prestigious district, one can only hope she had finally found peace.

She lived her life in close orbit with some of the most renowned artists, writers and musicians of her time: Gustav Mahler, Walter Gropius, Franz Werfel and Oskar Kokoschka. Alma had an extraordinary ability to recognise and nurture artistic talent, driving her partners to achieve greatness. These men – luminaries of their era – were captivated by her cunning intellect, charm and boundless energy. Driven by an insatiable hunger for life, Alma's existence was one of excess, passion and grandeur.

Admired for her beauty, wit and charisma, Alma was equally criticised for her imperious demeanour and the complexity of her relationships. Her passion for art and music was unparallelled, matched only by her determination to shape her own narrative – even if it meant altering the truth along the way. In her later years, as her body grew frail, she retained her aura of magnificence, continuing to draw both attention and admiration.

Her memoirs, and the controversies that surrounded them, solidified her as a fascinating and polarising figure. Alma's story continues to captivate and provoke to this day, a symbol of the complex interplay of genius, ambition and the eternal human drive to leave a legacy. She remains, even in the present, an enduring icon of cultural and personal complexity.

Epilogue

Alma Mahler-Werfel – A Legacy Beyond Her Relationships

Alma Mahler-Werfel was not just a muse – she was a force of nature. She navigated her personal and professional life in ways few could have imagined in her time. She was a symbol of intellectual power and artistic ambition, someone whose legacy extends far beyond her relationships with famous men. Alma's world was full of complex dynamics. She was fiercely independent, even as societal norms tried to constrain her. Alma's life story was one of defiance against expectations in both her art and her relationships.

How would Alma be perceived in today's world? As a woman who juggled family, art, and intense personal dynamics, she would likely face a mix of admiration and criticism. In an era of evolving gender roles, Alma would be celebrated as a figure of empowerment – a woman ahead of her time, even as she was inevitably condemned for her personal life. What is certain is that Alma would remain an influential voice in the arts and a champion of culture and music, while also carrying the aura of mystery and complexity that characterised her.

From her beginnings in Vienna, Alma's sphere of influence expanded widely. Her time in Austria established her as a cultural force, but she later gained recognition across Europe in France and England before the turmoil of the Second World War led her into exile in the United States. In California and New York, she found a new stage for her influence, mingling with the intellectual and artistic elite of the twentieth century. Alma's life was a testament to resilience, adaptability and a tireless commitment to creativity.

Alma was more than just a composer or a celebrity. She was a rebel, a formidable influencer, and a woman of extraordinary presence whose legacy transcends time. Her relationships were fundamental in shaping her life, but she was never defined solely by them. Each of the men she loved or married – whether Gustav Mahler, Walter Gropius, Oskar Kokoschka, or Franz Werfel – left an indelible mark on her story, as she did on theirs. Alma existed both in their shadow and as a force in her own right.

Gustav Mahler was Alma's first husband – a man she deeply admired, though their relationship was undeniably complicated. Mahler embodied the tormented artist, and Alma was both his muse and a woman who struggled to maintain her identity in the face of his genius and vulnerability. Despite his initial demands that she gives up her own composing, Alma later found her creative voice again, proving her resilience and determination.

Walter Gropius, Alma's second husband, was a visionary architect and one of the pioneers of modernist design. Their relationship reflected the tension between Gropius' professional ambitions and Alma's need for recognition and freedom. Although their marriage ultimately ended, it symbolised a meeting of minds at a time of seismic cultural change.

With Franz Werfel, Alma found a passionate and complex partnership. Werfel, a famous writer, brought a literary dimension to Alma's life, and although their relationship was one of love and loyalty, it was not without its challenges. Alma's role as his confidante, supporter and occasional critic reflected the dynamics she had with other outstanding figures in her life.

Oskar Kokoschka, the expressionist painter, offered Alma a relationship like no other. Their time together was stormy, and Kokoschka's obsession with Alma became the subject of his art. Their affair was brief but intense, leaving a lasting impression on both her life and her creative works.

Beyond the men she married, Alma attracted numerous other admirers – figures of artistic and intellectual stature who were deeply drawn to her but never chosen to share her life as husbands. Among them was composer Alexander Zemlinsky, whose admiration for Alma was intense but unreciprocated in marriage; Dr Emil Fraenkel, deeply enamoured yet ultimately outside the circle of her matrimonial decisions; and Gerhart Hauptmann, whose brief, intimate gesture left a memorable mark despite its complicated nature.

Alma's magnetic presence often made men fall deeply in love with her, yet she rarely returned those feelings. Many suitors were left disappointed, their affections met with laughter or dismissal when they failed to meet her exacting standards for a suitable husband. Admired by many, Alma remained fiercely selective, choosing only those who fitted her own vision and ambitions.

These lesser known relationships reveal Alma's power to inspire devotion and desire, as well as her unwavering agency in choosing her own path. They remind us that Alma's life was not defined solely by the men she married, but also by those who sought her, often unfulfilled, yet forever part of the wider constellation orbiting her formidable personality.

Few women had the audacity to marry – and exert a profound influence on – such monumental figures. Alma's relationships were dynamic, driven by her own ambitions and the demands of the men she loved. She was never just a wife in the traditional sense, but a partner, muse, and often a catalyst for brilliance.

Despite society's tendency to reduce her to a mere muse or accessory to her husbands, Alma was far more than that. She was a *salonnière*, a skilled networker, a composer, a mother, and a woman who shaped the intellectual and artistic discourse of her time. In an era when women were often defined only by their husbands, Alma defied convention by maintaining her independence and pursuing her own creative passions.

Her salons were legendary, hosting some of the greatest minds of her time. Imagine Alma in her Vienna salon, surrounded by politicians, entrepreneurs, artists, composers and writers, the scent of fresh lilies mingling with the hum of intellectual discourse. Imagine her later years in California, overlooking the Pacific, still a formidable presence in artistic and intellectual circles. Alma was a bridge between worlds – old Europe and the new American frontier, the classical and the modern, the personal and the universal.

Alma Mahler-Werfel's life is not just history; it is a testament to the power of resilience, creativity and individuality. She lived courageously, embracing the complexities of her life and defying the limitations imposed on her. Her legacy is one of strength and vulnerability, ambition and artistry.

Today, Alma would be celebrated as an artistic influencer, a socialite, a mentor, a rebel and a trailblazer and cultural icon – a woman who refused to be constrained by societal expectations.

She used her platform to spotlight the works of others while shaping her own creative identity, much like modern creators who navigate both personal expression and public expectation. And she always reminds us that art, love and ambition are timeless forces that transcend boundaries and eras. Whether in the salons of Vienna, the streets of Paris and London, the hills of Hollywood or the avenues in New York, Alma's voice echoes on, inspiring new generations to live boldly and create fearlessly.

Bibliography

Letter from Alban Berg to Helene Berg, 11 November, 1925

Letter from Franz Werfel to Alma Mahler, Fall 1918 / via Karen Monsoon: *Alma Mahler-Werfel – Die unbezahlbare Muse*, Wilhelm Heyne Verlag, München, 1985, Neuauflage: 2003

BAUER-LECHNER, Natalie, *Memories of Gustav Mahler*, Europäischer Literaturverlag, Leipzig, 1923

CANETTI, Elias, *Das Augenspiel. Lebensgeschichte 1931–1937*, 1985 (Memoire, Part 3), Fischer Verlag, Frankfurt am Main, 1988

DE LA GRANGE, Henry, WEIß, Günther, MARTNER, Knut, *Ein Glück ohne Ruh – Die Briefe Gustav Mahlers an Alma*, Siedler Verlag, München, 1995

FRY, Varian, *The Rescue of the Intellectuals: Varian Fry's Mission to Save Artists and Writers from the Nazis*, The Free Press, New York, 1997

FUCHS, Heinrich, *Emil Jakob Schindler – Zeugnisse eines ungewöhnl. Künstlerlebens. Werkkatalog*, Wien, 1970

GIROUD, Françoise, *Alma Mahler – oder die Kunst, geliebt zu werden*, aus dem Französischen von Ursel Schäfer, Paul Zsolnay Verlag, Wien, 1989

HILMES, Oliver, *Witwe im Wahn – Das Leben der Alma Mahler-Werfel*, Siedler Verlag, München, 2004

ISAACS, Reginald R., *Walter Gropius. Der Mensch und sein Werk*, Gebrüder Mann Verlag, Berlin 1984, Volume 1,

JUNGK, Peter Stephan, *Franz Werfel – A Life story*, Fischer Taschenbuch, 2001

KEEGAN, Susanne, *The Bride of the Wind: The Life of Alma Mahler,* Martin Secker & Warburg Ltd, 1. December 1991, London

KODEK, Günter K., *Die Kette der Herzen bleibt geschlossen. Mitglieder der österreichischen Freimaurer-Logen 1945 bis 1985*. Löcker Verlag, Wien, 2014

KOKOSCHKA, Oskar, *Mein Leben*, Bruckmann Verlag, Frankfurt am Main, 1971

KRENEK, Ernst, *Im Atem der Zeit – Erinnerungen an die Moderne,* Translated from American English by Friedrich Saathen. Rev. translation by Sabine Schulte, Hoffmann und Campe, Hamburg, 1998

MAHLER, Alma, SCHÖNBERG, Arnold, *Ich möchte so lange leben, als ich Ihnen dankbar sein kann – Der Briefwechsel*, Residenz Verlag, St. Pölten-Salzburg-Wien, 2012

MAHLER-WERFEL, Alma, *Mein Leben*, Fischer Verlag, Frankfurt am Main, 1963; 36th Edition in 2000

MAHLER-WERFEL, Alma, ASHTON, E.B. *And the Bridge is Love – Memories of a Lifetime*, Harcourt, Brace and Company, New York, 1958

MAHLER-WERFEL, Alma, *Diaries 1898–1902*, selected and translated by Anthony Beaumont, publisher Faber and Faber, London, 1998

MAHLER-WERFEL, Alma, *Tagebuch Suiten 1898–1902*, Antony Beaumont (Hrsg.), Susanne Rode-Breymann (Hrsg.), Fischer Taschenbuch, Berlin, 2001

MOLL, Carl, *Emil Jakob Schindler, 1842–1892. Eine Bildnisstudie*, Österreichische Staatsdruckerei, Wien, 1930

MONSOON, Karen, *Alma Mahler-Werfel – Die unbezahlbare Muse*, Wilhelm Heyne Verlag, München, 1985, Neuauflage: 2003

POLAK, Hans W., *Paul von Zsolnay*; In: *Neue österreichische Biographie ab 1815. Große Österreicher*. Volume XXII. Amalthea, Wien, 1987

RIETENAUER, Erich, *Alma meine Liebe – Persönliche Erinnerungen an eine Legende*, Amalthea Verlag, Wien, 2008

SCHMIDT, Werner, *Kokoschka und Dresden*, Verlag: E.A. Seemann, Leipzig 1996

TIETZE-CONRAT, Erica, *Tagebücher (1923–1926) – Volume I, Der Wiener Vasari*, Böhlau Verlag, Vienna-Köln-Weimar, 2015

TORBERG, Friedrich, *Die Tante Jolesch – Oder der Untergang des Abendlandes in Anekdoten*, Verlag Deutscher Taschenbuch Verlag, München, 1977

TORBERG, Friedrich, *Liebste Freundin und Alma – Briefwechsel mit Alma Mahler-Werfel*, Langen Müller Verlag, München-Wien, 1987

Van-Pelt-Library University of Pennsylvania, Philadelphia, *Mahler-Werfel – Mahler-Werfel Collection* (MWC), Ms. coll. 10.

WALDEN, Herwath, *Twenty Drawings*, Published by the publisher *Der Sturm*, Berlin, 1913

WERFEL, Franz, *Zwischen Oben und Unten*, Verlag Stockholm, Bermann-Fischer, 1. Auflage., 1946

Film and Media

Freund, Susanne *Big Alma,* Documentary-film, DOR-Film, Vienna, Austria, 2007

Interview Peter Stephan Jungk mit Marta Feuchtwanger (Transkript), Mechitaristenkloster Wien, Bibliothek, Depositum Peter Stephan Jungk (MKB)

Endnotes

Prologue

1. *And the bridge is Love – Memories of a Lifetime*, Alma Mahler-Werfel, with E.B. Ashton, p.307

Chapter 1

1. *Emil Jakob Schindler– Zeugnisse eines ungewöhnl. Künstlerlebens. Werkkatalog.* Heinrich Fuchs, Wien 1970
2. *Mein Leben,* Alma Mahler-Werfel, p.15
3. Ibid
4. Ibid, p.16
5. Ibid, p.17
6. Ibid, p.20
7. Ibid, pp.20-1
8. Ibid, p.21
9. Ibid

Chapter 2

1. *Mein Leben*, Alma Mahler-Werfel, p.26
2. *The Bride of the Wind: The Life of Alma Mahler,* Susanne Keegan, p.40
3. *Diaries 1898–1902, Alma Mahler-Werfel*, p.66
4. Ibid, p.68
5. Ibid, p.72
6. Ibid, p.73
7. Ibid
8. Ibid, p.103
9. Ibid, p.110
10. Ibid, p.111
11. Ibid
12. Ibid, p.125
13. Ibid
14. Ibid, p.126
15. Ibid

16. Ibid, p.133
17. Ibid, p.134
18. *Tagebuch Suiten 1898–1902, Alma Mahler-Werfel*, p.539
19. *Diaries 1898–1902, Alma Mahler-Werfel*, p.253
20. Ibid, p.396
21. Ibid
22. Ibid, p.397
23. Ibid
24. Ibid
25. Ibid, p.398
26. Ibid, p.398
27. Ibid
28. Ibid
29. Ibid
30. Ibid
31. Ibid, p.401
32. Ibid, p.441
33. Ibid, p.409
34. *Mahler-Werfel – Mahler-Werfel Collection* (MWC), Ms. coll. 10, Van-Pelt-Library University of Pennsylvania, Philadelphia

Chapter 3

1. *Diaries 1898–1902, Alma Mahler-Werfel*, p.443
2. *Mein Leben*, Alma Mahler, p.30
3. *Erinnerungen an Gustav Mahler*; Gustav Mahler *Briefe an Alma Mahler*, Alma Mahler-Werfel, p.39
4. *Diaries 1898–1902, Alma Mahler-Werfel*, p.443
5. Ibid, p.444
6. Ibid, p.445
7. Ibid, p.446
8. Ibid
9. Ibid
10. *Erinnerungen an Gustav Mahler*; Gustav Mahler *Briefe an Alma Mahler*, Alma Mahler-Werfel, p.44
11. Ibid, p.44
12. *Diaries 1898–1902, Alma Mahler-Werfel*, p.446
13. Ibid, p.448
14. Ibid
15. Ibid
16. Ibid, p.450
17. *Mein Leben*, Alma Mahler, p.32

18. Ibid, p.31
19. *Erinnerungen an Gustav Mahler*; Gustav Mahler *Briefe an Alma Mahler*, Alma Mahler-Werfel, p.47
20. *Memories of Gustav Mahler*, Natalie Bauer-Lechner, p.159
21. *Erinnerungen an Gustav Mahler*; Gustav Mahler *Briefe an Alma Mahler*, Alma Mahler-Werfel, p.83
22. Ibid, p.203
23. Ibid
24. Ibid
25. Ibid, p.231
26. Ibid

Chapter 4

1. *Mein Leben*, Alma Mahler, p.134
2. Ibid, p.52
3. *Alma Mahler-Werfel – Die unbezahlbare Muse*, Karen Monsoon, p.152
4. Ibid
5. Ibid, p.153
6. *Alma Mahler-Werfel – Die unbezahlbare Muse*, Karen Monsoon, p.155
7. *Kokoschka und Dresden*, Werner Schmidt, p.106
8. *Witwe im Wahn–Das Leben der Alma Mahler-Werfel*, Hilmes, Oliver, p.137
9. *Mein Leben*, Oskar Kokoschka, p.34
10. Ibid, p.39
11. Ibid, p.132
12. *Twenty Drawings*. Walden, Herwath, p.2
13. *And the Bridge is Love – Memories of a Lifetime*, Alma Mahler in collaboration with E.B. Ashton, p.84
14. *Mein Leben*, Alma Mahler, p.81
15. Ibid
16. Ibid, p.82
17. Ibid
18. Ibid, p.83

Chapter 5

1. *Mein Leben*, Alma Mahler, p.87
2. Ibid
3. Ibid
4. Ibid
5. Ibid, p.89

6. Ibid, p.90
7. Ibid, pp.90-1
8. *And the Bridge is Love – Memories of a Lifetime*, Alma Mahler in collaboration with E.B. Ashton, p.104–105
9. *Mein Leben*, Alma Mahler, p.114
10. Ibid, p.122
11. Karen Monson identifies this as a *'Letter from Franz Werfel to Alma Mahler'*, autumn 1918 / via Karen Monson: *Alma Mahler-Werfel – Die unbezahlbare Muse*, However, the content, voice and rhetorical stance of the letter indicate it was almost certainly written by Alma herself.
12. *Mein Leben*, Alma Mahler, p.127; Alma used the term 'genäschig', a somewhat unusual word in German. It refers to a child-like, indulgent desire for sweets, but in this context, it conveys a sense of temptation and longing. Her fingers, metaphorically described as 'greedy', are drawn to death as if enticed by something forbidden, yet dangerously close to it.
13. *Mein Leben*, Alma Mahler, p.127
14. The Albanian minister had described another mountain tribe's belief: 'It is not the murderer who is guilty, but the murdered.'

Chapter 6

1. *Mein Leben*, Alma Mahler, p.134
2. *Walter Gropius. Der Mensch und sein Werk*, Reginald R. Isaacs, p.175
3. *Im Atem der Zeit – Erinnerungen an die Moderne*, Ernst Krenek, p.394
4. Ernst Krenek to Ernst Josef Krenek, dateless (28.02.1922) Stadt und Landesbibliothek Wien (WSB), Ernst Krenek Estate
5. Ibid, p.394
6. Ibid, p.395
7. Ibid
8. *Tagebücher (1923–1926) – Volume I, Der Wiener Vasari*, Erica Tietze-Conrat, p.224
9. *Im Atem der Zeit – Erinnerungen an die Moderne*, Ernst Krenek, p.396
10. *Paul von Zsolnay*. In: *Neue österreichische Biographie ab 1815. Große Österreicher*, Hans W. Polak, p.134
11. *Die Tante Jolesch- Oder der Untergang des Abendlandes in Anekdoten*, Friedrich Torberg.
12. *Mein Leben*, Alma Mahler, p.162
13. Ibid, p.190
14. Ibid, p.163
15. Ibid
16. Ibid

17. Ibid, p.164
18. Letter from Alban Berg to Helene Berg, 11 November 1925
19. *Die Kette der Herzen bleibt geschlossen. Mitglieder der österreichischen Freimaurer-Logen 1945 bis 1985,* Günter K. Kodek
20. Milan Dubrovic, quoted after: *Franz Werfel – A Life story*, Peter Stephan Jungk, p.143
21. *Mein Leben*, Alma Mahler, p.171
22. Ibid, p.185
23. *And the Bridge is Love – Memories of a Lifetime*, Alma Mahler-Werfel with E.B. Ashton, p.196
24. *Mein Leben*, Alma Mahler, p.101

Chapter 7

1. *Mein Leben*, Alma Mahler, p.205
2. Ibid, p.214
3. *Emil Jakob Schindler: 1842–1892. Eine Bildnisstudie*, Carl Moll, Österreichischen Staatsdruckerei, 1930
4. *Mein Leben*, Alma Mahler, p.220
5. Ibid, p.228
6. Ibid, p.239
7. *Das Augenspiel. Lebensgeschichte 1931–1937*, Elias Canetti, p.52

Chapter 8

1. *Zwischen Oben und Unten*, Franz Werfel, p.743
2. Interview Peter Stephan Jungk mit Marta Feuchtwanger, MKB
3. *Mein Leben*, Alma Mahler, p.182
4. Ibid, p.283
5. Ibid, p.285
6. Ibid, p.283
7. *The Rescue of the Intellectuals: Varian Fry's Mission to Save Artists and Writers from the Nazis*, Varian Fry, p.81.
8. *Mein Leben*, Alma Mahler, p.320
9. Ibid, pp.320-1

Chapter 9

1. *Mein Leben*, Alma Mahler, p.321
2. Ibid, p.322
3. Ibid, pp.324-5
4. *Liebste Freundin und Alma – Briefwechsel mit Alma Mahler-Werfel*, Friedrich Torberg, p.21

5. Ibid, p.45
6. *Mein Leben*, Alma Mahler, p.327
7. Ibid, p.328
8. Ibid, p.337

Chapter 10

1. *Liebste Freundin und Alma – Briefwechsel mit Alma Mahler-Werfel*, Friedrich Torberg, p.249
2. *Mein Leben*, Alma Mahler, p.365
3. Alma Mahler-Werfel, undated diary fragment, Österreichische Nationalbibliothek
4. *Liebste Freundin und Alma – Briefwechsel mit Alma Mahler-Werfel*, Friedrich Torberg, p.255
5. Ibid, p.258
6. Ibid
7. Ibid
8. Ibid, p.261
9. *Mein Leben*, Alma Mahler, p.267
10. *Liebste Freundin und Alma – Briefwechsel mit Alma Mahler-Werfel*, Friedrich Torberg, p.265
11. Ibid
12. Ibid, p.266
13. Ibid, p.267
14. Ibid, p.269
15. *Mein Leben*, Alma Mahler, p.367
16. *Liebste Freundin und Alma – Briefwechsel mit Alma Mahler-Werfel*, Friedrich Torberg, p.269
17. *Mein Leben*, Alma Mahler, p.369
18. Ibid
19. Ibid
20. Ibid, pp.369-70
21. Ibid, p.370
22. *And the Bridge is Love – Memories of a Lifetime*, Alma Mahler-Werfel with E.B. Ashton, p.307
23. *Alma meine Liebe – Persönliche Erinnerungen an eine Legende*, Erich Rietenauer, p.266
24. Ibid
25. Documentary-film: *Big Alma,* by Susanne Freund, DOR-Film, 2007
26. Ibid
27. *Alma meine Liebe – Persönliche Erinnerungen an eine Legende*, Erich Rietenauer, p.274

Index of People